PROJECT MANAGEMENT FOR ENGINEERING AND CONSTRUCTION

McGraw-Hill Series in Construction Engineering and Project Management

CONSULTING EDITORS

Raymond E. Levitt, *Stanford University*
Jerald L. Rounds, *Arizona State University*

Barrie and Paulson: Professional Construction Management: Including CM, Design-Construct, and General Contracting
Callahan, Quackenbush, and Rowings: Construction Project Scheduling
Hinze: Construction Contracts
Jervis and Levin: Construction Law: Principles and Practice
Koerner: Construction and Geotechnical Methods in Foundation Engineering
Levitt and Samelson: Construction Safety Management
Oberlender: Project Management for Engineering and Construction
Oglesby, Parker, and Howell: Productivity Improvement in Construction
Peurifoy and Ledbettter: Construction Planning, Equipment, and Methods
Peurifoy and Oberlender: Estimating Construction Costs
Shuttleworth: Mechanical and Electrical Systems for Construction
Stevens: Techniques for Construction Network Scheduling

Also available from McGraw-Hill

Schaum's Outline Series in Civil Engineering

Most outlines include basic theory, definitions, and hundreds of solved problems and supplementary problems with answers.

Titles on the Current List Include:

Advanced Structural Analysis
Basic Equations of Engineering
Descriptive Geometry
Dynamic Structural Analysis
Engineering Mechanics, 4th edition
Fluid Dynamics, 2d edition
Fluid Mechanics & Hydraulics
Introductory Surveying
Mathematical Handbook of Formulas & Tables
Mechanical Vibrations
Reinforced Concrete Design, 2d edition
State Space & Linear Systems
Statics and Mechanics of Materials
Statics and Strength of Materials
Strength of Materials, 2d edition
Structural Analysis
Structural Steel Design, LRFD Method
Theoretical Mechanics

Schaum's Solved Problems Books

Each title in this series is a complete and expert source of solved problems containing thousands of problems with worked out solutions.

Related Titles on the Current List Include:

3000 Solved Problems in Calculus
2500 Solved Problems in Differential Equations
2500 Solved Problems in Fluid Mechanics & Hydraulics
3000 Solved Problems in Linear Algebra
2000 Solved Problems in Numerical Analysis
800 Solved Problems in Vector Mechanics for Engineers: Dynamics
700 Solved Problems in Vector Mechanics for Engineers: Statics

Available at your College Bookstore. A complete list of Schaum titles may be obtained by writing to: Schaum Division
McGraw-Hill, Inc.
Princeton Road, S-1
Hightstown, NJ 08520

PROJECT MANAGEMENT FOR ENGINEERING AND CONSTRUCTION

Garold D. Oberlender, Ph.D., P.E.

Professor of Civil Engineering
Oklahoma State University

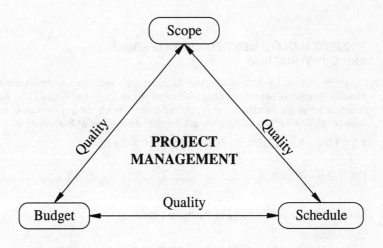

McGRAW-HILL, INC.

New York   St. Louis   San Francisco   Auckland   Bogotá   Caracas
Lisbon   London   Madrid   Mexico   Milan   Montreal   New Delhi
Paris   San Juan   Singapore   Sydney   Tokyo   Toronto

This book was set in Times Roman by Electronic Technical Publishing Services.
The editors were B. J. Clark and John M. Morriss;
the production supervisor was Denise L. Puryear.
The cover was designed by Joseph Gillians.
Project supervision was done by Electronic Technical Publishing Services.
R. R. Donnelley & Sons Company was printer and binder.

**PROJECT MANAGEMENT FOR ENGINEERING
AND CONSTRUCTION**

1 2 3 4 5 6 7 8 9 0   DOC   DOC   9 0 9 8 7 6 5 4 3 2

ISBN 0-07-048150-4

Library of Congress Cataloging-in-Publication Data

Oberlender, Garold D.
   Project management for engineering and construction / Garold D. Oberlender.
      p.   cm. — (McGraw-Hill series in construction engineering and project management)
   Includes bibliographical references and index.
   ISBN 0-07-048150-4
   1. Engineering—Management.   I. Title   II. Series.
TA190.024   1993   92-33745
658.4'04—dc20   CIP

ABOUT THE AUTHOR

Garold D. Oberlender is professor and coordinator of the graduate program in Construction Engineering and Management in the School of Civil Engineering at Oklahoma State University. He received his Ph.D. in civil engineering from the University of Texas at Arlington. Dr. Oberlender has conducted research and presented seminars on a variety of topics related to construction engineering and project management. A civil engineer with more than twenty-five years of experience, Dr. Oberlender has been a consultant to numerous companies in the application of computers in the design and construction of projects. He is coauthor with Robert L. Peurifoy of *Estimating Construction Costs, 4/e*. Dr. Oberlender is a registered professional engineer and a member of the American Society of Civil Engineers, the National Society of Professional Engineers, the American Society for Engineering Education, and the Project Management Institute.

CONTENTS

PREFACE

This book presents the principles and techniques of managing engineering and construction projects from the original plan, through design and construction, to completion. It emphasizes project management during the early stages of project development because the ability to influence the quality, cost, and schedule of a project can best be achieved during the early stages of development. Most books discuss project management during construction, after the scope of work is fully defined, the budget is fixed, and the completion date is firm. It is then too late to make any significant adjustments to the project to improve quality, cost, or schedule to benefit the owner.

Although each project is unique, there is certain information that must be identified and organized at the beginning of a project, before any work is started. Numerous tables and graphs are presented and discussed throughout this book to provide guidelines for management of the three basic components of a project: scope, budget, and schedule. The importance of achieving project quality to meet the owner's satisfaction is an integral part of project management. An entire chapter is devoted to the topic of total quality management.

The intended audience of this book is students of university programs in engineering and construction. It is also intended for persons in industry who aid the owner in the feasibility study, coordinate the design effort, and witness construction in the field. A common example is used throughout this book to illustrate project management of the design and construction process.

This book is based on the author's experience in working with hundreds of project managers in the engineering and construction industry. Much of the information in this book is based on formal and informal discussions with these project managers, who are actively involved in the practice of project management. Although the author has observed that no two project managers operate exactly the same, there are common elements that apply to all projects and all project managers. The author presents these common elements of effective project management that have been successfully applied in practice.

The author has referenced numerous publications related to project management. At the end of each chapter there is a list of references related to the subjects that are discussed. The author would like to thank the Construction Industry Institute for permission to use the contents of its publications and research findings related to project management, and The Construction Specification Institute for its permission to reproduce the titles and numbers of CSI Masterformat, which has become the industry standard for classification of information related to engineering and construction.

McGraw-Hill and the author would like to thank the following reviewers for their many comments and suggestions: Arthur Monsey, Washington University at St. Louis; Harold Pritchett, Oregon State University; and Jerald Rounds, Arizona State University.

The author would also like to thank Rock Spencer, Bill Smith, and Daryl Radcliffe of The Benham Group for their helpful comments and reference material that is used in this book. A special thanks is also given to Larry Vorba of Williams Engineering Company for his helpful comments related to integrating quality as a part of project management, and to Larry Neufeld of Canam Construction Company for his suggestions related to the contractor's perspective. The author also wishes to thank Robert Hughes for his review and suggestions, and to Oklahoma State University for its encouragement in the development of this book.

The author would like to thank the many project managers in industry who have shared their successes, and problems, and who have influenced the author's thoughts in the development of this book. Finally, the author greatly appreciates the patience and tolerance of his wife, Jana, and three sons, Dan, Tim, and Ron, for their support during the writing and editing phases in producing this finished book.

Garold D. Oberlender

PROJECT MANAGEMENT FOR ENGINEERING AND CONSTRUCTION

INTRODUCTION

PURPOSE OF THIS BOOK

The purpose of this book is to present the principles and techniques of project management beginning with the conceptual phase by the owner, through coordination of design and construction, to project completion.

Experienced project managers agree that the procedures used for project management vary from company to company and even among individuals within a company. Although each manager develops his or her own style of management, and each project is unique, there are basic principles that apply to all project managers and projects. This book presents these principles and illustrates the basic steps, and sequencing of steps, to develop a work plan to manage a project through each phase from conceptual development to completion.

Project management requires teamwork among the three principal contracting parties: the owner, designer, and contractor. The coordination of the design and construction of a project requires planning and organizing a team of people who are dedicated to a common goal of completing the project for the owner. Even a small project involves a large number of people who work for different organizations. The key to a successful project is the selection and coordination of people who have the ability to detect and solve problems to complete the project.

Throughout this book the importance of management skills is emphasized to enable the user to develop his or her own style of project management. The focus is to apply project management at the beginning of the project, when it is first approved. Too often the formal organization to manage a project is not developed until the beginning of the construction phase. This book presents the information that must be assembled and managed during the development and engineering design phase to bring a project to successful completion for use by the owner.

The intended audience of this book is students enrolled in university programs in engineering and construction. It is also intended for the design firms which aid the owner in the feasibility study, coordinate the design effort, and witness construction in the field. This book is also for persons in the owner's organization who are involved in the design and construction process.

ARRANGEMENT OF THIS BOOK

A discussion of project management is difficult because there are many ways a project can be handled. The design and/or construction of a project can be performed by one or more parties. Regardless of the method that is used to handle a project, the management of a project generally follows these steps:

Step 1: Project Definition (to meet the needs of the end user)
      Intended use by the owner after completion of construction
      Conceptual configurations and components to meet the intended use
Step 2: Project Scope (to meet the project definition)
      Define the work that must be accomplished
      Identify the quantity, quality, and tasks that must be performed
Step 3: Project Budgeting (to match the project definition and scope)
      Define the owner's permissible budget
      Determine direct and indirect costs plus contingencies
Step 4: Project Planning (the strategy to accomplish the work)
      Select and assign project staffing
      Identify the tasks required to accomplish the work
Step 5: Project Scheduling (the product of scope, budgeting, and planning)
      Arrange and schedule activities in a logical sequence
      Link the costs and resources to the scheduled activities
Step 6: Project Tracking (to ensure the project is progressing as planned)
      Measure work, time, and costs that are expended
      Compare "actual" to "planned" work, time, and cost
Step 7: Project Close-Out (final completion to ensure owner satisfaction)
      Final testing, inspection, and payment
      Turn over of the project to the owner

These steps describe project management in its simplest form. In reality, there is considerable overlap between the steps, because any one step may affect one or more other steps. For example, budget preparation overlaps project definition and scope development. Similarly, project scheduling relates project scope and budget to project tracking and control.

The topic of project management is further complicated because the responsibility for these steps usually involves many parties. Thus, the above steps must all be integrated together to successfully manage a project. Subsequent chapters of this book describe each of these steps.

Chapter 1 defines general principles related to project management. These basic principles must be fully understood because they apply to all of the remaining chapters. Many of the problems associated with project management are caused by the failure to apply the basic management principles that are presented in Chapter 1.

Chapter 2, Project Initiation, presents material that is generally performed by the owner. However, the owner may contract the services of a design organization to assist with the feasibility study of a project. The project manager should be involved at the project development or marketing phase to establish the scope. This requires input from experienced technical people that represent every aspect of the proposed project.

Chapter 3, Project Budgeting, applies to all parties in a project: the owner, designer, and contractor. The budget must be linked to the quantity, quality, and schedule of work to be accomplished. A change in scope or schedule almost always affects budget, so the project manager must continually be alert to changes in a project and to relate any changes to the budget.

Chapter 4, Development of the Work Plan, applies to the project manager who is responsible for the management of the design effort. Generally, he or she is employed by the professional design organization which may be an agency of the owner or under contract by the owner to perform design services. The material presented in this chapter is important because it establishes the work plan which is the framework for guiding the entire project effort. The information in this chapter relates to all of the steps and to all of the chapters of this book.

Chapter 5, Project Scheduling, provides the base against which all activity is measured. It relates the work to be accomplished to the people who will perform the work as well as to the budget and schedule. Project scheduling can not be accomplished without a well-defined work plan that is described in Chapter 4, and it forms the basis for Project Tracking described in Chapter 6.

Chapter 6, Project Tracking, can not be accomplished without a well-defined work plan as described in Chapter 4, and a detailed schedule as described in Chapter 5. This chapter is important because there is always a tendency for scope growth, cost overrun, or schedule delays. A control system must simultaneously monitor the three basic components of a project: the work accomplished, the budget, and the schedule. These components must be collectively monitored, not as individual components, because a change in any one component usually will affect the other two components.

Chapter 7, Design Coordination, applies to the project manager of the design organization. The quality, cost, and schedule of a project is highly dependent on the effectiveness of the design effort. The end result of the design process is to produce plans and specifications in a timely manner that meet the intended use of the project by the owner. The product of the design must be within the owner's approved budget and schedule, and must be constructable by the construction contractor.

Chapter 8, Construction Phase, is important because most of the cost of a project is expended in the construction phase, and the quality of the final project is highly dependent upon the quality of work that is performed by the construction contractor. Most of the books that have been written on project management have been directed toward a project in the construction phase. This book emphasizes project management from the initial conception of the project by the owner, through coordination of design and development of the construction documents, and into the construction phase until project close out.

Chapter 9, Project Close Out, discusses the steps required to complete a project and turn it over to the owner. This is an important phase of a project because the owner will have expended most of the budget for the project, but will not receive any benefits from the expenditures until it is completed and ready for use. Also it is sometimes difficult to close a project because there are always many small items that must be finished.

Chapter 10, Tips for Making Things Happen, addresses the human aspects of project management. Although the primary emphasis of this book is on the techniques of project management; it is people who ensure the successful completion of a project.

Chapter 11, Total Quality Management, presents the management philosophy that has gained much attention in the engineering and construction industry in recent years. Most of the attention has been attributed to the success of TQM in the manufacturing and electronics industries. However, many of the topics related to TQM are applicable to good project management of design and construction.

DEFINITION OF A PROJECT

A project consists of three components: scope, budget, and schedule. When a project is first assigned to a project manager, it is important that all three of these components be clearly defined. Throughout this book, the term *Scope* represents the work to be accomplished, i.e., the quantity and quality of work. *Budget* refers to costs, measured in dollars and/or labor-hours of work. *Schedule* refers to the logical sequencing and timing of the work to be performed. The quality of a project must meet the owner's satisfaction and is an integral part of project management as illustrated in Figure 1-1.

The source of many problems associated with a project is failure to properly define the project scope. Too often the focus is just on budget or schedule. Not only should the scope, budget, and schedule be well defined, but each must be linked together since one affects the other, both individually and collectively.

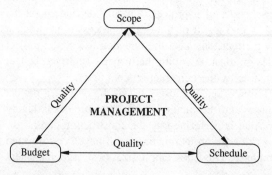

FIGURE 1-1
Quality is an integral part of Scope, Budget, and Schedule.

Since the project scope defines the work to be accomplished, it should be the first task in the development of a project, prior to the development of either the budget or the schedule. Experienced project managers agree that the budget and schedule are derived from the scope. Too often, top management specifies a project budget or schedule and then asks the project team to define a scope to match the budget. This is the reverse order of defining a project and is not a good project management practice. It is the duty of a project manager to ensure that the project scope, budget, and schedule are linked together.

Budgeting is important because it establishes the amount of money the owner will spend to obtain the project and the amount of money that the design and construction organizations will be compensated for performing the work. Each party is concerned about project cost overrun because it adversely affects profitability and creates adverse relationships between the parties.

Scheduling is important because it brings together project definition, people, cost, resources, timing, and methods of performing work to define the logical sequence of activity for the project. The schedule is the final product of scope definition, budgeting, and planning and forms the base against which all activity is measured. Project tracking and control can not be accomplished without a good plan and schedule.

Quality is an element that is integrated into and between all parts of a project: scope, budget, and schedule. It should not be construed as merely creating drawings with a minimum number of errors, furnishing equipment that meets specifications, or building a project to fulfill the requirements of a contract. Certainly these factors are a part of quality, but it involves much more. Quality is meeting the needs and satisfaction of the ultimate end user of the project, the owner.

Quality is the responsibility of all participants in a project, including all levels of management and workers in each of the principal parties. An attitude of achieving quality must be instilled in everyone and perpetuate throughout the work environment. The attitude should not be "what can we do to pass quality control or final inspection?" Instead, it should be "what can we do to improve our work and what is the best way that we can furnish a project that meets the needs and satisfaction of the owner?"

RESPONSIBILITIES OF PARTIES

Each of the three principal parties in a project has a role to fulfill in the various phases of design development and construction. A team approach between the owner, designer, and contractor must be created with a cooperative relationship to complete the project in the most efficient manner. Too often an adverse relationship develops that does not serve the best interest of anyone.

The owner is responsible for setting the operational criteria for the completed project. Examples are usage of a building, barrels per day of crude oil to be refined, millions of cubic feet per hour of gas to be transported in a pipeline, and so on. Any special equipment, material, or company standards that are to apply to the project must also be defined. Owners also need to identify their level of involvement in the project, e.g., the review process, required reports, and levels of approval. The owner is also responsible for setting parameters on total cost, payment of costs, major milestones, and the project completion date.

The designer is responsible for producing design alternatives, computations, drawings, and specifications that meet the needs of the owner. In addition there may be other duties that are delegated to the designer by the owner, e.g., on-site or periodic inspection, review of shop drawings and in some instances the acquisition of land and/or permits. It is the duty of the designer to produce a project design that meets all federal, state, and local codes; standards; and environmental and safety regulations. In addition a budget for the design should be prepared, along with a design schedule that matches the owner's schedule. The design schedule should be directly correlated to the construction schedule so the project can be completed by the construction contractor when the owner needs it.

Generally the designers are not obligated under standard-form contracts to guarantee the construction cost of a project, although there have been some cases where the designer has been held legally responsible for the construction price. As part of their design responsibility, designers usually prepare an estimate of the probable construction cost for the design they have prepared. Major decisions by the owner to proceed with the project are made from the designer's cost estimate.

The cost and operational characteristics of a project are influenced most, and are more easy to change, during the design phase. Because of this, the designer plays a key role during the early phase of a project by working with the owner to keep the project on track so the owner/contractor relationship will be in the best possible form.

The construction contractor is responsible for the performance of all work in accordance with the contract documents that have been prepared by the designer. This includes furnishing all labor, equipment, material, and know-how necessary to build the project. The construction phase is important because most of the project budget is expended during construction. Also, the operation and maintenance of the completed project is highly dependent on the quality of work that is performed during construction. The contractor must prepare an accurate estimate of the project, develop a realistic construction schedule, and establish an effective project control system for cost, schedule, and quality.

WHO DOES THE PROJECT MANAGER WORK FOR?

The project manager works for the project, although he or she may be employed by the owner, designer, or contractor. For large projects a team consisting of a project manager for the owner, designer, and contractor form a group of people who work together to manage the design, procurement, and construction activities. For small projects the owner may delegate overall project management responsibility to a design consultant, or a professional construction manager, and assign an owner's representative as a liaison to represent the owner's interest.

The Construction Industry Institute (CII) has sponsored research and published numerous papers on a variety of topics related to project management. *Organizing for Project Success*, a CII publication, provides a good description of the interface between project managers for the owner, designer, and contractor. The following paragraphs are a summary of the project management teams that are discussed in the publication.

After commitment has been made by an owner to invest in a project an Investment Management Team is formed, within the owner's organization to provide overall project control. The major functions, such as marketing, engineering, finance, and manufacturing, are usually represented. A Project Executive usually leads the team and reports to the head of the business unit which made the decision to proceed with the project. A member of this team is the Owner's Project Manager.

The Owner's Project Manager leads a Project Management Team which consists of each Design Project Manager and Construction Project Manager that is assigned a contract from the owner. Their mission is to accomplish the work, including coordinating the engineering, procurement, and construction phases. The Owner's Project Manager leads this team which is one of the most important management functions of the project. The Owner's Project Manager is responsible for the accomplishment of all work, even though he or she has limited resources under their direct control because the work has been contracted to various organizations.

Reporting to each Design Project Manager and Construction Project Manager are the Work Managers who fulfill the requirements of their contracts. Each Design and Contractor Project Manager reports to the Owner's Project Manager for contractual matters, and to his or her parent organization for business matters.

The Work Managers are the design leaders and supervisors who lead the teams actually accomplishing the work. They are directly responsible for the part of the contract assigned to them by their Project Manager. They must also communicate and coordinate their efforts with Work Managers from other organizations. Usually this communication does not flow vertically through a chain of command, but instead flows horizontally between people actually involved in the work. It is their responsibility to also work with their Project Manager and keep them informed. This is further discussed in Chapter 8.

PURPOSE OF PROJECT MANAGEMENT

For the purpose of this book, project management may be defined as:

> The art and science of coordinating people, equipment, materials, money, and schedules to complete a specified project on time and within approved cost.

Much of the work of a project manager is organizing and working with people to identify problems and determine solutions to problems. In addition to being organized and a problem solver, a manager must also work well with people. It is people who have the ability to create ideas, identify and solve problems, communicate, and get the work done. Because of this, people are the most important resource of the project manager. Thus, the project manager must develop a good working relationship with people in order to benefit from the best of their abilities.

It is the duty of a project manager to organize a project team of people and coordinate their efforts in a common direction to bring a project to successful completion.

Throughout the project management process there are four questions that must be addressed: Who? Does What? When? and How much?

The work required often involves people outside of the project manager's organization. Although these individuals do not report directly to the project manager, it is necessary that effective working relationships be developed.

A manager must be a motivated achiever with a "can do" attitude. Throughout a project there are numerous obstacles that must be overcome. The manager must have perspective with the ability to forecast methods of achieving results. The drive to achieve results must always be present. This attitude must also be instilled in everyone involved in the project.

Good communication skills are a must for a manager. The management of a project requires coordination of people and information. Coordination is achieved through effective communication. Most problems associated with project management can be traced to poor communications. Too often the "other person" receives information that is incorrect, inadequate, or too late. In some instances the information is simply never received. It is the responsibility of the project manager to be a good communicator and to ensure that people involved in a project communicate with each other.

TYPES OF MANAGEMENT

Management may be divided into at least two different types: functional management (sometimes called discipline management) and project management. Functional management involves the coordination of repeated work of a similar nature by the same people. Examples are management of a department of design engineering, surveying, estimating, or purchasing. Project management involves the coordination of one time work by a team of people who often have never previously worked together. Examples are management of the design and/or construction of a substation, shopping center, refinery unit, or water treatment plant. Although the basic principles of management apply to both of these types of management, there are distinct differences between the two.

Most individuals begin their career in the discipline environment of management. Upon graduation from college, a person generally accepts a position in a discipline closely related to his or her formal education. Typical examples are design engineers, estimators, schedulers, or surveyors. The work environment focuses on how and who will perform the work, with an emphasis on providing technical expertise for a single discipline. Career goals are directed toward becoming a specialist in a particular technical area.

Project management requires a multi-discipline focus to coordinate the overall needs of a project, with reliance on others to provide the technical expertise. The project manager must be able to delegate authority and responsibility to others and still retain focus on the linking process between disciplines. Project managers cannot become overly involved in detailed tasks or take over the discipline they are educated in, but should focus on the project objectives.

A fundamental principle of project management is to organize the project around the work to be accomplished. The work environment focuses on what must be performed,

TABLE 1-1
DISTINGUISHING BETWEEN PROJECT AND DISCIPLINE
MANAGEMENT

Project Management is concerned with	Discipline Management is concerned with
What must be done	How it will be done
When it must be done	Who will do it
How much will it cost	How well it will be done
Coordinating overall needs	Coordinating specific needs
Multi-discipline focus	Single-discipline focus
Reliance on others	Providing technical expertise
Project quality	Technical quality
Administrative viewpoint	Technical viewpoint
A generalist's Approach	A specialist's Approach

when it must be accomplished, and how much will it cost. Career development for project managers must be directed toward the goal of becoming a generalist with a broad administrative viewpoint.

The successful completion of a project depends upon the ability of a project manager to coordinate the work of a team of specialists who have the technical ability to perform the work. Table 1-1 illustrates the relationship between project management and discipline management.

FUNCTIONS OF MANAGEMENT

Management is often summarized into five basic functions: planning, organizing, staffing, directing, and controlling. Although these basic management functions have been developed and used by managers of businesses, they apply equally to the management of a project.

Planning is the formulation of a course of action to guide a project to completion. It starts at the beginning of a project, with the scope of work, and continues throughout the life of a project. The establishment of milestones and consideration of possible constraints are major parts of planning. Successful project planning is best accomplished by the participation of all parties involved in a project. There must be an explicit operational plan to guide the entire project throughout its life.

Organizing is the arrangement of resources in a systematic manner to fit the project plan. A project must be organized around the work to be performed. There must be a breakdown of the work to be performed into manageable units, that can be defined and measured. The work breakdown structure of a project is a multi-level system that consists of tasks, subtasks, and work packages.

Staffing is the selection of individuals who have the expertise to produce the work. The persons that are assigned to the project team influence every part of a project. Most managers will readily agree that people are the most important resource on a project. People provide the knowledge to design, coordinate, and construct the project. The numerous problems that arise throughout the life of a project are solved by people.

Directing is the guidance of the work required to complete a project. The people on the project staff that provide diverse technical expertise must be developed into an effective team. Although each person provides work in his or her area of expertise, the work that is provided by each must be collectively directed in a common effort and in a common direction.

Controlling is the establishment of a system to measure, report, and forecast deviations in the project scope, budget, and schedule. The purpose of project control is to determine and predict deviations in a project so corrective actions can be taken. Project control requires the continual reporting of information in a timely manner so management can respond during the project rather than afterwards. Control is often the most difficult function of project management.

KEY CONCEPTS OF PROJECT MANAGEMENT

Although each project is unique, there are key concepts that a project manager can use to coordinate and guide a project to completion. A list of the key concepts is provided in Table 1-2.

TABLE 1-2
KEY CONCEPTS OF PROJECT MANAGEMENT

1. Ensure that one person, and only one person, is responsible for the project
2. Don't begin work without a signed contract, regardless of the pressure to start
3. Confirm that there is an approved scope, budget, and schedule for the project
4. Lock in the project scope at the beginning and ensure there is no scope growth without approval
5. Make certain that scope is understood by all parties, including the owner
6. Determine who developed the budget and schedule, and when they were prepared
7. Verify that the budget and schedule are linked to the scope
8. Organize the project around the work to be performed, rather than trying to keep people busy
9. Ensure there is an explicit operational work plan to guide the entire project
10. Establish a work breakdown structure that divides the project into definable and measurable units of work
11. Establish a project organizational chart that shows authority and responsibilities for all team members
12. Build the project staff into an effective team that works together as a unit
13. Emphasize that quality is a must, because if it doesn't work it is worthless, regardless of cost or how fast it is completed
14. Budget all tasks; any work worth doing should have compensation
15. Develop a project schedule that provides logical sequencing of the work required to complete the job
16. Establish a control system that will anticipate and report deviations on a timely basis so corrective actions can be taken
17. Get problems out in the open with all persons involved so they can be resolved
18. Document all work, because what may seem irrelevant at one point in time may later be very significant
19. Prepare a formal agreement with appropriate parties whenever there is a change in the project
20. Keep the client informed; they pay for everything and will use the project upon completion

Each of the key concepts shown in Table 1-2 is discussed in detail in subsequent chapters of this book. It is the responsibility of the project manager to address each of these concepts from the beginning of a project and through each phase until completion.

ROLE OF THE PROJECT MANAGER

The role of a project manager is to lead the project team to ensure a quality project within time, budget, and scope constraints. A project is a single, non-repetitive enterprise and because each project is unique, its outcome can never be predicted with absolute confidence. A project manager must achieve the end results despite all the risks and problems that are encountered. Success depends on carrying out the required tasks in a logical sequence, utilizing the available resources to the best advantage. The project manager must perform the five basic functions of management: planning, organizing, staffing, directing, and controlling.

Project planning is the heart of good project management. It is important for the project manager to realize that he or she is responsible for project planning, and it must be started early in the project (before starting any work). Planning is a continuous process throughout the life of the project, and to be effective it must be done with input from the people involved in the project. The techniques and tools of planning are well established. Table 1-3 provides guidelines for planning.

A project organizational chart should be developed by the project manager for each project. The chart should clearly show the appropriate communication channels between the people working on the project. Project team members must know the authority of every other team member in order to reduce miscommunications and rework. Organized work leads to accomplishments and a sense of pride in the work accomplished. Unorganized work leads to rework. Rework leads to errors, low productivity, and frustrated team members. Table 1-4 provides guidelines for organizing.

TABLE 1-3
PROJECT MANAGER'S ROLE IN PLANNING

1. Develop planning focused on the work to be performed
2. Establish project objectives and performance requirements early so everyone involved knows what is required
3. Involve all discipline managers and key staff members in the process of planning and estimating
4. Establish clear and well-defined milestones in the project so all concerned will know what is to be accomplished, and when it is to be completed
5. Build contingencies into the plan to provide a reserve in the schedule for unforeseen future problems
6. Avoid reprogramming or replanning the project unless absolutely necessary
7. Prepare formal agreements with appropriate parties whenever there is a change in the project and establish methods to control changes
8. Communicate the project plan to clearly define individual responsibilities, schedules, and budgets
9. Remember that the best-prepared plans are worthless unless they are implemented

TABLE 1-4
PROJECT MANAGERS' ROLE IN ORGANIZING

1. Organize the project around the work to be accomplished
2. Develop a work breakdown structure that divides the project into definable and measurable units of work
3. Establish a project organization chart for each project to show who does what
4. Define clearly the authority and responsibility for all project team members

Project staffing is important because people make things happen. Most individuals will readily agree that people are the most important resource on a project. They create ideas, solve problems, produce designs, operate equipment, and install materials to produce the final product. Because each project is unique, the project manager must understand the work to be accomplished by each discipline. The project manager should then work with his or her supervisor and appropriate discipline managers to identify the persons who are best qualified to work on the project. Table 1-5 provides guidelines for project staffing.

The project manager must direct the overall project and serve as an effective leader in coordinating all aspects of the project. This requires a close working relationship between the project manager and the project staff to build an effective working team. Because most project team members are assigned (loaned) to the project from their discipline (home) departments, the project manager must foster the development of staff loyalty to the project while they maintain loyalty to their home departments. The project manager must be a good communicator and have the ability to work with people at all levels of authority. The project manager must be able to delegate authority and responsibility to others and concentrate on the linking process between disciplines. He or she cannot become overly involved in detailed tasks, but should be the leader of the team to meet project objectives. Table 1-6 provides guidelines for directing the project.

Project control is a high priority of management and involves a cooperative effort of the entire project team. It is important for the project manager to establish a control system that will anticipate and report deviations on a timely basis, so corrective action can be initiated before more serious problems actually occur. Many team members

TABLE 1-5
PROJECT MANAGER'S ROLE IN STAFFING

1. Define clearly the work to be performed, and work with appropriate department managers in selecting team members
2. Provide an effective orientation (project goals and objectives) for team members at the beginning of the project
3. Explain clearly to team members what is expected of them and how their work fits into the total project
4. Solicit each team member's input to clearly define and agree upon scope, budget, and schedule

TABLE 1-6
PROJECT MANAGER'S ROLE IN DIRECTING

1. Serve as an effective leader in coordinating all important aspects of the project
2. Show interest and enthusiasm in the project with a "can do" attitude
3. Be available to the project staff, get problems out in the open, and work out problems in a cooperative manner
4. Analyze and investgate problems early so solutions can be found at the earliest possible date
5. Obtain the resources needed by the project team to accomplish their work to complete the project
6. Recognize the importance of team members, compliment them for good work, guide them in correcting mistakes, and build an effective team

TABLE 1-7
PROJECT MANAGER'S ROLE IN CONTROLLING

1. Maintain a record of planned and actual work accomplished to measure project performance
2. Maintain a current milestone chart that displays planned and achieved milestones
3. Maintain a monthly project cost chart which displays planned expenditures and actual expenditures
4. Keep records of meetings, telephone conversations, and agreements
5. Keep everyone informed, ensuring that no one gets any "surprises", and have solutions or proposed solutions to problems

resist being controlled, therefore the term *monitoring a project* may also be used as a description for anticipating and reporting deviations in the project. An effective project control system must address all parts of the project: quality, work accomplished, budget, schedule, and scope changes. Table 1-7 provides guidelines for project control.

PROFESSIONAL AND TECHNICAL ORGANIZATIONS

Due to the increased cost and complexity of projects, the interest in developing and applying good project management principles has gained considerable attention by owners, designers, and contractors. Numerous organizations have made significant contributions related to project management by conducting research, sponsoring workshops and seminars, and publishing technical papers. The following paragraphs describe some of these organizations.

The American Society of Civil Engineers (ASCE), founded in 1852, is the oldest national engineering society in the United States. Membership comprises over 100,000 civil engineers working in government, education, research, construction, and private consulting. The construction division of ASCE has many councils and technical committees that have published technical papers related to project management in its *Journal of Construction Engineering and Management*.

The National Society of Professional Engineers (NSPE), founded in 1936, is the national engineering society of registered professional engineers from all disciplines of engineering. NSPE membership comprises over 50,000 engineers who are organized in five practice divisions: construction, education, government, industry, and private practice. The construction practice division has numerous committees that have contributed to contract documents and legislation related to engineers in the construction industry.

The Project Management Institute (PMI), founded in 1969, consists of members from all disciplines and is dedicated to advancing the state-of-the-art in the profession of project management. PMI has a certification program for project management professionals and publishes a *Project Management Book of Knowledge* (PMBOK).

The Construction Management Association of America (CMAA), founded in 1981, is an organization of corporate companies, public agencies, and individual members who promote the growth and development of construction management (CM) as a professional service. CMAA publishes documents related to CM, including the *Standard CM Services and Practice*.

The Construction Industry Institute (CII), founded in 1983, is a national research organization consisting of an equal number of owner and contractor member companies, and research universities from across the United States. CII is organized into committees, councils, and research task forces which are comprised of owners, contractors, and academic members who work together as a team to conduct research and produce publications on a variety of topics related to project management.

The following list of organizations is provided to the reader as sources for information related to project management:

American Association of Cost Engineers
American Institute of Architects
American Society of Civil Engineers
American Society of Military Engineers
Construction Industry Institute
Construction Management Association of America
National Institute for Engineering Management & Systems
National Society of Professional Engineers
Project Management Institute
Society of American Value Engineers

QUESTIONS FOR CHAPTER 1—INTRODUCTION

1 As presented in this chapter, quality is an integral part of project management. Because there are different levels of quality, it is important for the owner, designer, and contractor to have a mutual understanding of the quality that is expected in a project. Describe methods that can be used to ensure that quality is adequately defined, understood, and properly included a the project.

2 Give an illustrative example of an adverse relationship that may arise when an owner fails to fulfill his or her responsibility of clearly defining the operational criteria of a project.

3 Give an illustrative example of an adverse relationship that may arise when a designer fails to give adequate attention to the impact of a design selection on the cost or schedule during the construction phase.

4 Give an illustrative example of an adverse relationship that may arise when a contractor fails to perform his or her work in accordance with the contract documents.

5 In actuality, there are at least three project managers that are involved in a project, one each working for the owner, designer, and contractor. Since each of these individuals work for a different organization, describe methods that you would suggest to ensure good working relationships between these three individuals.

6 Interview three project managers, one working for an owner, designer, and contractor, respectively, to identify factors that each manager believes is important for the successful completion of a project.

7 A definition of project management is given in this chapter. Review this definition and expand it to include additional items that you feel are important to the function of project management.

8 Consult publications from one or more of the references at the end of this chapter to compare and contrast the differences between "project management" and "functional management."

9 The five basic functions of management discussed in this chapter are derived from the basic principles of business management. Review two sources of publications that describe the role and functions of management, one from a journal of business management and one from a journal of engineering management. Compare the business perspective of management to the engineering perspective of management.

10 Throughout the project management process, there are four questions that must be addressed: Who? Does What? When? and How much? Expand this list to include other questions that may be appropriate for some situations in the management of a project.

REFERENCES

1 Adams, J. R. and Campbell, B., *Roles and Responsibilities of the Project Manager*, Project Management Institute, Drexel Hill, PA, 1982.

2 Adams, J. R., Bilbro, C. R., and Stockert, T. C., *An Organization Development Approach to Project Management*, Project Management Institute, Drexel Hill, PA, 1986.

3 "Organizing for Project Success", Publication No. 12-2, Construction Industry Institute, Austin, TX, February, 1991.

4 Stuckenbruck, L. C., *The Implementation of Project Management: The Professional's Handbook*, Project Management Institute, Drexel Hill, PA, 1981.

CHAPTER 2

PROJECT INITIATION

CONTRACTURAL ARRANGEMENTS

Project management requires teamwork among the three principal contracting parties. The owner's team must provide the project's needs, the level of quality expected, a permissible budget, and the required schedule. They must also provide the overall direction of the project. The designer's team must develop a set of contract documents that meets the owner's needs, budget, required level of quality, and schedule. In addition, the work specified in the contract documents must be constructable by the contractor. The contractor's team must efficiently manage the physical work required to build the project in accordance with the contract documents.

There are numerous combinations of contract arrangements for handling a project. Figure 2-1 illustrates the fundamental arrangements in their simplest form. Each of these arrangements are briefly described in the following paragraphs.

A design/bid/build contract is commonly used for projects that have no unusual features and a well-defined scope. It is a three party arrangement involving the owner, designer, and contractor. This method involves three steps: a complete design is prepared, followed by solicitation of competitive bids from contractors, and the award of a contract to a construction contractor to build the project. Two separate contracts are awarded, one to the designer and one to the contractor. Since a complete design is prepared before construction, the owner knows the projects configuration and approximate cost before commencing construction. Considerable time can be required because each step must be completed before starting the next step. Also changes during construction can be expensive because the award of the construction contract is usually based upon a lump-sum, fixed-price bid before construction, rather than during construction.

FIGURE 2-1
Contracting Arrangements.

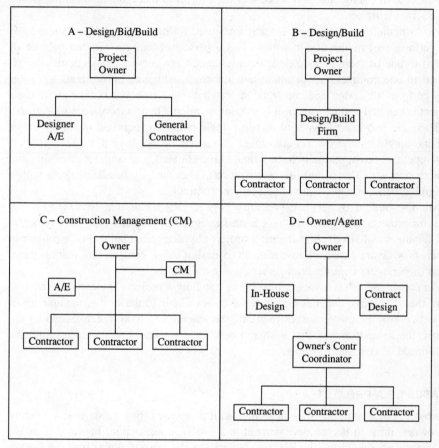

A design/build contract is often used to shorten the time required to complete a project or to provide flexibility for the owner to make changes in the project during construction. It is a two party arrangement between the owner and the design/build firm. Since the contract with the design/build firm is awarded before starting any design or construction, a cost reimbursable arrangement is normally used instead of a lump-sum fixed-cost arrangement. This method requires extensive involvement of the owner for decisions that are made during the selection of design alternatives, and the monitoring of costs and schedules during construction.

A construction management contract can be assigned to a construction management (CM) firm to coordinate the project for the owner. The CM contract is a four party arrangement involving the owner, designer, construction management firm, and the contractor. During the past twenty years there has been considerable debate regarding the CM process and the amount of responsibility assigned to the CM by the owner. The basic CM concept is that the owner assigns a contract to a firm that is knowledgable and capable of coordinating all aspects of the project to meet the intended use of the project by the owner.

An owner/agent arrangement is sometimes used for handling a project. Some owners perform part of the design with in-house personnel and contract the balance of design to one or more outside design consultants. Construction contracts may be assigned to one contractor or to multiple contractors. Although uncommon, an owner may perform all design and construction activities with in-house personnel. When a project is handled in this manner, it is sometimes refered to as a force-account method.

There are two general types of owners: single-builder owners and multiple-builder owners. Single-builder owners are organizations that do not have a need for projects on a repetitive basis, normally have a limited project staff, and contract all design and construction activities to outside organizations. They usually handle projects with a design/bid/build or construction management contract.

Multiple-builder owners are generally large organizations that have a continual need for projects, and generally have a staff assigned to project work. They typically will handle small-sized, short-duration projects by design/bid/build. For a project in which they desire extensive involvement, a design/build, construction management, or an owner/agent contract arrangement is often used.

An owner can select a variety of ways of handling a project. The contract arrangement that is selected depends on the resources available to the owner, the amount of project control the owner wishes to retain, the amount of involvement desired by the owner, the amount of risk that is shared between the owner and contractor, and the importance of cost and schedule.

PHASES OF A PROJECT

A project is in a continual state of change as it progresses from its start, as a need by the owner, through design development and finally, construction. Figure 2-2 shows the various phases during the life of a project. As the project moves from one phase to another, additional parties become involved and more information is obtained to better identify the scope, budget, and schedule. There are times when a project recycles through a phase before gaining management approval to proceed to the subsequent phase. During each phase, it is the responsibility of the project manager to keep all work within the approved scope, budget, and schedule.

In the early phases of design development, there may not be sufficient information to define the scope accurately enough to know the work to be performed. A characteristic of most project managers is "I can do it." This characteristic often leads to assignment of work to the project manager before the work is completely defined or officially approved. This applies to the project manager in either the owner, designer, or contractor organization. The people who work around the project manager include clients, subordinates, project team members, upper management, and colleagues who are themselves project managers. A project manager can not efficiently utilize his or her time or effectively manage when special requests are made for work that is not well defined. If these conditions exist, the work should be performed on a time

FIGURE 2-2
Phases of a Project.

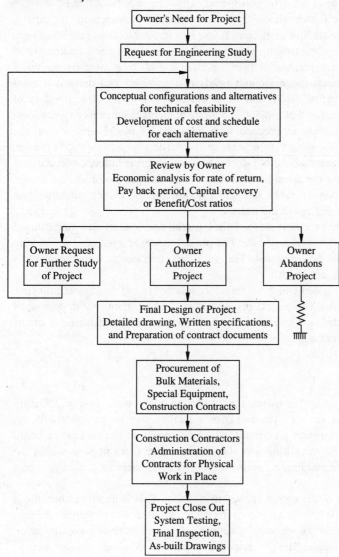

and material basis for actual work accomplished, until an adequate scope, budget, and schedule can be determined. Another option is to define a scope, with a matching budget and schedule. Then when there is a deviation from the defined scope, the project manager can advise the owner of the readjusted budget and schedule caused by the change in scope and obtain their approval before proceeding with the work.

During the development of conceptual configurations and alternatives, the quality and total cost of the project must be considered. This can only be achieved through extensive input from the owner who will ultimately use the project, since the cost to operate and maintain the facility after completion is a major factor in project design. Sometimes the budget is a controlling factor which causes the owner's contemplated scope to be reduced, or expanded. If this condition exists, care must be exercised to ensure the project meets the minimum needs of the owner and there is a clear understanding of the level of quality that is expected by the owner. It is the duty of the project manager to ensure that project development meets the owners expectations.

The owner's authorization to proceed with final design places pressure on the designer to complete the contract documents at the earliest possible date. However, the quality and completeness of the bid documents have a great influence on the cost of the project. Adequate time should be allocated to the designer to produce a design for the project that is constructable and will perform for the owner with the least amount of maintenance and operating costs.

For large projects the procurement of bulk material and special equipment has a large impact on the construction schedule. The project manager must ensure that long lead-time purchase items are procured. This must be coordinated with the owner's representative on the project team.

The type of contract chosen and the contractors selected to bid the project influence cost, schedule, and quality. The project manager plays an important role in process of pre-qualification of contractors, the evaluation of bids, and recommendations of the award of construction contracts.

OWNER'S STUDY

A project starts as a need by the owner for the design and construction of a facility to produce a product or service. The need for a facility may be recognized by an operating division of the owner, a corporate planning group, a top executive, a board of directors, or an outside consulting firm. Generally one or more persons within the owner's organization are assigned to perform a needs assessment to study the merits of pursuing the project.

The first requirement of the owner is objective-setting. This is important because it provides a focus for scope definition, guides the design process, and influences the motivation of the project team. The process of setting objectives involves an optimization of quality, cost, and schedule. The owner's objectives must be clearly communicated and understood by all parties, and serve as a benchmark for the numerous decisions that are made throughout the duration of the project.

The magnitude of the owner's study varies widely, depending on the complexity of a project and the importance of the project to the owner. It is an important study because the goals, objectives, concepts, ideas, budgets, and schedule that are developed will greatly influence the design and construction phases.

The owner's study must conclude with a well-defined set of project objectives and needs, the minimum requirements of quality and performance, an approved maximum budget, and a required project completion date. Failure to provide any of the above

FIGURE 2-3
Importance of Clear Project Definition During the Early Phases of a Project.

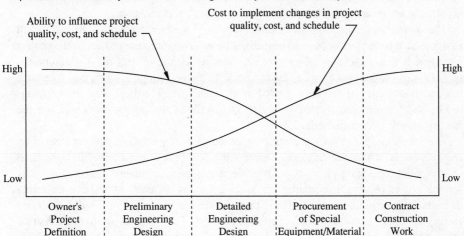

items starts a project in the wrong direction and leads to future problems. Sometimes an owner will contract parts of the study to an outside consulting firm. If an outside firm is utilized, the owner must still be involved to be certain his or her needs are represented.

The thoroughness and completeness of the owner's study has a significant impact on total project cost. An inadequately defined project scope leads to changes during design and/or construction. An incomplete scope leads to costly change orders and, frequently, to claims and disputes which lead to major cost overruns, delays, and other problems. Experienced managers agree the time to achieve savings and reduce changes is in the early life of the project, not at the start of construction. This concept is illustrated in Figure 2-3.

OWNER'S NEEDS AND PROJECT OBJECTIVES

An owner must know his or her needs and objectives before any productive project work can be started. If the owner doesn't know what the project requires, then no one knows what to do. Defining owner needs is the first step in a broad range of preproject activities that lead to scope definition. A project manager cannot form the project team to execute the project without a clear scope definition.

The process of identifying owner needs and objectives requires the involvement of a wide range of people within the owner's organization. This includes top managers and investors, financial personnel, and in particular the people who will use and/or operate the project after it is constructed. The process of identifying owner needs and objectives usually involves numerous activities and discussions. It is important that "what is needed" be separated from "what is wanted." Without constraints of cost and schedule, focus easily shifts from what is needed to what is wanted. This makes a project unaffordable and nonfeasible. Because there are always constraints of cost and schedule, the owner must develop a project definition based upon need. This process involves a an optimization of quantity, quality, cost, and schedule.

The owner's organization must realize that it is their responsibility to resolve all issues related to project needs and objectives before assigning the project to the project manager. It is not the duty of the project manager or the project team to define the owner needs. Vague owner needs lead to project changes, scope growth, cost overruns, rework, and misunderstandings among team members. The best way to determine needs, and information related to needs, is to talk to the people who will use the facility after it is constructed.

The following paragraphs present a hypothetical example of the development of an owner's needs. An owner may define a company goal of centralization of its operations to streamline operating efficiency. To achieve this goal, company management may set the objective of consolidating the service facility of each of its five operating districts into a single location. Thus, there is a need to design and build a service facility that will serve the five operating districts. Key people, from each district, must meet and agree on what is needed in a facility that satisfies the intended usage by each operating district. Negotiations between the people should focus on what is best overall for the company in order to achieve efficiency of operations, which is the company's goal. Compromise is often necessary to separate "what is needed" from "what is wanted." The end result should be a facility that meets the needs of all five districts and can be operated more efficiently than five separate service facilities. For example, agreement may be reached that the owner needs a facility consisting of three buildings: an employee's office building, a warehouse, and a maintenance shop. Additionally, an outside heavy equipment and bulk materials storage area may be needed. These minimum requirements of the facility then initiate the process of project definition and scope.

A part of the owner's needs and objectives study is assessment of the total project budget because management generally will not approve starting the design of a project unless the probable total cost is known. The project budget at this stage of development is based on parameter costs, such as cost per square foot of building or cost per acre of site development. If the anticipated project cost exceeds the amount that management is willing to approve, then it is necessary to reduce the scope of work. For example, the employee's office building and maintenance shop may be retained in the project and the warehouse eliminated. This decision would be made if the warehouse is the lowest priority of the three buildings. Consideration would be given to adding the warehouse at a future date when funds are available, after completion of the site-work, the employee's office building, and the maintenance shop. The project management of this type of project is further discussed in Chapters 4, 5, 6 and Appendix E.

PROJECT SCOPE DEFINITION

Project scope identifies those items and activities that are required to meet the needs of the owner. For example, a project may need three buildings consisting of an employee's office building, a warehouse, and a maintenance shop. In addition, the project may need a crushed aggregate area for storage of heavy equipment and bulk materials. Each of the above items should be defined in further detail, such as number of employees in each building, type and amount of storage needed in the warehouse, type of maintenance required, size and weight of equipment, etc. This type of information is needed by the project manager and team to define the work required to meet the owner's needs and objectives.

The purpose of project scope definition is to provide sufficient information to identify the work to be performed, to allow the design to proceed without significant changes that may adversely affect the project budget and schedule. Just to state that a project consists of three buildings and an outside storage area is not enough information to start the design phase. To assist the owner in this effort, a comprehensive check list of items should be prepared. Table 2-1 is an abbreviated check list for

TABLE 2-1
ABBREVIATED CHECK LIST FOR PROJECT SCOPE DEFINITION OF
A PETROCHEMICAL PROJECT

1. General
    1.1 Size of plant capacity
    1.2 Process units to be included
    1.3 Type of plant feedstock
    1.4 Products to be made, initial and future
    1.5 Should plant be designed for minimum investment
    1.6 Horizontal vs. stacked arrangement of equipment
    1.7 Layout and provisions for future expansion
    1.8 Any special relationships, (e.g. involvements of other companies)

2. Site Information
    2.1 Access to transportation; air, waterway, highway, railway
    2.2 Access to utilities; water, sewer, electrical, fire protection
    2.3 Climate conditions; moisture, temperature, wind
    2.4 Soil conditions; surface, subsurface, bearing capacity
    2.5 Terrain; special precautions for adjacent property
    2.6 Acquisition of land; purchase, lease, expansion potential
    2.7 Space available for construction

3. Buildings
    3.1 Number, types, and size of each
    3.2 Occupancy; number of people, offices, laboratories
    3.3 Intended usage; offices, conferences, storage, equipment
    3.4 Special heating and cooling requirements
    3.5 Quality of finish work and furnishings
    3.6 Landscaping requirements
    3.7 Parking requirements

Regulatory Requirements
    4.1 Permits; construction, operation, environmental, municipal
    4.2 Regulations and codes; local, state, federal
    4.3 Safety; detection systems, fires, emergency power
    4.4 Environmental; air, liquids, solids, wetlands
    4.5 Preservations restrictions

project scope definition of a petrochemical project. The table is provided for illustrative purposes only and does not include all of the items that should be considered. A similar check list should be prepared for other types of projects. Experienced design and construction personnel can provide valuable input to assist an owner in the development of a check list for project scope.

Before design is started, the scope must adequately define deliverables, that is, what will be furnished. Examples of deliverables are: design drawings, specifications, assistance during bidding, construction inspection, record drawings, reimbursable expenses, etc. All of this information must be known before starting design because it affects the project budget and schedule. To accomplish this, the project manager from the design organization must be involved early in the project; and he or she will require input from experienced technical people who represent every aspect of the proposed project.

A realistic budget and schedule cannot be determined for a project without a well-defined scope of work. Thus, the project scope should be developed first, then a project budget and schedule developed that matches the scope. It is the responsibility all project managers to keep all work within the approved scope, and all costs and schedule within approved limits.

There are times when an owner may become excited about the merits of a project and anxious to begin work as soon as possible. This usually occurs when a new product is developed or a government official decides a facility should be built at a particular time or location. The project manager must thoroughly review the project scope and be certain that it is sufficiently well defined before starting work on the project. If this is not done, the project team is forced into defining scope while work is being performed, which leads to frustration and adverse relationships. The simple solution to this problem is to lock in the scope at the beginning of the project, before starting work, to make certain that all parties know the full extent of the required work.

PROJECT STRATEGY

In the early stages of project development the owner must develop the project strategy, a plan to carry out tasks in a timely manner. Project strategy forms the framework for handling the project. It includes the contracting strategy, the roles and responsibilities of the project team, and the schedule for design, procurement, and construction.

Contract strategy identifies the overall organizational structure and the allocation of risk among the contracting parties. In the early stages of project development the owner must decide the work that can be performed by in-house personnel, and the work that must be contracted to outside organizations. The owner may have a large engineering staff that can handle the entire project; design, procurement, and construction. In other cases the owner may only have a limited staff for projects, which requires the assignment of contracts to outside organizations that have the capability to perform the work that is required.

Although a large organization may have the in-house capability, it may not be able to schedule the work when it is needed due to prior commitments. The owner's organization must make a realistic assessment of the work that can be accomplished in-house and an outside firm's capability to perform the work, then evaluate the cost and schedule trade-offs of purchasing outside services.

The type of contract chosen defines the allocation of responsibilities and risks for each party and influences the project schedule. If a fast-track schedule is important in order to obtain an early return on the project investment, then a cost-plus-fee contracting strategy may be desirable. Government projects of an emergency nature are sometimes handled in this manner. If there is ample time to complete the entire design, a traditional design/bid/build approach with a lump-sum contract may be desirable. The owner must evaluate all possibilities, identify the advantages and disadvantages, and consider what best meets his or her needs, objectives, budget constraints, and schedule requirements.

The project strategy includes a schedule for the timing of design, procurement, and construction tasks. The purpose of the owner's schedule is to identify and interface overall project activities: design, procurement, and construction. A workable schedule must be developed that integrates the activities of all parties involved in the project. Any change in the project schedule should be approved by all parties.

PARTNERING

The competitive environment and the rigid requirements of contracts have, at times, caused adverse relationships in the construction industry. Traditionally, contractors and vendors have been selected on a competitive-bid basis to provide construction services, under formal contracts, to meet the requirements specified in the drawings and specifications. A short-time commitment is made for the duration of the project. Thus, contractors and vendors work themselves out of a job.

A relatively new concept called *partnering* is an approach which focuses on making long-term commitments, with mutual goals for all parties involved, to achieve mutual success. The Construction Industry Institute (CII) established a task force on partnering to evaluate the feasibility of this method of doing business in the construction industry. CII publication 17-1, entitled *In Search of Partnering Excellence*, is a report that discusses the research findings on partnering practices. The following paragraphs are excerpts from the report.

Partnering is a business strategy that offers many advantages to the parties involved; however its success depends on the conduct of the parties and their ability to overcome barriers related to doing business differently than the past. Companies agree to share resources in a long-term commitment of trust and shared vision, with an agreement to cooperate to an unusually high degree to achieve separate yet complementary objectives. Partnering is not to be construed as a legal "partnership" with the associated joint liabilities.

The first known partnering relationship in the construction industry was between an oil company and a contractor. The owner approached the contractor and proposed that some of the existing engineering blanket work be accomplished using a new set of relationships and accountabilities. Hence, both agreed to enter into a "partnering relationship" to perform multiple-projects in different locations. The services provided by the contractor included project-execution related services, while the owner provided technical assurance and approved only primary funding documents and scoping documents developed by the contractor. Twenty-five different projects were performed with this relationship.

From a contractual point of view, this first partnering relationship differed from traditional contracts because the bureaucratic procedures were removed and all issues were open for negotiations. In this relationship the owner agreed to carry the financial burden of any risks that might occur during the duration of the relationship. The parties agreed to set performance evaluation criteria for major areas that were important to the projects. An incentive system based on the performance criteria was utilized, including monetary awards given by the owner to the contractor for doing a good job. Contractor incentives to employees included both monetary and non-monetary incentives.

A cultural change is required by all parties in a partnering relationship. The three key elements of any successful partnering relationship are trust, long-term commitment, and shared vision. As these three elements are developed, other sub-elements are achieved and the benefits to all parties are maximized. Both customer and supplier can profit from reduced overhead and workload stability. Competitive advantage is enhanced through improved cost, quality, and schedule. Growth and balance are important to the continual improvement of the partnering agreement. For example, in developing long-term commitment, a partnering agreement may grow from single to multiple projects. Likewise, trust may evolve from competitive bidding through complete disclosure of project costs in a cost-plus relationship. Shared vision can expand to open sharing and mutual development of business objectives.

The CII publication discusses applications of partnering to small businesses and projects, guidelines for selecting partners, and guidelines for implementing a partnering relationship.

QUESTIONS FOR CHAPTER 2—PROJECT INITIATION

1 There are many contractual arrangements for handling a project. This chapter describes the arrangements in four basic forms: design/bid/build, design/build, construction management, and owner/agent. Describe the advantages and disadvantages of each of these arrangements, considering factors such as the cost, time, and level of involvement desired by the owner of the project.

2 Review one of the references at the end of this chapter, or from another reference, and briefly describe the many forms of construction management that is currently being used in the engineering and construction industry.

3 The various phases for development of a project are shown in Figure 2-2. Review each phase and indentify the party that most likely would be involved in performing the work of the phase, and the party whose work will be most influenced by the results of the phase. Identify parties as one of the following: owner, consultant to the owner, designer, construction manager, or construction contractor.

4 A part of the owner's study is defining the requirements of the project. Identify and describe methods that can be used to assist an owner with this important study assuming that the owner does not have the expertise to perform the study.

5 Review the list of references at the end of this chapter and summarize the process of setting project objectives to assure the successful completion of a project.

6 Describe the differences between project objectives and project scope definition. Define the interactive role of the owner and designer in this process to ensure a well-defined understanding between the two parties.

7 Review published articles that describe the concept and process of partnering, and list major differences between partnering and traditional methods of contracting strategies.

REFERENCES

1 Barrie, D. S. and Paulson, B. C., *Professional Construction Management*, 3rd ed., McGraw-Hill, Inc., New York, 1992.

2 Barrie, D. S., *Directions in Managing Construction*, Wiley, New York, 1981.

3 Haltenhoff, C. E., *Construction Management: A State-of-the-Art Update*, Proceedings of the Construction Division, American Society of Civil Engineers, New York, 1986.

4 Hancher, D. E., *In Search of Partnering Excellence*, Publication No. 17-1, Construction Industry Institute, Austin, TX, July, 1991.

5 Laufer, A., *Owner's Project Planning: The Process Approach*, Source Document No. 45, Construction Industry Institute, Austin, TX, March, 1989.

6 *Organizing for Project Success*, Publication No. 12-2, Construction Industry Institute, Austin, TX, February, 1991.

7 Rowings, J. E., *Project Objective Setting*, Publication 12-1, Source Document No. 31, Construction Industry Institute, Austin, TX, April, 1989.

8 *Scope Definition and Control*, Publication No. 6-2, Construction Industry Institute, Austin, TX, July, 1986.

9 *Standard CM Services and Practice*, Construction Management Association of America, Washington, D.C., 1988.

CHAPTER 3

PROJECT BUDGETING

DEVELOPMENT OF PROJECT ESTIMATES

The budget for a project is the maximum amount of money the owner is willing to spend for design and construction to economically justify the project. Estimating is a prerequisite to project budgeting. The preparation of estimates for budgeting is one of the most difficult tasks in project management because it must be done before the work is accomplished. It is a process that involves a series of successive approximations beginning with the owner's feasibility study through design development and construction.

The preparation of cost estimates for budgeting is important to each party because the decision to proceed, at each phase in the project, is based on the estimated cost that was determined in the preceding phase. The owner's organization must determine a realistic maximum and minimum cost of the entire project which includes the cost of design and construction. The designer's organization must determine the cost of performing design tasks and producing the contract documents. It must also determine the probable cost of construction as a part of the design process. The construction contractor's organization must determine the cost of all material, labor, and equipment to build the project on the job-site.

Project budgeting begins with the owner during the study of needs, priorities, and scope. As discussed in Chapter 2, the project budget is derived from scope definition, therefore a special effort should be made early in the development of a project to define the scope as detailed and accurately as possible. The control of project scope growth and cost overruns can be greatly enhanced if the owner obtains the early advice and expertise of experienced design and construction professionals, who have the knowledge of construction costs. All parties must realize that the estimated cost, at any time, is based upon the amount of information that is known about the project when the estimate was prepared. Too often this concept is not fully recognized. A project manager can play an important role as mediator in the early stages of the development of a project by testing, scrutinizing, and identifying the variances that should be applied to an estimate.

The owner's organization must prepare estimates to determine the overall project budget, which includes the approved cost for design and construction. If the scope is not well defined or the owner's organization does not have the expertise to perform such an estimate, the owner can enlist a designer to perform these services on a cost-reimbursable basis. Because this budget is prepared prior to any detailed design work, it should include a reasonable amount of contingency funds to allow some flexibility in decision making during design development.

The designer's organization must prepare a budget based on the estimated costs to provide design services. In addition, as a part of the design process the designer must prepare the estimated construction costs of the various design alternatives that are being evaluated to meet the owner's needs for the project. This is necessary before completion of the contract documents. It is the designer's responsibility to keep design costs and estimated construction costs within the owner's overall approved project budget. This requires extensive cooperation and involvement with the owner because the scope must sometimes be readjusted to meet the owner's approved budget, or the budget must be readjusted to meet the owner's needs. This decision must be made by the owner's organization.

The construction contractor's organization must prepare a bid that is submitted to the owner, based on the estimated costs to build the project in accordance with the contract documents. For competitive-bid projects, the contractor is not obligated to a cost that is within the owner's approved budget because this information is usually not known to the contractor. For negotiated cost-reimbursable projects the contractor's organization works closely with the owner to determine construction alternatives with costs that are within the owner's overall approved budget.

LEVELS OF ACCURACY

A range of accuracy, usually a plus or minus percentage, should be assigned to any estimate by the estimator based on his or her best assessment of the projects true cost. There is no industry standard that has been agreed on regarding the amount of plus or minus percentage that should be applied to an estimate. To discuss this issue it is helpful to divide projects into two general categories: building projects and industrial projects.

Building projects generally have two types of estimates: approximate estimates (sometime called preliminary, conceptual, or budget estimates) and detailed estimates (sometimes called final, definitive, or contractor's estimates). For large owner organizations the approximate estimate is prepared by the owner during the feasibility study of the project's needs, priorities, and scope definition. For small owner organizations it is usually prepared in cooperation with the design organization that is contracted by the owner to design the project and prepare the contract documents. The level of accuracy of the approximate estimate can vary significantly, depending upon the amount of information that is known about the project. With no design work it may range from +40% to −20%. After preliminary design work, it may range from +25% to −10%. On completion of detailed design work it may range from +10% to −5%.

For building projects, the detailed estimate is prepared by the construction contractor from a complete set of contract documents prior to submittal of the bid or formal proposal to the owner. The detailed estimate is important to both the owner and the contractor because it represents the bid price, the amount of money the owner must pay for completion of the project, and the amount of money the contractor will receive for building the project. For a building project that has a complete set of well-defined contract documents and no unusual features, the competitive bidding of numerous contractors will often result in less than a 1% variation in the lowest two bids.

For petrochemical and processing projects, estimating is difficult because of the wide range of variations in the number and sizes of piping, instrumentation, equipment, and other components that are required to process the product that the plant is built to produce. Because of the complexity of the project, estimating is done in stages as the design progresses and more information becomes known about the project.

Although there is no industry agreement, the petrochemical and processing industry generally develops project budget estimates in stages. For example, the feasibility estimate is the first estimate and is usually done within an owner's organization as a part of the feasibility plan. Estimates at this stage are commonly referred to as "order of magnitude" cost estimates. The estimate is prepared as a ratio of costs of previously completed similar projects, contractor quotes, or owner cost records, such as cost per horsepower, cost per barrel of throughput, or cost per pound of finished product. The level of accuracy is usually ±50%.

After the major equipment is identified and process flow sheets are developed, an "equipment factored" estimate can be prepared. This estimate is based on applying factors to in-house priced major equipment in order to compensate for piping, instrumentation, electrical, and other construction costs that are required to complete the cost estimate. The level of accuracy at this stage is usually ±35%.

After completion of piping and instrumentation drawings a preliminary "control estimate" can be developed. The documents and data for this estimate usually include equipment sizing and layout, process flow sheets, piping and instrumentation drawings, building sizes, and a milestone schedule. The level of accuracy is usually ±15%.

The final estimate is performed near the end of engineering design when most of the costs have been identified and is called the definitive estimate, commonly referred to as an Approved for Expenditure estimate, AFE Definitive estimate. It is based on process flow sheets, mechanical flow sheets, equipment layout, isometrics, and building plans. The level of accuracy of an AFE Definitive estimate is usually ±10%.

OWNER'S ESTIMATE FOR BUDGETING

Every project must be shown as economically feasible before it is approved by the owner's management. Economic feasibility is determined by an economic analysis for projects in the private sector or by a benefit/cost ratio for projects in the government sector. To perform an economic analysis an owner's estimate must be prepared.

Estimating costs during the inception of a project by the owner, prior to any design, is difficult because only limited detailed information is known about the project. However, this cost estimate is important because it is used to set the maximum project budget that will be approved for design and construction. At this stage of project development the only known information is the number of units or size of the project, such as number of square feet of building area, number of cars in a parking garage, number of miles of 345-KV transmission line, or number of barrels of crude oil processed per day. At some point in time an estimate has to be frozen and converted to a project budget.

Preparation of the owner's estimate requires knowledge and experience of the work required to complete the project. Cost information from professionals who are knowledgeable about design and construction is essential. Cost information for preparation of the owner's budget is usually derived from one of two sources: cost records from previous projects of similar type and size, or pricing manuals that are published annually by several organizations.

For buildings, public works, and heavy construction projects, the R. S. Means *Cost Guide* is commonly used. The Richardson's Manual for construction estimating is a common reference for petrochemical and processing projects. These pricing manuals provide costs per unit for various types of projects, such as cost per square foot of building area for offices, warehouses, maintenance buildings, etc. The costs are derived from previous projects that have been completed at numerous geographic locations. Figure 3-1 illustrates the type of information that is available for several types of buildings. It shows the low, average, and high cost per square foot, based on the level of quality. The budget for a proposed project can be calculated by multiplying the cost per square foot by the total square feet in the project. The cost of land, permits, and design fees should be added to the calculated cost of construction. A reasonable percentage multiplier should also be applied for contingency since the design is not prepared for the project during the owner's budgeting process. Adjustments for time and location should also be made as discussed in the following paragraphs.

The other source of cost information is company records from previous projects. Although the total cost of previously completed projects will vary between projects, unit costs can be calculated to forecast the cost of future projects. The term of "weighting" is commonly used to refer to the procedure of analyzing historical cost data to determine a unit cost for forecasting future project costs. A unit cost should be developed that emphasizes the average value, yet accounts for extreme maximum and minimum values. Equation 3.1 can be used for weighting cost data from previous projects:

$$UC = \frac{A + 4B + C}{6} \qquad \text{(Eq 3.1)}$$

where UC = forecast unit cost
  A = minimum unit cost of previous projects
  B = average unit cost of previous projects
  C = maximum unit cost of previous projects

FIGURE 3-1
Illustrative Examples of Cost per-Square-Foot Information Available from Pricing Manuals.

Component	Office Buildings			Shopping Centers		
	Low $/SF	Average $/SF	High $/SF	Low $/SF	Average $/SF	High $/SF
Foundation	3.10	3.55	3.90	0.70	0.90	0.95
Floors on Grade	2.45	2.80	3.15	3.10	3.15	3.20
Superstructure	11.70	14.95	16.50	8.60	8.40	12.85
Roofing	0.15	0.25	0.15	1.90	2.15	2.05
Exterior Walls	3.85	8.65	10.60	2.20	2.80	3.30
Partitions	3.40	4.70	5.75	2.05	2.30	3.10
Wall Finishes	1.85	3.35	4.10	0.60	1.65	1.65
Floor Finishes	1.60	3.45	4.20	1.90	2.25	2.70
Ceiling Finishes	1.20	2.50	3.05	1.60	2.90	2.90
Conveying Systems	4.35	5.90	6.70	0.90	1.15	1.40
Specialties	0.50	0.70	2.15	0.85	0.85	2.35
Fixed Equipment	0.80	2.50	3.05	0.90	1.05	1.15
Heat/Vent/Air Cond.	6.95	8.40	9.85	2.45	3.50	3.70
Plumbing	2.75	3.25	3.95	3.50	3.40	3.60
Electrical	3.60	4.20	5.10	3.30	4.70	4.85
	$48.25	$69.15	$82.20	$34.55	$41.15	$49.75

Component	Secondary Schools			General Hospitals		
	Low $/SF	Average $/SF	High $/SF	Low $/SF	Average $/SF	High $/SF
Foundation	1.20	1.50	1.65	3.70	4.15	4.30
Floors on Grade	3.20	3.55	3.65	0.25	0.35	0.40
Superstructure	9.50	9.95	10.50	14.40	16.10	16.45
Roofing	1.45	1.65	1.65	2.75	3.20	3.35
Exterior Walls	3.25	4.50	4.90	13.50	16.10	16.20
Partitions	5.15	5.30	5.20	6.10	9.55	15.90
Wall Finishes	2.65	2.75	3.15	5.70	6.90	7.15
Floor Finishes	2.70	3.20	3.20	2.20	2.40	2.60
Ceiling Finishes	2.80	2.95	2.85	1.80	1.90	2.30
Conveying Systems	0.00	0.00	0.00	10.95	11.30	12.60
Specialties	1.50	1.55	1.60	2.60	2.80	2.95
Fixed Equipment	2.50	2.70	3.65	4.40	4.55	4.90
Heat/Vent/Air Cond.	7.85	8.45	8.80	18.30	22.10	23.20
Plumbing	4.40	4.85	5.60	7.60	9.25	10.60
Electrical	8.90	9.70	10.05	11.35	15.15	15.75
	$57.05	$62.60	$66.45	$105.60	$125.80	$138.65

Example 3-1 illustrates the weighting procedure. The procedure can be applied to other types of projects and their parameters. Examples are apartment units, motel rooms, miles of electric transmission line, barrels of crude oil processed per day, square yards of pavement, etc.

Example 3-1

Cost information from eight previously completed parking garage projects is shown below.

Project	Cost	No. Cars	Unit Cost	
1	$466,560	150	$3,110	
2	290,304	80	3,629	
3	525,096	120	4,376	← highest value
4	349,920	90	3,888	
5	259,320	60	4,322	
6	657,206	220	2,987	← lowest value
7	291,718	70	4,167	
8	711,414	180	3,952	

Total = $30,431

Average cost per car = $3,804 ← average value

From Eq 3.1 the forecast unit cost can be calculated as:

$$UC = \frac{\$2,987 + 4(\$3,804) + \$4,376}{6} = \$3,763/\text{car}$$

For a project with 135 cars the estimated cost can be calculated as:

$$135 \text{ cars @ } \$3,763 = \$508,005$$

It is necessary to adjust the cost information from previously completed projects for differences in size, time and location. The previous example illustrates adjustment relative to size. Time adjustments represent variation in costs due to inflation, deflation, interest rates, etc. Location adjustments represent variation in costs between locations due to geographical differences in costs of materials, equipment, and labor.

An index can be used to adjust previous cost information for use in preparation of the owner's estimate. Various organizations publish indices that show economic trends. The *Engineering News Record* (ENR) annually publishes indices of construction costs for both time and location. Example 3-2 illustrates the combination of adjustments of cost estimates for size, time, and location. *Estimating Construction Costs*, 4th Edition, published by McGraw-Hill presents a comprehensive discussion of estimating project costs.

Example 3-2

Use the time and location indices below to calculate the forecast cost for a building with 62,700 SF of floor area. The building is to be constructed 3 years from now in city B. A similar type building that cost $2,197,540 and contained 38,500 SF was completed 2 years ago in city D.

Year	Index	Location	Index
3 yr ago	358	City A	1025
2 yr ago	359	City B	1170
1 yr ago	367	City C	1260
Current year	378	City D	1240

An equivalent compound interest can be calculated based on the change in the cost index during the 3-yr period:

$$\frac{378}{358} = (1+i)^3 \longrightarrow i = 1.83\%$$

Estimated Cost	Previous Cost	Time Adjustment	Location Adjustment	Size Adjustment
"	= $2,197,540 ×	$(1+.0183)^5$ ×	(1170/1240) ×	(62,700/38,500)
"	= $2,197,540 ×	1.095 ×	0.944 ×	1.629
"	= $3,700,360			

ECONOMIC FEASIBILITY STUDY

Regardless of its size or type, a project must be economically feasible. There are at least two ways to determine economic feasibility, depending on whether the owner is in the private sector or government sector. For a private project the economic feasibility can be determined by an economic analysis of the monetary return on the investment to build the project. For a government project the economic feasibility for public projects is usually determined by a benefit/cost ratio.

There are three methods that are commonly used by the private sector to evaluate the monetary return on a potential investment: capital recovery, pay back period, and rate of return. Each method uses the fundamental equations of the time value of money. There are numerous books that have been published that describe the development and use of these equations for economic analysis. For convenience, each of the six basic equations are shown in equations 3.2–3.7, following.

Fundamental Equations of Time Value of Money

$P =$ Present Worth

$F =$ Future Sum

$A =$ Equal Payment Series

$i =$ Annual Interest Rate

$n =$ Study Period (years)

Single Payment Series:

Compound Amount $\qquad F = P(1 + i)^n = P(\overset{F/P i-n}{\quad})$ $\qquad$ Eq. 3.2

Present Worth $\qquad P = F\dfrac{1}{(1 + i)^n} = F(\overset{P/F i-n}{\quad})$ $\qquad$ Eq. 3.3

Equal Payment Series:

Compound Amount $\qquad F = A\left[\dfrac{(1 + i)^n - 1}{i}\right] = A(\overset{F/A i-n}{\quad})$ $\qquad$ Eq. 3.4

Sinking Fund $\qquad A = F\left[\dfrac{i}{(1 + i)^n - 1}\right] = F(\overset{A/F i-n}{\quad})$ $\qquad$ Eq. 3.5

Present Worth $\qquad P = A\left[\dfrac{(1 + i)^n - 1}{i(1 + i)^n}\right] = A(\overset{P/A i-n}{\quad})$ $\qquad$ Eq. 3.6

Capital Recovery $\qquad A = P\left[\dfrac{i(1 + i)^n}{(1 + i)^n - 1}\right] = P(\overset{A/P i-n}{\quad})$ $\qquad$ Eq. 3.7

The factor designation at the right of the preceding interest equations represents an abbreviated form of the equation illustrated in the following:

$(\overset{F/P i-n}{\quad})$ means find the Future Sum, F, from a known Present Worth, P, and Interest Rate i during a Study Period of n.

In general, an economic analysis involves the process of solving for one of the variables. For example, capital recovery solves for A, pay back period solves for n, and rate of return solves for i. A more complex analysis using one or more of the basic six equations is required when multiple sums of money are distributed over the study period, or when tax advantages are included.

The capital recovery method evaluates the amount of annual money, A, that must be obtained throughout the study life, n, of a project in order to obtain a recovery on the original capital investment, P. A simple illustration is given in Example 3-3. There may be other considerations that should be evaluated, such as tax advantages, nonuniform generation of revenue, and the disposal of the facility after its useful life. The pay back period method evaluates the number of years, n, that a project must be operated in order to obtain an interest rate, i, for a given investment, P, with an annual generated income of, A. This method is illustrated in Example 3-4. A rate of return analysis evaluates the interest rate, i, that equates the initial investment, P, to the yearly net cash flow as illustrated in Example 3-5. A trial and error solution is required in this example because the annual payments are not uniform. All of these examples are simple illustrations of the methods that can be used to determine the economic feasibility of a project.

Example 3-3

This example illustrates the capital recovery method for determining economic feasibility. Suppose the feasibility estimate for a project is $7.0M with an expected operating life of 12 years. Annual maintenance and operating expenses are forecast as $560K per year. Using a 10% interest rate, what net annual income must be received to recover the capital investment of the project?

$$A = P\left[\frac{i(1+i)^n}{(1+i)^n - 1}\right] + \$0.56M$$

$$= \$7.0M\left[\frac{0.10(1+0.10)^{12}}{(1+0.10)^{12} - 1}\right] + \$0.56M$$

$$= \$1.588M \text{ per year}$$

If the project can be built for $7.0M, operated for $560K per year, and earn $1.5876M per year the project is economically feasible, neglecting any tax advantages. If the project can be built for less than $7.0M, or can be built to operate more efficiently than $560K per year, it is even more economically attractive.

Example 3-4

This example illustrates the pay back period method for determining the economic feasibility of a project. The initial investment for a project is $18.0M. A net annual profit of $3.5M is anticipated. Using a 15% desired rate of return on the investment, what is the pay back period for the project.

$$P = A\left[\frac{(1+i)^n - 1}{i(1+i)^n}\right]$$

$$\$18.0M = \$3.5M\left[\frac{(1+0.15)^n - 1}{0.15(1+0.15)^n}\right]$$

$$n = 10.5 \text{ years}$$

Example 3-5

This example illustrates the rate-of-return method for determining the economic feasibility of a project. An initial project investment of $1.05M is being considered for a 5 year study period. It is anticipated the project will be sold after the 5 year period for $560K. Determine the rate of return with the anticipated net profit shown below.

End of Year	Net Profit ($1,000)
0	0
1	−350
2	−120
3	+420
4	+735
5	+680

Using Equation 3-2 to transfer the costs from each year to an equivalent present worth:

Try $i = 15\%$

$$P = [-\$350\overset{P/F15-1}{(0.8695)} - \$120\overset{P/F15-2}{(0.7562)} + \$420\overset{P/F15-3}{(0.6575)} + \$735\overset{P/F15-4}{(0.5718)}$$

$$+ \$680\overset{P/F15-5}{(0.4972)} + \$560\overset{P/F15-5}{(0.4972)}] \times 1000$$

$1.05M > \$0.92M$, therefore try a lower rate of return

Try $i = 10\%$

$$P = [-\$350\overset{P/F10-1}{(0.9090)} - \$120\overset{P/F10-2}{(0.8264)} + \$420\overset{P/F10-3}{(0.7513)} + \$735\overset{P/F10-4}{(0.6830)}$$

$$+ \$680\overset{P/F10-5}{(0.6209)} + \$560\overset{P/F10-5}{(0.6209)}] \times 1000$$

$1.05M < \$1.17M$, therefore try a higher rate of return

Try $i = 12\%$

$$P = [-\$350\overset{P/F12-1}{(0.8929)} - \$120\overset{P/F12-2}{(0.7972)} + \$420\overset{P/F12-3}{(0.7118)} + \$735\overset{P/F12-4}{(0.6355)}$$

$$+ \$680\overset{P/F12-5}{(0.5674)} + \$560\overset{P/F12-5}{(0.5674)}] \times 1000$$

$1.05M \doteq \$1.06M$, therefore the rate of return is slightly over 12%.

It is important for the project manager and his or her team to realize that an owner's economic study, similar to one of those illustrated, is used by the owner to approve the project budget, which is the capital investment, P. When a project exceeds its budget, then the economic justification that was used by the owner to proceed with the project is impaired.

A popular method for deciding on the economic justification of a public project is to compute the benefit/cost ratio, which is simply the ratio of the benefits to the public divided by the cost to the government. If the ratio is 1, the equivalent benefits and equivalent costs are equal. This represents the minimum justification for an expenditure by a public agency. Generally, the first step is to determine the benefits that can be derived from a project. This is in contrast to the consideration of profitability as a first step in evaluating the merits of a private enterprise. The second step in evaluating a public project involves an analysis of cost to the governmental agency. When a public project is being considered, the question is: Will this project result in the greatest possible enhancement of the general welfare in terms of economic, social, environmental, or other factors that serve the needs of the general public? The measurement of benefits is sometimes difficult because they cannot always be expressed in dollars.

Many government agencies have a list of projects that are waiting for approval, but for which funds are not yet available. The decision as to which project to approve may be based upon the amount of money that is allocated in a fiscal year, rather than economic feasibility.

DESIGN BUDGETS

The design organization has a difficult task of estimating the cost of providing design services and/or producing contract documents for the project before the design and construction phases begin. For many projects the magnitude of work that is required by the designer can not be fully anticipated, because design is a creative process that involves the evaluation of numerous alternatives. The evaluation of design alternatives is a necessary part of the design process required to select the best design that satisfies the owner's need for the project.

Compensation for design services is usually by one of the following methods: lump-sum, salary cost times a multiplier, cost plus a fixed payment, or percent of construction. The method that is used depends on the accuracy of the scope definition that is provided to the design organization.

For projects that have a well-defined scope with no unusual features, and are similar to projects that a designer has handled in the past, a lump-sum design contract is commonly used. Preparation of the design budget can be developed by defining tasks, and grouping of tasks, in a work breakdown structure. The development of a project work breakdown structure and design work packages is discussed in Chapter 4. A design work package, shown in Figure 4-7, can, then be prepared for each task. Based upon the past experience of the designer with similar projects, the estimated labor-hours of design calculations, number of drawings, labor-hours per drawing, travel, and other expenses can be estimated for each task. The total cost for design can be calculated by adding the cost of all design work packages. The final design budget is usually broken down by discipline with the labor-hours based on the number of drawings to be produced. Figure 3-2 illustrates the summary of a design engineering budget. Figure 3-3 shows an example of time distribution for design calculations as well as the development of drawings and specifications for a project.

The salary cost times a multiplier method is used for projects when it is difficult to accurately define the scope of work at the time the designer is retained for the project. For these types of projects, preliminary services, such as process studies, development of alternate layout plans, or other services are required to establish information that is needed for the final design. The designer provides a fee schedule to the owner that lists the classification and salary costs of all personnel, and a rate schedule for all other costs that are directly chargeable to the project. Work is then performed based on the actual time expended in the design effort. A multiplier, usually within a range from 2.0 to 3.0, is applied to direct salary costs which compensate the design organization for overhead, plus a reasonable margin for contingencies and profit. A larger multiplier may be used for unusual projects that require special expertise, or for projects of short duration or small size. Travel, subsistence, supplies, and other direct non-salary expenses are generally reimbursed at actual costs, plus a 10% to 15% service charge.

The cost plus a fixed payment method is used for projects that have a general description or statement of the scope of contemplated work, such as the number, size and character of buildings or other facilities, the extent of utilities, and other items. The design organization is reimbursed for the actual cost of all salaries, services, and

FIGURE 3-2
Illustrative design engineering budget.

DATE:____/____/____

PROJECT BUDGET FORM

Project Name

Dept. Number	Department	HOURS							DOLLARS
		ADMIN	MTGS	SHED	SPECS	CALCS	DWGS	TOTAL	
0100	Project Management							12,000	$840,000
		3,000	2,400	900				6,300	
		1,500	1,200	3,000				5,700	
0200	Architecture		350	100	350	250	800	1,850	$111,000
0300	Mechanical		350		480	360	1,760	2,950	$177,000
0400	Electrical		350		2,100	3,200	7,450	13,100	$786,000
0500	Structural							26,360	$1,581,600
	Project Engineer	2,500	750					3,250	
	CADDS Coord.		160				2,800	2,960	
	Department		550		1,300	6,700	11,600	20,150	
0600	Environmental	400						400	$28,000
0700	Civil							7,140	$428,400
	Turb./Gen. Spec				340			340	
	Department		190	100	1,310	2,000	3,200	6,800	
0800	CADDS		100	100			1,000	1,200	$60,000
0900	Clerical	7,000	400		600			8,000	$200,000
1000	Document Control	1,000			200		800	2,000	$50,000
1100	Reproduction				200		800	1,000	$26,000
1200	Project Control	1,000	200	500				1,700	$102,000
1300	Management	400						400	$36,000
1400	Subcontractor A	100	100		86	114	200	600	$60,000
1500	Subcontractor B	50	100		50		200	400	$40,000
1600	Record Drawings					1,000	2,000	3,000	$150,000
1700	Support Buildings		100		400	500	1,500	2,500	$150,000
WORK–HOUR SUBTOTAL		16,950	7,300	4,700	7,416	14,124	34,110	84,600	$4,826,000

Task #	Description								
1800	Contingency								$500,000
1900	General Expenses								$24,000
2000	Travel								$100,000
2100	Office Budget								$50,000
EXPENSES SUBTOTAL									$674,000
TOTAL									$5,500,000

FIGURE 3-3
Example of time distribution for design calculations, drawings, and specifications.

DRAWINGS

	50% Drawings	20% Drawing Review	20% Drawing Submittals	10% Final Record	Total
Architecture	400	160	160	80	800
Mechanical	880	352	352	176	1,760
Electrical	3,725	1,490	1,490	745	7,450
Structural	5,800	2,320	2,320	1,160	11,600
Civil	1,600	640	640	320	3,200
	12,405	4,962	4,962	2,481	24,810

CALCULATIONS

	70% Drawings	20% Drawing Review	10% Drawing Submittals	Total
Architecture	175	50	25	250
Mechanical	252	72	36	360
Electrical	2,240	640	320	3,200
Structural	4,690	1,340	670	6,700
Civil	1,400	400	200	2,000
	8,757	2,502	1,251	12,510

DRAWINGS

	25% Drawings	25% Drawing Review	25% Drawing Submittals	25% Final Record	Total
Reproduction	200	200	200	200	800
Doc. Control	200	200	200	200	800
	400	400	400	400	1,600

SPECIFICATIONS

	80% Specs	20% Review	Total
Architecture	280	70	350
Mechanical	384	96	480
Electrical	1,680	420	2,100
Structural	1,040	260	1,300
Civil	1,048	262	1,310
Turbine/Gen.	272	68	340
Consultants	108	28	136
Clerical	480	120	600
	5,292	1,324	6,616

SPECIFICATIONS

	50% Specs	50% Review	Total
Reproduction	100	100	200
Doc. Control	100	100	200
	200	200	400

supplies plus a fixed fee that is agreed on between the designer and owner. The fixed fee usually varies from 10% for large projects to 25% for small projects that are short in duration.

Design work may also be compensated based on a percentage of the construction cost of a project, although this method is not as common today as it was in the past. Generally the percentage is on a sliding scale that decreases as the construction cost increases. The percentage also varies depending on the level of design services that are provided, such as design only, design and preparation of drawings, or full design services which include design, preparation of drawings, and observation during construction. The percentage generally will range from 5% to 12% of the anticipated construction cost.

The percentage data given in the above paragraphs are not fixed, nor should the ranges be considered as absolute maximums or minimums. Instead, it is presented as a guide to establish the approximate costs that may be incurred for the design of a project.

CONTRACTOR'S BID

Most of the cost of a project is expended during the construction phase when the contractor must supervise large work forces who operate equipment, procure materials, and physically build the project. The cost of construction is determined by the contractor's bid that has been accepted by the owner before starting the construction process. Depending on the completeness of the design and the amount of risk that is shared between the owner and contractor, there are many methods that have been developed to compensate the construction contractor.

The pricing format for providing construction services can be divided into two general categories: fixed price and cost reimbursable. Fixed price contracts usually are classified as lump-sum, unit-price, or a combination of lump-sum and unit-price. Cost reimbursable contracts can be classified as cost-plus a fixed fee or cost-plus a percentage. An incentive is often built into cost reimbursable contracts to control the total cost of a project. Examples of incentives are "target price" and "guaranteed maximum price."

For projects with a complete set of plans and specifications that have been prepared prior to construction, the contractor can prepare a detailed estimate for the purpose of submitting a lump-sum bid on the project. Only one total-cost figure is quoted to the owner, and this figure represents the amount the owner will pay to the contractor for the completed project, unless there are revisions in the plans or specifications. The contractor's bid is prepared from a detailed estimate of the cost of providing materials, labor, equipment, subcontract work, overhead, and profit.

The preparation of lump-sum detailed estimates generally follows a systematic procedure that has been developed by the contractor for his or her unique construction operations. Building contractors organize their estimates in a format that closely follows The Construction Specification Institute's (CSI) masterformat. The CSI masterformat organizes project information into 16 major divisions and is recognized as the industry standard for building construction. Appendix D provides a listing of the

CSI masterformat titles and numbers. A typical summary of an estimate of a building construction project is shown in Figure 3-4. Each major division is subdivided into smaller items of work referred to as either broadscope, medium scope, and narrow scope. For example, the work required for division 2, site-work, is subdivided into clearing, excavation, compaction, etc. as illustrated in Figure 3-5.

Heavy engineering construction contractors generally organize their estimates in a work breakdown structure (WBS) that is unique to the project to be constructed. An example of the WBS organization of an estimate for an electric power construction project is illustrated in Figures 3-6 to 3-8. Each group is subdivided into divisions of the work required to construct the group; likewise, each division of that work is subdivided into the components shown in Figures 3-7 and 3-8.

The unit-price bid is similar to the lump-sum bid, except that the contractor submits a cost per unit of work in place, such as a cost per cubic yard of concrete. The contract documents define the units the owner will pay the contractor. The final cost is determined by multiplying the bid cost per unit by the actual quantity of work that is installed by the contractor. Thus, the price that the owner will pay to the contractor is not determined until the project has been completed, when the actual quantities are known.

FIGURE 3-4
Example of building construction project bid summary using the CSI organization of work.

Item	Division	Material	Labor	Subcontract	Total
1	General requirement	$ 16,435.00	$ 36,355.00	$ 4,882.00	$ 57,672.00
2	Site-work	15,070.00	20,123.00	146,186.00	181,389.00
3	Concrete	97,176.00	51,524.00	0.00	148,700.00
4	Masonry	0.00	0.00	212,724.00	212,724.00
5	Metals	212,724.00	59,321.00	0.00	272,045.00
6	Woods and plastics	38,753.00	10,496.00	4,908.00	54,157.00
7	Thermal and moisture	0.00	0.00	138,072.00	138.072.00
8	Doors and windows	36,821.00	32,115.00	0.00	68,936.00
9	Finishes	172,587.00	187,922.00	0.00	360,509.00
10	Specialties	15,748.00	11,104.00	9,525.00	36,377.00
11	Equipment	0.00	0.00	45,729.00	45,729.00
12	Furnishings	0.00	0.00	0.00	0.00
13	Special construction	0.00	0.00	0.00	0.00
14	Conveying systems	0.00	0.00	0.00	0.00
15	Mechanical	0.00	0.00	641,673.00	641,673.00
16	Electrical	0.00	0.00	354,661.00	354,661.00
	Total direct costs	$605,314.00	$408,960.00	$1,558,360.00	$2,572,644.00
	Material tax (5%)	30,266.00			2,602,910.00
	Labor tax (18%)		73,613.00		2,676,523.00
	Contingency (2%)			53,530.00	2,730,053.00
	Bonds/Insurance			34,091.00	2,764,144.00
	Profit (10%)			276,414.00	3,040,558.00

Bid price = $3,040,558.00

FIGURE 3-5
Division 2 estimate for site-work.

Cost code	Description	Quantity	Material	Labor	Subcontract	Total
2110	Clearing	L.S.	$ 0.00	$ 0.00	$ 3,694.00	$ 3,694.00
2220	Excavation	8,800 yd³	0.00	11,880.00	9,416.00	21,296.00
2250	Compaction	950 yd³	0.00	2,223.00	722.00	2,945.00
2294	Handwork	500 yd²	0.00	1,750.00	0.00	1,750.00
2281	Termite control	L.S.	0.00	0.00	3,475.00	3,475.00
2372	Drilled piers	1,632 lin ft	14,580.00	2,800.00	14,525.00	31,904.00
2411	Foundation drains	14 ea.	490.00	1,470.00	0.00	1,960.00
2480	Landscape	L.S.	0.00	0.00	8,722.00	8,722.00
2515	Paving	4,850 yd²	0.00	0.00	105,633.00	105,633.00
			$15,070.00	$20,123.00	$146,186.00	$181,389.00

FIGURE 3-6
Example of electric power construction bid summary using the WBS organization of work[†].
Group-level report

No.	Group	Material	Labor and equipment	Subcontract	Total
1100	Switch station	$1,257,295.00	$ 323,521.00	$3,548,343.00	$ 5,128,167.00
2100	Transmission line A	3,381,625.00	1,260,837.00	0.00	4,641,462.00
2300	Transmission line B	1,744,395.00	0.00	614,740.00	2,358,135.00
3100	Substation at spring creek	572,874.00	116,403.00	1,860,355.00	2,549,632.00
4200	Distribution line A	403,297.00	54,273.00	215,040.00	672,610.00
4400	Distribution line B	227,599.00	98,675.00	102,387.00	427,661.00
4500	Distribution line C	398,463.00	21,498.00	113,547.00	532,508.00
		$7,985,548.00	$1,872,215.00	$6,453,412.00	$16,311,175.00

[†] For large projects the costs are sometimes rounded to the nearest $100 or $1,000. Figures 3-6 to 3-8 show full dollars to illustrate the transfer of costs among the component, division, and group levels of an estimate.

Cost reimbursable contracts for construction may be used for several reasons; to start construction at the earliest possible date, to allow the owner to make changes in the scope of work without substantial modifications in the contract, or because the project is unique with features that prevent a reasonable approximation of the actual cost of construction. The estimate for this type of project is usually prepared by the

FIGURE 3-7
Example of electric power construction estimate using the WBS organization of work.
Division-level report for transmission line A

Cost item	Description	Material	Labor	Equipment	Total
2100	TRANSMISISON LINE A				
2210	Fabrication of steel towers	$ 692,775.00	$ 0.00	$ 0.00	$ 692,775.00
2370	Tower foundations	83,262.00	62,126.00	71,210.00	216,598.00
2570	Erection of steel towers	0.00	144,141.00	382,998.00	527,139.00
2620	Insulators and conductors	2,605,588.00	183,163.00	274,744.00	3,063,495.00
2650	Shield wire installation	0.00	78,164.00	63,291.00	141,455.00
	Total for 2100	$3,381,625.00	$467,594.00	$792,243.00	$4,641,462.00

FIGURE 3-8
Example of electric power construction estimate using the WBS organization of work.
Component-level report for tower foundations

Cost item	Description	Quantity	Material	Labor	Equipment	Total
2370	TOWER FOUNDATIONS					
2372	Drilling foundations	4,196 lin ft	$ 0.00	$25,428.00	$44,897.00	$ 70,325.00
2374	Reinforcing steel	37.5 tons	28,951.00	22,050.00	15,376.00	66,377.00
2376	Foundation concrete	870 yd^3	53,306.00	13,831.00	10,143.00	77,280.00
2378	Stub angles	3,142 lb	1,005.00	817.00	794.00	2,616.00
	Total for 2370		$83,262.00	$62,126.00	$71,210.00	$216,598.00

contractor as an approximate estimate. The owner and contractor agree on a cost rate for all labor, equipment, and other services that may be charged to the project by the contractor. The contractor is reimbursed for all costs that are accrued during the construction phase of the project plus a percentage of the costs or a fixed fee.

To maintain some degree of control over the total cost of a project, an incentive is often placed on cost reimbursable contracts. For example, the contract may be awarded on a cost plus basis with a guaranteed maximum price, commonly called a GMP contract. For a GMP contract, the owner and contractor agree on a guaranteed maximum price prior to the start of construction. They also agree on the distribution of costs that each will incur if the final cost is above or below the guaranteed maximum price. Then, during construction, the contractor is reimbursed for actual costs plus a fixed fee or percentage of actual costs. If the actual final cost is above or below the guaranteed maximum price, then the predetermined distribution of the difference of costs is distributed between the owner and contractor. To illustrate, if the cost exceeds the guaranteed maximum price, the contractor may pay 70% of the cost and the owner pays 30% of the cost. If the cost is less than the guaranteed maximum price, the contractor receives 60% of the reduced costs and the owner receives 40%.

QUESTIONS FOR CHAPTER 3—PROJECT BUDGETING

1 Usually each of the three principal parties (the owner, designer, and contractor) prepares a cost estimate at different times during the life of a project. Describe the purpose of each estimate and the impact the estimate may have on the other two parties.

2 Why is it important to define the range of accuracy, in percentage, that should be applied to any estimate? Who should set this range and who should be informed of the selected range?

3 Prepare a cost estimate for the construction of a small, high quality, office building that contains 18,525 square feet of floor area. Use the data in Table 3-1 to prepare the estimate. Assume the cost of design for the project is 12% of construction, and a site-work cost of $80,000. What range of percentage of this cost would you recommend to define the level of accuracy?

4 Use the time and location indices in Example 3-2 to estimate the cost of a building that contains 64,500 square feet of floor area. The building is to be constructed two years from now in city A. The cost of a similar type building that contains 95,000 square feet was completed last year in city C for a cost of $6,507,400.

5 During the feasibility study of a project, the initial estimated cost for design and construction is $3.7 million. It is anticipated that the cost to maintain and operate the facility after completion of construction will be $250,000 per year. Assuming the owner must obtain a return on the initial investment of 15%, what net annual income must be received to economically justify the project.

6 The cost estimate of a project is $3.5 million. Annual costs for maintaining and operating the facility are forecast as $250,000 per year. After 8 years, it is anticipated the facility will be sold for $2.0 million. If the owner requires a 15% return on his or her investment, what net annual income must be received to recover the capital investment of the project?

7 The initial investment for a project is $4.7 million. A net annual profit of $1.5 million is anticipated. Using a 12% desired rate of return on the investment, what is the pay back period for the project?

REFERENCES

1 Ahuja, H. N. and Campbell, W. J., *Estimating: From Concept to Completion*, Prentice-Hall, Englewood Cliffs, NJ, 1987.

2 *Building Estimator's Reference Book*, The Frank R. Walker Company, Chicago.

3 *Consulting Engineering A Guide for the Engagement of Engineering Services*, Manual No. 45, American Society of Civil Engineers, New York, 1988.

4 *Current Practice in Cost Estimating and Cost Control*, Conference Proceedings, American Society of Civil Engineers, New York, 1983.

5 *Means Cost Guide*, Robert Snow Means Company, Duxbury, MA, published annually.

6 Neil, J. M., *Construction Cost Estimating for Project Control*, Prentice-Hall, Englewood Cliffs, NJ, 1982.

7 Parker, A. D., Barrie, D. S., and Snyder, R. N., *Planning and Estimating Heavy Construction*, McGraw-Hill Inc., New York, 1984.

8 Peurifoy, R. L. and Oberlender, G. D., *Estimating Construction Costs*, 4th ed., McGraw-Hill Inc., New York, 1989.

9 "The Richardson Rapid System" Process Plant Construction Estimating Standards, Richardson's Engineering Services, Inc., Mesa, AZ, published annually.

10 White, J. A, Agee, M. H., and Case, K. E., *Principles of Engineering Economic Analysis*, Wiley, New York, 1989.

CHAPTER 4

DEVELOPMENT
OF WORK PLAN

PROJECT MANAGER'S INITIAL REVIEW

The discussion of developing the project work plan in this chapter is based on handling the project in its early stage of development, prior to design. It is presented from this perspective because the ability to influence the overall quality, cost, and schedule of a project can best be achieved during design. Most books and articles discuss project management during the construction phase, after design is completed. At this time in the life of a project the scope of work is fully defined, the budget is fixed, and the completion date is firm. It is then too late to make any significant adjustments in the project to improve quality, cost, or schedule to benefit the owner.

When a project manager is assigned to a project, his or her first duty is to gather all of the background material that has been prepared by the sponsoring organization. This includes the owner's study and the contract that has been signed by the project manager's organization. These documents must be thoroughly reviewed to be certain that there is a well-defined scope, an approved budget, and a schedule that shows major milestones for the project, in particular the required completion date.

The purpose of this initial review process is to become familiar with the owner's objectives, the overall project needs, and to identify any additional information that may be needed to begin the process of developing a work plan to manage the project. To organize the review process it is best to divide the questions into the three categories that define a project: scope, budget, and schedule. To guide this initial review, the project manager should continually ask questions like those shown in Table 4-1.

TABLE 4-1
GUIDELINES FOR PROJECT MANAGER'S INITIAL
PROJECT REVIEW

Scope
1. What is missing?
2. Does it seem reasonable?
3. What is the best way to do this?
4. What additional information is needed?
5. What technical expertise is needed?
6. How is the best way to handle construction?
7. What is the owner's expected level of quality?
8. What codes and regulations are applicable?

Budget
1. Does the budget seem reasonable?
2. How was the budget determined?
3. Who prepared the budget?
4. When was the budget prepared?
5. Should any portion of the budget be re-checked?
6. Has the budget been adjusted for time & location?

Schedule
1. Does the schedule seem reasonable?
2. How was the schedule determined?
3. When was the schedule prepared?
4. Who prepared the schedule?
5. How firm is the completion date?
6. Are there penalties or bonuses?

OWNER'S ORIENTATION

After the project manager has performed the initial project review and become familiar with the project, the owner's authorized representative should be identified and a meeting scheduled to set up the necessary coordination arrangements with the owner. The owner's representative serves two roles in a project: as a participant in providing information and clarifying project requirements, and as a reviewer and approver of all team decisions. The owner must be considered an integral part of the project team, beginning at the start of the project and continuing through all phases until completion.

During this initial meeting, the owner's authorized representative should set priorities for the project. There are four elements of concern for a project: quality, scope, time, and cost. It is understood that quality is an element that must be satisfied. The owner should set the level of quality that is expected in the project. There must be a mutual understanding of quality between the project manager and the owner's representative. Scope is the fixed quantity of work to be performed. It may be expanded or reduced by the owner as the project proceeds, generally depending on the costs. The priority of time or cost is set by the owner. Frequently, time is initially set as a priority over cost. However, cost may take precedence over time if the market for the product changes or other conditions arise. If a priority is not set, the project manager must attempt to optimize time and cost.

The level of involvement required by the owner's representative must be determined at the beginning of the project. If he or she wants to sign everything, then the project manager must include time in the project schedule and cost into the budget for the owner's involvement. Two-way communication is an absolute requirement. The project manager should also inform the owner's representative of how he or she plans to create a project team that will be coordinated to represent each part of the project.

This initial meeting also gives both the owner's representative and the project manager the opportunity to meet each other. At this meeting it may be desirable to visit with others in the owner's organization that may be concerned with the project. Issues to discuss might include clarification of goals and requirements, desired level of quality, any uniqueness about the project, financing, regulatory agencies, and approval process.

In some instances this meeting may be the project managers first introduction to the owner's representative. Because many owners expect an all-knowing project manager, some precautions need to be taken. Since the project team has not yet been formed, all discussions should focus on the work to be performed rather than work that has been completed. Ideally, the project manager should have assisted in the proposal preparation that was approved by the owner to proceed with the project. This gives the project manager a better understanding of the history behind the project and previous contact with the owner's representative.

ORGANIZATIONAL STRUCTURES

Each project manager is affected by the environment in which he or she works. The organization of a company can have a large impact on the ability to manage a project. Figures 4-1 through 4-5 show various organizational structures of companies. A project manager may work for a company that is organized as shown in these figures, or he or she may manage a project for a client whose company organization is similar to one of these organizational structures.

If a company is product oriented, it will be organized around manufacturing and marketing of the product, with the priority of decisions focused on products. A company that is service oriented will be organized around providing customer service. The design and construction of a project is a means to an end for the company to provide a product or service, and does not represent the primary function of that company. This secondary emphasis on a project can hamper the work of a project manager.

The organizational structure shown in Figure 4-1 is an example of a business with an emphasis on manufacturing and marketing of products. The engineering portion of the company exists to support the manufacturing operation. Manufacturing exists to produce the product for the marketing group to sell. Questions related to the engineering/construction of a project for this company would typically be directed to the engineering department. However, the answers to these questions often come from the manufacturing department, which in turn may have to obtain input from the marketing group. This requires a channel of communications between various parties which can

FIGURE 4-1
Traditional Management Organization (Production Line/Business Oriented).

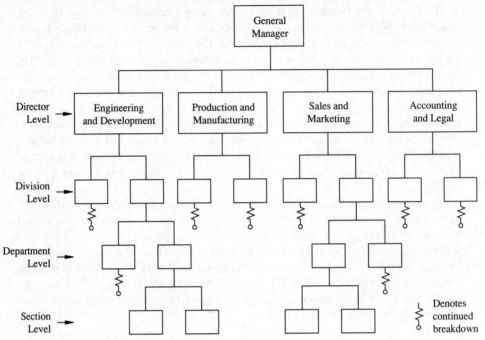

cause misinterpretation of information and a delay in obtaining answers. A project manager performing work for a company that is organized as shown in Figure 4-1 should include a contingency in the project schedule for delays of owner responses, and should be alert to the potential for scope growth.

An example of a functional organization is illustrated by the electrical power company shown in Figure 4-2. The company emphasis is on generation, transmission, and distribution of electrical power services. Utilities and governmental agencies are usually organized in functional departments. This type of organization is efficient for the design and construction of projects involving a single function, such as the design and construction of a transmission line or a substation. However, if a project involves design and construction of a unit of a power station, plus two transmission lines and a substation, it can be difficult to identify the project within the organization. There is a tendency for the project to pass from one department to another if a single project manager is not assigned overall responsibility. This can lead to lost information and schedule delays. Even if a single project manager is assigned, coordinating across departments lines can be difficult.

Figure 4-3 shows a typical work environment of a consulting engineering company that provides design services for projects. The company emphasis is discipline oriented, involving a group of specialists who share knowledge and technical expertise.

FIGURE 4-2
Functional Organization (Electrical Power Company).

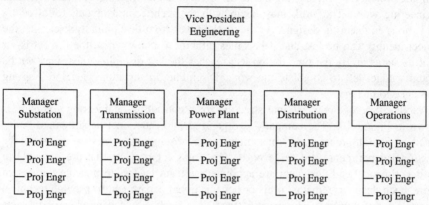

Over-emphasizing separate disciplines can encourage competition and conflicts at the expense of the whole organization, resulting in focus on internal department operations rather than external relations and project work. When emphasis is focused on internal departments, decision making and communication channels tend to be vertical, rather than horizontal, with little attention paid to costs, schedules, and coordination.

Many consulting engineering companies are organized as shown in Figure 4-3. For small projects with short durations this type of organization is efficient. However, project management can be hindered because some of the engineers have a dual role, as both a designer and a project manager. As the number of disciplines

FIGURE 4-3
Discipline Organization (Design Firm).

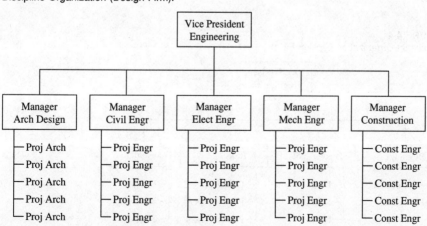

increase, coordination of complex projects becomes more difficult. For example, a complex project may involve architectural, civil, structural, mechanical, and electrical engineering work. The work may begin with the architectural layout, followed by the various engineering designs. As the work moves from discipline to discipline, the project identity can be lost and it becomes difficult to know where the project is, or what its status is. By the time the project reaches the last discipline there may not be enough budget left to complete the work. Discipline organizations develop a strong resistance to change.

Another type of organizational structure for a consulting engineering company is shown in Figure 4-4. The company is organized into functional departments: buildings, heavy/civil, process, and transportation. The disciplines are dispersed among the functional departments and serve on design teams for projects that are assigned to the department. Lead designers are appointed as team leaders to manage the design effort. Each designer remains in his or her functional department to provide technical expertise for the project. However, if there is a decline in the number of projects in one or more departments, one or more designers may be transferred to another functional department. This can be disruptive to the management of projects.

To increase emphasis on project cost, schedule, and general coordination, a matrix organization as shown in Figure 4-5 is often used. The objective is to retain the design disciplines in their home departments so technical expertise is not lost, and to create a projects group that is responsible for overall project coordination. To accomplish this the designer has two channels of communications, one to the technical supervisor and another to the project manager. Issues related to technical expertise are addressed vertically while issues related to the project are addressed horizontally.

The matrix organization provides a work environment with emphasis on the project. Each project is defined by a horizontal line on the matrix. The project manager is responsible for overall project coordination, interfacing of disciplines, client relations, and monitoring of overall project costs and schedules. The various design disciplines are responsible for providing technical expertise, quality performance, and the cost and schedule for their particular part of the project. No one person works for the other

FIGURE 4-4
Functional Organization (Design Firm).

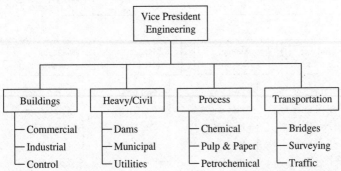

FIGURE 4-5
Matrix Organization (Design Firm).

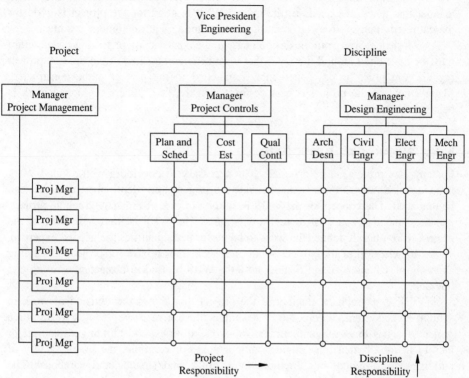

on the project team, instead everyone works for the project. The project manager is the leader of the team and serves as a focal point for integrating responsibility.

A matrix defines lines of communications but does not indicate the authority for conflict resolution. A matrix may be defined as a "strong matrix," where project managers have the authority to decide what is good for the overall project. At the opposite end of the spectrum is the "weak matrix," where discipline managers have the authority in decision making. A discipline supervisor may be more concerned with his or her technical area than the overall project. Designers are usually concerned with producing the best design possible, sometimes at the expense of project cost or schedule and without regard to the effect on other departments.

The success of project management in the matrix organization depends on the philosophy of the company and the attitude of the employees. Too much emphasis on disciplines can lead to time and cost problems. Likewise, too much emphasis on projects can lead to inefficiencies and quality problems due to losing control of and contact with the technical departments. Therefore, there must be a balance between managing the project and providing technical expertise. Mutual respect among disciplines is essential. The project manager relies on the expertise of each team member and recognizes that everyone is a key player on the team of a successful project. A "can do" attitude must exist, with a drive to complete a quality project in an efficient manner that meets the needs of the owner. What is good for the project is good for the entire company. Effective communications among team members is a must.

As a project moves from the design phase to the construction phase, a work structure must be developed around the work that must be accomplished in the field. A project organization must be developed that is matched to the project to be constructed. Management of the project is best performed in the field, where the actual work is being performed.

WORK BREAKDOWN STRUCTURE

For any size project, large or small, it is necessary to develop a well-defined Work Breakdown Structure (WBS) that divides the project into identifiable parts that can be managed. The concept of the WBS is simple; in order to manage a whole project, one must manage and control each of its parts. The WBS is the cornerstone of the project work plan. It defines the work to be performed, identifies the needed expertise, assists in selection of the project team, and establishes a base for project scheduling and control. Chapters 5 and 6 show how the WBS is used in project scheduling and tracking.

A WBS is a graphical display of the project that shows the division of work in a multi-level system. Figure 4-6 is a simple illustrative example of a WBS for a project that has three major facilities: site-work, utilities, and buildings. Each major facility is sub-divided into smaller components. For example, the major facility of buildings is sub-divided into three buildings: office, maintenance, and warehouse. The project is further broken down so the components at each level are subsets of the next higher level. The number of levels in a WBS will vary depending upon the size and complexity of the project. The smallest unit in the WBS is a work package. A work package must be defined in sufficient detail so the work can be measured, budgeted, scheduled, and controlled. Development of work packages is discussed later in this chapter.

The development of the WBS is a continuing process that starts when the project is first assigned to the project manager and continues until all work packages have been defined. The project manager starts the process of developing the WBS by identifying major areas of the project. As members of the project team define the work to be performed in more detail, the WBS is adjusted accordingly. Thus, the WBS is used from the start to the finish of the project for planning and controlling. It is an effective means of defining the whole project, by parts, and providing effective communication channels for exchange of information that is necessary for management of the project.

The WBS is the foundation of a project management system. Code numbers can be used to relate the WBS to the Organizational Breakdown Structure (OBS) for management of people. Code numbers can also be used to relate the WBS to the Cost Breakdown Structure (CBS) for management of costs. Similarly, code numbers can relate the WBS to the Critical Path Method (CPM) schedule to manage time. Thus, the WBS provides a systematic approach for identifying work, compiling the budget,

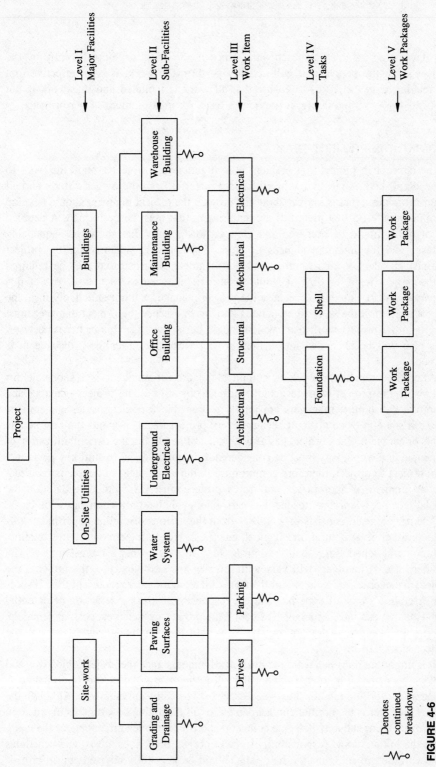

Level I
Major Facilities

Level II
Sub-Facilities

Level III
Work Item

Level IV
Tasks

Level V
Work Packages

Denotes
continued
breakdown

FIGURE 4-6
Illustrative Work Breakdown Structure (WBS).

55

and developing an integrated schedule. Since the WBS is developed jointly by the project team, the people that will actually perform the work, it is an effective tool for relating work activities to ensure that all work is included and that work is not duplicated. Most importantly, it provides a basis for measurement of performance.

FORMING THE PROJECT TEAM

A key concept in project management is to organize the project around the work to be accomplished. After review of all backup material from the owner's study and all other information that is known about the project, the project manager should develop a preliminary WBS that identifies the major tasks that must be performed. A detailed list of tasks should be prepared and grouped into phases that show the sequencing of tasks and the interdependences of work. This provides identity for the project to assist in selection of resources and the technical expertise that will be required of the project team. A time schedule should be attached to each task. All of this preparatory work is required because the project manager can not effectively form the project team until the work to be done is known. In essence the project manager must develop a pre-project work plan, which should be reviewed by his or her supervisor. This plan will be expanded into a final project work plan after the project team is formed.

After the preparatory work is complete the project manager is responsible for organizing the project team to achieve project objectives. The project manager and appropriate discipline managers are jointly responsible for selecting team members. This can sometimes be difficult because every project manager wants the best people on his or her team. Each project has a specific list of needs, but the overall utilization of all people in the company must be considered. It is not practical to shift key personnel from project to project, therefore compromise in the assignment of people is required. The assignment of appropriate staff for a project must take into consideration the special technical expertise needed and personnel available on a company-wide basis.

The project team consists of members from the various discipline departments (architectural, civil, structural, mechanical, electrical, etc.), project controls (estimating, planning and scheduling, quality control, etc.), and the owner's representative. The number of team members will vary with the size and complexity of the project. The project manager serves as leader of the team. All team members represent their respective discipline's area of expertise and are responsible for early detection of potential problems that can have an adverse effect on the project's objectives, cost, or schedule. If a problem occurs, each team member is to notify his immediate supervisor and the project manager.

It is important that each team member clearly understands the project objectives and realizes his or her importance in contributing to the overall success of the project. A cooperative working relationship is necessary between all team members. Although the project manager is the normal contact person for all discipline departments involved in the project, he or she may delegate contact responsibility to lead members of the team. Since the initiative and responsibility to meet project objectives, costs, and schedules rests with the project manager, he or she should be kept fully advised and informed.

The project manager must organize, coordinate, and monitor the progress of team members to ensure the work is completed in an orderly manner. He or she should also maintain frequent contact with the owner's representative.

KICK-OFF MEETING

After formation of the project team the project manager calls the first team meeting, commonly called the kick-off meeting. It is one of the most important meetings in project management and is held prior to starting any work. The purpose of the kick-off meeting is to get the team members together to identify who is working the project and to provide them with the same base of knowledge about the project so they will feel like they are a part of the team. It is important for the project manager to fully understand the project objectives, needs, budget, and schedule and to transmit this information to team members early in the project. In particular the scope of work must be closely reviewed.

The kick-off meeting allows the team to set priorities, identify problem areas, clarify member responsibilities, and to provide general orientation so the team can act as a unit with a common set of goals. At the meeting the project manager should present the project requirements and the initial work plan, discuss working procedures, and establish communication links and working relationships. Every effort should be made to eliminate any ambiguities or misunderstandings related to scope, budget, and schedule. These three elements of a project can not be changed without approval of both the project manager and the owner's representative.

Prior to the meeting the project manager should prepare general project information data, including the project name (that will be used for all documents and correspondence), project location, job account number, and other information needed by the project team. Standards, CADD requirements, policies, procedures, and any other requirements should also be presented. It is important to provide this information to key people on the project so they know the project is approved for work and feel that they are a part of the team. The project manager should visit with key team members prior to the meeting to identify and resolve any peculiar problems and clarify any uncertainties.

In general the meeting is short in duration, but it is the first step in understanding what needs to be done, who is going to do it, when it is to be done, and what the costs will be. This is not a design meeting but an orientation meeting. The project manager must keep the meeting moving and not get overly involved in details. Minutes of the meeting must be recorded and distributed to team members. In particular, there should be documentation of the information that is distributed, the agreements among the team members, and the identification of team concerns or questions that require future action by the project manager or team members.

There are three important purposes of the kick-off meeting: to orient team members regarding project objectives and needs, to distribute the project manager's overall project plan, and to assign to each team member the responsibility of preparing work packages for the work required in his or her area of expertise. Work packages should be prepared and returned to the project manager within two weeks of the kick-off

TABLE 4-2
KICK-OFF MEETING CHECKLIST

1. Review the agenda and purpose of the meeting
2. Distribute the project title, account number, and general information needed by the project team
3. Introduce team members and identify their areas of expertise and responsibility
4. Review project goals, needs, requirements, & scope (including guidelines, limitations, problems)
5. Review project feasibility estimate of the owner & the approved budget for the project team
6. Review project preliminary schedule & milestones
7. Review initial project work plan:
   How to handle design
   How to handle procurement
   How to handle construction
8. Discuss assignments to team members:
   Ask each member of the team – – – – – – – – – – –> (who?)
   To review the scope of work required in their area – – –> (what?)
   To develop a preliminary schedule for their work   – – –> (when?)
   To develop a preliminary estimate for their work – – – –> (how much?)
9. Ask each team member to prepare design work packages for their responsible work and report this information to the project manager within two weeks
10. Establish the next team meeting, write minutes of kick-off meeting, and distribute to each team member and management

meeting. To facilitate orderly conduct of the meeting and to ensure that important items are covered, the project manager should use a checklist for the kick-off meeting as illustrated in Table 4-2.

WORK PACKAGES

The project manager is responsible for organizing a work plan for the project, however he or she can not finalize the project plan without extensive input from each team member. The kick-off meeting should serve as an effective orientation for team members to learn the project requirements and restrictions of budget and schedule. At that meeting the project manager assigns each team member to review the scope of work required of his or her respective expertise, to identify any problems, and to develop a budget and schedule required to meet the scope. This can be accomplished by preparing a design work package that describes the work to be provided.

Each team member is responsible for the development of one or more work packages for the work he or she is to perform. A work package provides a detailed description of the work required to meet project needs and to match the project manager's initial work plan. The work packages should be assembled by each team member and supplied to the project manager within two weeks of the kick-off meeting.

A work package is divided into three categories: scope, budget, and schedule. Figure 4-7 illustrates the contents of a work package. The scope describes the required work and services to be provided. It should be described in sufficient detail so other team members, who are providing related work, can interface their work accordingly. This is important because a common problem in project management is coordinating related work. There is a risk of the same work being done by two persons, or work not being done at all, because two people are each thinking the other person is providing the work. Team members must communicate among themselves during the process of preparing the work packages for a project.

A work package is the lowest level in the Work Breakdown Structure (WBS) and establishes the baseline for project scheduling, tracking, and cost control. The work package is extremely important for project management because it relates the work to be performed to time, cost, and people. As shown in the budget section of Figure 4-7, a code account number relates the work to the Cost Breakdown Structure (CBS). Likewise, the schedule section has a code number that relates the work to the Organizational Breakdown Structure (OBS). The CBS is used for management of project costs and is further discussed in Chapter 6. The OBS code number identifies and links the work to the people. Many articles have been published that discuss the relationship of the work packages to the WBS, OBS, and the CBS.

The preparation of the budget portion of a work package requires a careful evaluation of all resources needed to produce the work. All work tasks and items must be budgeted, including personnel, computer services, reproduction expenses, travel, expendable supplies, and incidental costs.

Team members must consider their overall work load when they prepare the schedule portion of a work package. Since a team member is generally assigned to one or more projects, the preparation of a work package for a new project must consider other assigned duties and future commitments to other projects. The failure of team members to carefully integrate the schedule of all projects for which they are assigned is a common source of late completion of projects. Too often team members over commit their time without making allowances for potential interruptions and unforeseen delays in their work. All tasks should be identified and scheduled.

FOLLOW-UP WORK

After the exchange of information at the kick-off meeting and a review of the required work by each team member there may be a need to readjust the work breakdown structure of the initial project plan. A team member may have the capability to perform the work, but may determine that the magnitude of the work is in excess of what he or she can schedule because of prior commitment to other projects. Thus, a part or all of his or her portion of the project may require assignment to outside contract work. Another option would be a re-staffing of the project based on the overall available resources of the project manager's organization. These situations should be resolved within two weeks of the kick-off meeting.

An accumulation of the budgets from all of the team's work packages provides an estimated cost for the total project. If the estimated cost exceeds the approved

FIGURE 4-7
Team Member's Work Package.

WORK PACKAGE

Title: _____

WBS Code: _____

1. SCOPE

Required Scope of Work: _____
_____
_____

Services to Be Provided: _____
_____
_____
_____
_____
_____
_____

2. BUDGET

Personnel Assigned to Job	Work Hours	$ Cost	CBS Code Acct	Computer Services Type	Hours	$ Cost
___	___	___	___	___	___	___
___	___	___	___	___	___	___
___	___	___	___	___	___	___
___	___	___	___	___	___	___

Total Work Hours = ____   Personnel Costs = $ ____
Computer Hours = ____   Computer Costs = $ ____

Travel Expenses _____ + Reproduction Expenses _____ + Other Expenses _____ = $ _____

Total Budget = $-Labor + $-Computer + $-Travel + $-Other = $ _____

3. SCHEDULE

OBS Code	Work Task	Responsible Person	Start Date	End Date
___	___	___	___	___
___	___	___	___	___
___	___	___	___	___

Work Package: Start date: _____ End date: _____

ADDITIONAL COMMENTS: _____
_____
_____

Prepared by: _____ Date: _____
Approved by: _____ Date: _____

budget, the project manager is made aware of this situation early in the project, within two weeks of the kick-off meeting. The team as a whole must then work together to determine alternative methods of handling the project to keep the estimated cost within the approved budget. If it can not be resolved within the team, the project manager must work with his or her supervisor to determine a workable solution. If a solution can not be found, the owner must be advised so an agreeable solution can be determined for a scope of work that matches the approved budget. It is important to resolve issues of this nature at the beginning of the project, when choices of alternatives can be made, rather than later when it is too late.

After receipt of all work packages, the project manager must integrate the schedules of all team members to develop a schedule for the entire project. If the project schedule exceeds the required completion date, the team as a whole must work together to determine alternative methods of scheduling the work. If the discrepancy between the planned schedule and required schedule can not be resolved within the team, the project manager must then resolve the issue with his or her supervisor. If the required schedule can not be achieved, then the owner must be advised so that acceptable agreements can be reached.

Issues related to project scope, budget, and schedule must be resolved early. Effective communication and cooperation among team members is necessary. The results of the team assignments and definitions of work packages allow the project manager to finalize the work breakdown structure that forms the foundation of the project work plan. After receipt of all information, the project manager can finalize the overall plan to manage the project.

PROJECT WORK PLAN

The project manager must develop a written work plan for each project that identifies the work that needs to be done, who is going to do it, when it is to be done, and what the costs will be. The level of detail should be of sufficient detail to allow all project participants to understand what is expected of them in each phase and time period of the project, otherwise there is no basis for control. It is important that a participatory approach be used and that team members understand project requirements, jointly resolve conflicts, and eliminate overlaps or gaps in related work. There must be agreements on priorities, schedule, and budget.

Upon receipt of all of the team members' work packages the project manager can assemble the final project work plan. Table 4-3 provides the basic components of a work plan: the directory, tasks, schedule, and budget. The project directory contains all pertinent information, such as project title, number, objectives, scope, etc. The project organization chart shows all participants, including the owner's representative. The detailed list of tasks, and grouping of tasks, is derived from the work breakdown structure. The sequencing and scheduling of tasks can be obtained by integrating the schedules of work packages provided by team members. Likewise, the budget can be obtained from a summary of the costs from all work packages.

Once the work plan is finalized it serves as a document to coordinate all work and as a guide to manage the overall effort of the project. It becomes the base for control

TABLE 4-3
COMPONENTS OF A PROJECT WORK PLAN

Directory
- Project Title and Number
- Project Objectives and Scope
- Project Organizational Chart

Tasks
- Detailed Listing of Tasks
- Grouping of Tasks
- Work Packages

Schedule
- Sequencing and Interdependences of Tasks
- Anticipated Duration of each Task
- Calendar Start and Finish Date of Tasks

Budget
- Labor-hours and Cost of Staff for each Task
- Other Expenses Anticipate for each Task
- Billing Approach and Anticipated Revenue by Month

Measurement
- Accomplishment of Tasks
- Completion of Work Packages
- Number of Drawings Produced

of all work. Appendix E illustrates the components of a work plan for a project: work breakdown structure, project organizational chart, sample work package, and project schedule. Note the transfer of information from one component to another to form the integrated work plan.

The first step in organizing a project is development of a Work Breakdown Structure (WBS). The WBS defines the work to be accomplished, but does not define who is responsible for performing the work. A successful project depends on people to make things happen. However, merely selecting good people is not enough. A key function in project management is to organize the project around the work to be accomplished, then select the right people to perform the work within the approved budget and schedule.

After the WBS is complete, the next step is to link the Organizational Breakdown Structure (OBS) from the company to the required work that is defined in the WBS. Figure 4-8 illustrates the linking of the WBS and OBS to identity the various disciplines that are responsible for each part of the WBS. The project manager, with the assistance of discipline managers, can then begin the process of selecting individuals from the various discipline departments who will form the project team.

The linking of the WBS and OBS establishes the project framework for management of the project. After the project framework is defined, a project schedule can be developed to guide the timing of activities and interface related work. The time

FIGURE 4-8
Linking the WBS and OBS.

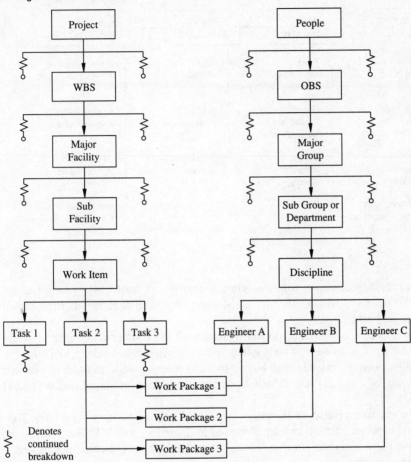

required to accomplish each activity can be obtained from the work packages. The critical path method (CPM) technique is the most common network scheduling system that is used in the engineering and construction industry. Techniques for project scheduling are discussed in Chapter 5.

On completion of the project framework, a coding system, often referred to as a Cost Breakdown System (CBS), can be developed to identify each component of the WBS. The coding system provides a common code of accounts used by all participants in the project because it is directly related to the WBS, that is, the work to be performed. Coding systems are discussed in Chapters 5 and 6.

The integration of the WBS, OBS, and CPM forms the project plan which is the base for project tracking and control. A code of accounts can be developed that relates the required work (defined in the WBS), to the people (shown on the OBS) who will

FIGURE 4-9
Phases of Development of Work Plan.

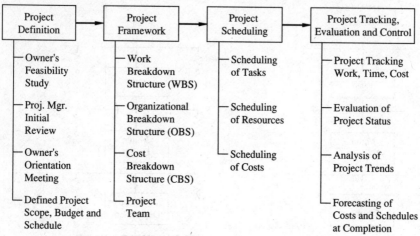

do the work, in accordance with the schedule (shown on the CPM) to complete the project. Thus, the WBS, OBS, and CPM must be linked together to form an all encompassing project plan.

To be effective, a system of project management must integrate all aspects of the project; the work to be done, who is going to do it, when it is to be done, and what the cost will be. Actual work can then be compared to planned work, in order to evaluate the progress of a project and to develop trends to forecast at completion costs and schedules.

The development phases of the project work plan are illustrated in Figure 4-9. Topics related to project definition were discussed in Chapters 2 and 3. Project framework is presented in this chapter. Project scheduling and tracking is presented in Chapters 5 and 6 respectively.

QUESTIONS FOR CHAPTER 4—DEVELOPMENT OF WORK PLAN

1 As discussed in this chapter, the work environment of a project manager can have a significant impact on his or her ability to manage projects. Describe factors that may help or hinder the work of a project manager in each of the following organizational structures: functional organization, discipline organization, and matrix organization.

2 You are the project manager of a project that has the following facilities: security entrance, driveways, parking, landscape, small office building, fabrication building, communication building, and a recreational building. Develop a preliminary work breakdown structure for the project. Identify the engineering disciplines required for the design of the project.

3 Describe the purpose of a kick-off meeting for a project. What are typical items that are presented and discussed during the meeting, including specific assignments that a project manager should ask of team members.

4 Briefly describe the contents of a design work package, who assigns it, when is it assigned, who completes it, and when should it be completed.

5 As the project manager for a project, discuss options that might be considered for one of your team members who is having difficulty completing a design work package. Discuss options for each of the following situations: difficulty in defining the scope of work, difficulty in finding experienced personnel that can be assigned to tasks in the work package, and difficulty in estimating the time that it may take to complete the work.

6 You are the project manager for a project and have just compiled all of the design work packages and found that the costs exceed the approved budget. Describe the options that you would consider to manage the discrepancy.

7 The basic contents of a project work plan are shown in Table 4-3. Identify the contents that relate to the fundamental questions of Who? Does what? When? and How much?

8 For the basic components of a project work plan shown in Table 4-3, identify the components that relate to the organization structure, work breakdown structure, cost breakdown structure, and the critical path methods for project scheduling.

9 The development of a work plan for a project follows four phases: project definition, framework, schedule, and tracking. Identify and briefly describe the parts that make up each of these four phases.

REFERENCES

1 Cable, D., and Adams, J. R., *Organizing for Project Management*, Project Management Institute, Drexel Hill, PA, 1982.

2 Eldin, N. N., "Management of Engineering/Design Phase," *Journal of Construction Engineering and Management*, ASCE, New York, Vol. 117, No. 1, March, 1991.

3 Emling, R. E., "A Code-of-Accounts from an Owner's Point of View," *Transactions of the American Association of Cost Engineers*, Morgantown, WV 1970.

4 *Handbook for Preparation of Work Breakdown Structures*, NHB 5610, National Aeronautics Space Agency, Washington, D.C., 1975.

5 Johnston, D. C., "Planning Engineering and Construction Projects," *Engineering Management Division Symposium*, ASCE, New York, 1986.

6 Neil, J. N., *Manual for Special Project Management*, Construction Industry Institute, Austin, TX, July, 1991.

7 *Quality in the Constructed Project: A Guide for Owners, Designers, and Contractors*, Volume 1, Manual No. 73, ASCE, New York, 1990.

5

PROJECT SCHEDULING

DESIRED RESULTS OF PLANNING

Project planning is the heart of good project management because it provides the central communication that coordinates the work of all parties. Planning also establishes the benchmark for the project control system to track the quantity, cost, and timing of the work required to successfully complete the project. Although the most common desired result of planning is to finish the project on time, there are other benefits that can be derived from good project planning, see Table 5-1.

TABLE 5-1
DESIRED RESULTS OF PROJECT PLANNING

---

1. Finish the project on time
2. Continuous (uninterrupted) flow of work (no delays)
3. Reduced amount of rework (least amount of changes)
4. Minimize confusion and misunderstandings
5. Increased knowledge of status of project by everyone
6. Meaningful and timely reports to management
7. You run the project instead of the project running you
8. Knowledge of scheduled times of key parts of the project
9. Knowledge of distribution of costs of the project
10. Accountability of people, defined responsibility/authority
11. Clear understanding of who does what, when, and how much
12. Integration of all work to ensure a quality project for the owner

---

Planning is the first step to project scheduling. Planning is a process and not a discrete activity. As changes occur, additional planning is required to incorporate the changes into the schedule. There are many situations or events that can arise that can impact a project schedule. Examples are changes in personnel, problems with permits, change in a major piece of equipment, or design problems in structures. Good planning detects changes and adjusts the schedule in the most efficient manner.

A common complaint of many design engineers is they can not efficiently produce their work because of interruptions and delays. The cause of this problem is usually a lack of planning, and in some instances no planning at all. Planning should clearly identify the work that is required by each individual and the interface of work between individuals. It should also include a reasonable amount of time for the exchange of information between project participants, including the delay time for reviews and approvals.

Another common complaint of many designers is the amount of rework they must do because of changes in the project. This also leads to confusion and misunderstandings that further hinder productive work. Planning should include a clear description of the required work before the work is started. However, it must be recognized that changes are a necessary part of project work, especially in the early development phases. If changes in the work are expected, or probable, then project planning should include provisions for a reasonable allowance for the anticipated changes. Too often people know that changes will occur, but fail to include them in the project planning.

Project planning and scheduling can serve as an effective means of preventing problems. It can prevent delays in work, a major cause of late project completion and cost overrun, which often leads to legal disputes. It can also prevent low worker morale and decline in productivity that is caused by lack of direction.

PRINCIPLES OF PLANNING AND SCHEDULING

There must be an explicit operational plan to guide the entire project. The plan must include and link the three components of the project: scope, budget, and schedule. Too often, planning is focused only on schedule without regard to the important components of scope and budget.

To develop an integrated total project plan, the project must be broken down into well-defined units of work that can be measured and managed. This process starts with the work breakdown structure (WBS). Once this is completed, the project team members who have the expertise to perform the work can be selected. Team members have the ability to clearly define the magnitude of detail work that is required. They also have the ability to define the time and cost that will be required to produce the work. With this information a complete project plan can be developed.

The project plan and schedule must clearly define individual responsibilities, schedules, budgets, and anticipated problems. The project manager should prepare formal agreements with appropriate parties whenever there is a change in the project. There should be equal concern given to schedule and budget, and the two must be linked. Planning, scheduling, and controlling begin at the inception of the project, and are

TABLE 5-2
KEY PRINCIPLES FOR PLANNING AND SCHEDULING

1. Begin planning before starting work, rather than after starting work
2. Involve people who will actually do the work in the planning and scheduling process
3. Include all aspects of the project; scope, budget, schedule, and quality
4. Build flexibility into the plan, include allowance for changes and time for reviews and approvals
5. Remember the schedule is the plan for doing the work, and it will never be precisely correct
6. Keep the plan simple, eliminate irrelevant details that prevent the plan from being readable
7. Communicate the plan to all parties, any plan is worthless unless it is known

continuous throughout the life of the project until completion. Table 5-2 lists key principles for planning and scheduling.

RESPONSIBILITIES OF PARTIES

The principal parties of owner, designer, and contractor all have a responsible role in project planning and scheduling. It is erroneous to assume this role is the responsibility of any one party. Each must develop a schedule for his or her required work and that schedule must be communicated and coordinated with the other two parties, because the work of each affects the work of the others.

The owner establishes the project completion date, which governs the scheduling of work for both the designer and contractor. The owner should also set priorities for the components that make-up the project. For example, if the project consists of three buildings, the relative importance of the buildings should be identified. This assists the designer in the process of organizing his or her work and developing the design schedule to produce drawings that are most important to the owner. It also assists in the development of specifications and contract documents that communicate priorities to the construction contractor.

The design organization must develop a design schedule that meets the owner's schedule. This schedule should include a prioritization of work in accordance with the owner's needs and should be developed with extensive input from all designers who will have principal roles in the design process. Too often, a design schedule is produced by the principal designer, or the project manager of the design organization, without the involvement of those who will actually do the work.

The construction contractor must develop a schedule for all construction activities in accordance with the contract documents. It should include procurement and delivery of materials to the job, coordination of labor and equipment on the job, and interface the work of all sub-contractors. The objective of the construction schedule should be to effectively manage the work to produce the best quality project for the owner. The purpose of construction scheduling should *not* be to settle disputes related to project work, but to manage the project in the most efficient manner.

For some projects, it may be desirable for one party to maintain the schedule and the other parties to participate in monitoring it. Ultimately each one of the parties will be responsible for his or her portion of the schedule. Maintaining one common schedule as a cooperative effort between parties can reduce problems associated with maintaining three separate schedules.

PLANNING FOR MULTIPLE PROJECTS

Many project managers are assigned the responsibility of simultaneously managing several small projects that have short durations. A small project is usually staffed with a few people who perform a limited number of tasks to complete the project. For projects of this type, there is a tendency for the project manager to forgo any formal planning and scheduling because each project is simple and well defined. However, the problem that the project manager has is not the management of any one project at a time; instead, the problem is managing all of the projects simultaneously. The task of simultaneously managing multiple small projects can be very difficult and frustrating. Thus, the need for good planning and scheduling is just as important for the management of multiple small projects as it is for the management of a single large project.

To manage multiple small projects, the project manager must develop a plan and schedule that includes all projects for which he or she is assigned, even though the projects may be unrelated. This is necessary because the staffing of small projects requires assigning individuals to several projects at the same time so they will have a full-time work load. Thus, their work on any one project affects their work on other projects. For this type of work environment the project manager must develop a plan and schedule that interfaces the work of each individual that is working on all the projects for which the project manager is responsible. In particular, the plan should clearly show how the work of each person progresses from one project to another.

A large project is commonly assigned to one project manager who has no other responsibilities than management of the single project at one time. It is staffed by persons who provide the diverse technical expertise that is required to accomplish the numerous tasks to complete the project. For projects of this type, the problem of the project manager is identifying and interfacing related tasks to ensure the work is accomplished in a continuous manner. He or she relies on the input of team members to develop the project plan and schedule. Much of the work of the project manager involves extensive communications with team members to ensure that work is progressing in a continuous and uninterrupted manner.

Regardless of the project size, large or small, planning and scheduling must be done. Perhaps the greatest mistake a project manager can make is to assume that planning and scheduling is not required for some reason, such as, he or she is too busy, there will be too many changes, the project is too small, or some other reason.

TECHNIQUES FOR PLANNING AND SCHEDULING

The technique used for project scheduling will vary depending upon the project's size, complexity, duration, personnel, and owner requirements. The project manager must choose a scheduling technique that is simple to use and is easily interpreted by all project participants. There are two general methods that are commonly used: the bar chart (sometimes called the *Gantt chart*) and the critical path method (sometimes called CPM or network analysis system).

The bar chart, developed by Henry L. Gantt during World War I, is a graphical time-scale of the schedule. It is easy to interpret; but it is difficult to update, does not show interdependences of activities, and does not integrate costs or resources with the schedule. It is an effective technique for overall project scheduling, but has limited application for detailed construction work because the many interrelationships of activities, that are required for construction work, are not defined. Many project managers prefer the bar chart for scheduling engineering design work because of its simplicity, ease of use, and because it does not require extensive interrelation of activities. However, it can require significant time for updating since the interrelationship of activities are not defined. A change in one activity on the bar chart will not automatically change subsequent activities. Also, the bar chart does not integrate costs with the schedule, nor does it provide resources, such as labor-hours, which are important for management of design.

Some designers argue that they cannot define the interrelationships between the activities which make up a design schedule. They use this argument to support the use of a bar chart. They also argue that resources change constantly on a design project, resulting in a schedule which is too difficult to maintain. Either of these situations may occur at times on some projects. However, if these situations exist on every project it is likely that the projects are not well planned, managed, or controlled.

The Critical Path Method (CPM) was developed in 1956 by the DuPont Company, with Remington Rand as consultants, as a deterministic approach to scheduling. The CPM method is commonly used in the engineering and construction industry. A similar method, Program Evaluation and Review Technique (PERT) was developed in 1957 by the U.S. Navy, with Booz, Allen, & Hamilton Management consultants, as a probabilistic approach to scheduling. It is more commonly used by the manufacturing industry; however, it can be used for risk assessment of highly uncertain projects. Both methods are often referred to as a network analysis system (NAS). The CPM provides interrelationship of activities and scheduling of costs and resources. It also is an effective technique for overall project scheduling and detailed scheduling of construction. However, it does have some limitations when applied to detailed engineering design work during the early stages of a project because it requires an extensive description of the interrelationship of activities.

Although the CPM technique requires more effort than a bar chart, it provides more detailed information that is required for effective project management. Using a network schedule to plan a project forces the project team to break a project down into identifable tasks and to relate the tasks to each other in a logical sequence in much greater detail than a bar chart. This up-front planning and scheduling helps the project team to identify conflicts in resources before they occur. The project manager must use his or her own judgement and select the method of scheduling that best defines the work to be done and that communicates project requirements to all participants.

NETWORK ANALYSIS SYSTEMS

The network analysis system (NAS) provides a comprehensive method for project planning, scheduling, and controlling. NAS is a general title for the technique of defining and coordinating work by a graphical diagram that shows work activities and the interdependences of activities. Many books and articles have been written that describe the procedures and applications of this technique. It is not the purpose of this book to present the details of network methods because so much material has already been written. The following paragraphs and figures present the basic fundamentals of NAS to guide the project manager in the development of the project plan and schedule. The basic definitions shown in Figure 5-1 are presented to clarify the following paragraphs because there are variations in terminology used in network analyses.

For project management the CPM is the most commonly used NAS method. The concept is simple, the computations only require basic arithmetic; and a large number of computer programs are available to automate the work required of CPM scheduling. The most difficult task in the use of CPM is identifying and interfacing the numerous activities that are required to complete a project, that is, development of the CPM network diagram. If a well-defined WBS is developed first, the task of developing a CPM diagram is greatly simplified.

There are two basic methods of drawing CPM diagrams: the arrow diagram (sometimes called activity on arrow) and the precedence diagram (sometimes called activity on node). Although both methods achieve the same results, most project managers prefer the precedence method because it does not require the use of dummy activities. The precedence method can also provide the start-to-start, finish-to-finish, start-to-finish, and finish-to-start relationship of activities, which can significantly reduce the number of activities that are required in a network diagram. However, many individuals prefer to not use these relationships because of potential confusion in the network scheduling.

Figure 5-2 is a simple precedence diagram that is presented to illustrate the time computations for analysis of a project schedule by the critical path method. Each activity is described by a single letter. The number at the top of the activity is the assigned activity number and the number at the bottom of each activity represents the duration in working days. A legend is shown in the lower left hand corner to define the start and finish days. All calculations for starts and finishes are based on end-of-day.

After the CPM diagram has been prepared the duration of each activity can be assigned and the forward pass calculations performed to calculate the early start and early finish of each activity. The largest early finish of all preceding activities defines the early start of all following activities. For example, activity "H" can not be started until activities "E" and "F" are both completed. Since the largest early finish of the two preceding activities is 12, the early start for activity "H" is 12. The forward pass calculations are performed on all activities from the first activity "A," to the last activity "Q." The early finish of the last activity defines the project completion, which is 41 days for this particular project. This project duration is a calculated value based upon the duration and interdependences of all activities in the project.

FIGURE 5-1
Basic Definitions for CPM.

Activity — The performance of a task required to complete the project, such as, design of foundations, review of design, procure steel contracts, or form concrete columns. An activity requires time, cost, or both time and cost.

Network — A diagram to represent the relationship of activities to complete the project. The network may be drawn as either an "arrow diagram" or a "precedence diagram."

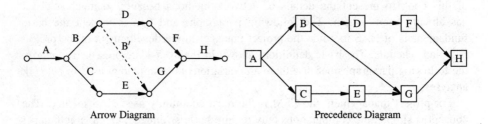

Arrow Diagram   Precedence Diagram

Duration (D) — The estimated time required to perform an activity. The time should include all resources that are assigned to the activity.

Early Start (ES) — The earliest time an activity can be started.

Early Finish (EF) — The earliest time an activity can be finished and is equal to the early start plus the duration.

$$EF = ES + D$$

Late Finish (LF) — The latest time an activity can be finished.

Late Start (LS) — The latest time an activity can be started without delaying the completion date of the project.

$$LS = LF - D$$

Total Float (TF) — The amount of time an activity may be delayed without delaying the completion date of the project.

$$TF = LF - EF = LS - ES$$

Free Float (FF) — The amount of time an activity may be delayed without delaying the early start time of the immediately following activity.

$FF_i = ES_j - EF_i$, where the subscript i represents the preceding activity and the subscript j represents the following activity

Critical Path — A series of interconnected activities through the network diagram, with each activity having zero, free and total float time. The critical path determines the minimum time to complete the project

Dummy Activity — An activity (represented by a dotted line on the arrow network diagram) that indicates that any activity following the dummy cannot be started until the activity or activities preceding the dummy are completed. The dummy does not require any time.

A backward pass can be performed to calculate the late start and late finish of each activity. The smallest late start of all following activities defines the late finish of all preceding activities. For example activities "H" and "I" cannot both be started until activity "F" is completed. Since the smallest early start of the two following activities

FIGURE 5-2
Time Computations for Simple Precedence Diagram.

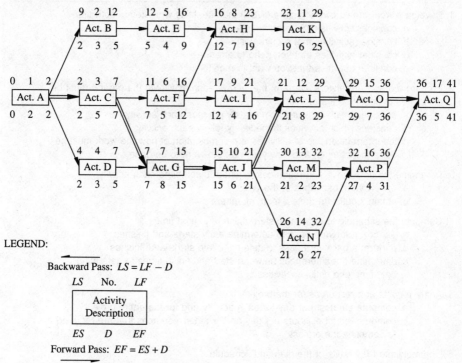

is 16, the late finish for "F" is 16. The backward pass calculations are performed on all activities from the last activity "Q" to the first activity "A."

The difference between starts and finishes determines the amount of free and total float. For example, the total float for activity "M" is 9 days, the difference between its late start (30) and early start (21). The free float for activity "M" is 4 days, the difference between its early finish (23) and the early start (27) of the immediately following activity "P."

The critical path, as noted by the double line on Figure 5-2, is defined by the series of interconnected activities that have zero total float. Since these activities have no float time available, any delay in their completion will delay the completion date of the project. Therefore, they are called critical activities.

Table 5-3 lists the basic steps to guide the process of developing a CPM diagram for project planning and scheduling. It is not always possible to complete a step without some readjustments. For example, the CPM diagram of step 2 may need readjusting after evaluation of the time and resources of steps 4 and 5. Some activities that were originally planned in a series may need to occur in parallel in order to meet a time requirement. Each project manager and his or her team must work together to develop

TABLE 5-3
STEPS IN PLANNING AND SCHEDULING

1. Develop a work breakdown structure (WBS) that identifies work items (activities)
   a. consider activities that require time
   b. consider activities that require cost
   c. consider activities that you need to arrange
   d. consider activities that you want to monitor

2. Prepare a drawing (network diagram) that shows each activity in the order it must be performed to complete the project
   a. consider which activities immediately precede each activity
   b. consider which activities immediately follow each activity
   c. the interrelationship of activities is a combination of how the work must be done (constraints) and how you want the work to be done

3. Determine the time, cost, and resources required to complete each activity
   a. review work packages of the WBS
   b. obtain input from project team members

4. Compute the schedule to determine start, finish, and float times
   a. perform a forward pass to determine early starts and finishes
   b. perform a backward pass to determine late starts and finishes
   c. determine the differences between start and finish times to determine float time and critical activities

5. Analyze costs and resources for the project
   a. compute the cost per day for each activity and for the entire project
   b. compute the labor-hours per day and/or other resources that are required to complete the project

6. Communicate the results of the plan and schedule
   a. display time schedule for activities
   b. display cost schedule for activities
   c. display schedule for other resources

a project plan and schedule that achieves the required project completion date with the resources that are available.

DEVELOPMENT OF CPM DIAGRAM FROM THE WBS

Table 5-3 provided the list of basic steps that can be used to guide the process of developing a network analysis system for project planning and scheduling. The development of the WBS is an important first step that is often neglected. Attempting to draw the CPM diagram without a WBS usually leads to numerous revisions to the diagram.

Figure 5-3 is an example of a WBS for the design of a service facility project that consists of two buildings, site-work, and on-site utilities. A discussion of a typical owner's study for this type of project was presented in Chapter 2. To handle this project the contracting strategy is to use in-house personnel to design the on-site utilities, site-work, and the industrial maintenance building (denoted as Building A). This is commonly called performing work by the force-account method. A contract is

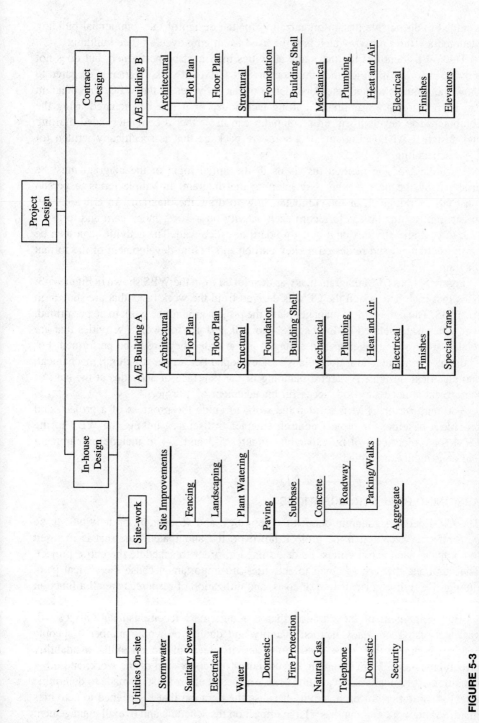

FIGURE 5-3
Work Breakdown Structure for Design of Service Facility Project.

assigned to an outside design organization for the design of the commercial building (denoted as Building B), which is to be used as an employee's office building.

The WBS identifies the tasks and activities that must be performed, but does not provide the order in which they must occur. The CPM network diagram is prepared to show the sequencing and interdependence of the activities in the WBS. The diagram can be prepared by traditional drafting techniques or it can be prepared using the computer. The development on a computer can use either a computer aided drafting and design (CADD) program, or a software package that is specifically written for CPM scheduling.

Regardless of the method that is used, the initial logic of the diagram must be arranged by the person who is developing the diagram. In simple terms, a person must tell a draftsman, or the computer, how to draw the diagram. An efficient way to accomplish this task is to record each activity on a 3 × 5 index card and to use a tack to post all activities on a bulletin board or office wall. The activities can then be easily rearranged and reviewed by key participants before development of the formal diagram.

Figure 5-4 is a CPM diagram that was developed from the WBS shown in Figure 5-3. Note that each activity on the CPM is derived from the work tasks that are shown on the WBS. Thus, the project manager plans the project around the work to be performed, which has been defined by the people who will perform the work. Activities that are related are grouped together and arranged in the order they are to be performed. For example, the architectural floor plans are developed before the structural, mechanical, and electrical designs. A careful planning of the interface of activities at the start of the project is necessary for successful management of a project.

The purpose of CPM is to plan the work to guide the progress of a project, and provide a baseline for project control. Chapter 6 discusses linking the WBS to the CPM for project control by expanding Figures 5-3 and 5-4 to include procurement and construction activities.

ASSIGNING REALISTIC DURATIONS

The CPM network diagram defines the activities, and sequencing of activities, to be performed to accomplish the project; however, the anticipated time that is required to complete each activity must be determined in order to schedule the entire project. The durations that are assigned to activities are important because the critical path, timing of activities, distribution of costs, and utilization of resources are all a function of activity durations.

The assignment of the duration that is required to accomplish an activity will vary depending on many factors: quantity and quality of work, number of people and/or equipment that is assigned to the activity, level of worker skills, availability of equipment, work environment, effectiveness of supervision of the work, and other conditions. Although these variations exist, a special effort must be made to determine a realistic duration for each activity because the duration that is assigned to activities in a CPM network diagram has a large impact on the schedule and overall management of a project.

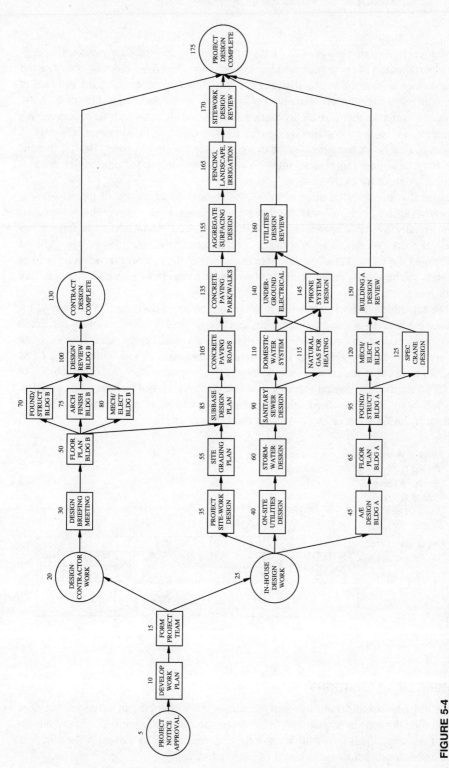

FIGURE 5-4
CPM Diagram for Design Engineering.

Many activities in a project are routine in nature which enables a reasonably accurate determination of the probable time of completion. For these types of activities the duration can be determined by dividing the total quantity of work by the production rate, which is a function of the number of individuals that are assigned to the activity. A common mistake that is made by many people is to calculate the time to accomplish an activity assuming a continuous flow of uninterrupted work. However, all work is subject to delays, interruptions, or other events that can impact time. Thus, a reasonable amount of time (allowance) must be added to the calculated time to determine a realistic duration for each activity.

Generally, the duration of an activity can be determined by one of three methods; by analyzing historical records from previously completed projects, by referencing commercially available manuals that provide costs and production rates for various types of work, or from the experience and judgement of the person who will be performing the work. It is often desirable to determine the probable duration by several methods so the results can be compared to detect any significant variations that may occur.

The schedule for the design work is the total time to produce the final drawings, including the overlap of design calculations and design drafting. As previously discussed most engineers prefer a bar chart for scheduling individual design tasks. However, for project control the individual bar charts must be developed into activities on the CPM diagram to develop the total project schedule. The start and finish of each activity of the CPM engineering design schedule is a composite of all tasks of the work package. The following illustrates the evaluation of overlapping tasks of the work package to determine the duration of an activity on the CPM diagram.

Tasks of Work Package	Duration
Project Engineering	5 days
Structural Design	16 days
CADD Operator	9 days
Total Design Days	30 days

Project Engineering
Structural Design
CADD Operator

24 day duration for
CPM scheduling
control diagram

COMPUTER APPLICATIONS

The CPM network diagram, by itself, identifies the sequencing of activities but does not provide the scheduled start and finish dates, the distribution of costs, or the allocation of resources. This information can easily be determined by assigning the duration, cost, and resources that are required of each activity.

There are many CPM computer programs available to perform the numerous calculations necessary to determine the scheduled time, cost, and resources of activities. Although the number, type, and format of the computer generated output reports vary widely, depending on the software, the basic input data required for each is the same information. The information required for the input data consists of activity number, description, duration, cost, and resources, such as, labor-hours. The sequencing, or interrelationship of activities, is defined by the CPM network diagram. The input data is the same information that is compiled during preparation of the design work packages for the WBS, or during preparation of the estimate for a project by the construction contractor. Thus, the computer application of CPM is appropriate for both the design and construction phase of a project.

The information that must be assembled for a CPM computer analysis is illustrated in Figures 5-5 and 5-6. Figure 5-5 is a simple CPM precedence network diagram for a sewer and water line construction project. Construction activities are selected for this illustrative example because they are easily recognizable by most readers. Each activity is Figure 5-5 is shown with its time and cost information. Resources are excluded for simplicity of this presentation and are discussed in the following section. A hand analysis of starts and finishes is shown in Figure 5-5 to illustrate the calculations and to relate them to the computer output reports discussed in the following paragraphs. The times that are shown on the diagram all represent end-of-day. A listing of the computer input data for this project is shown in Figure 5-6.

For this project, two surveying crews are available which allows Activities 130 and 140 to occur simultaneously. Only one trenching machine is available, therefore trenching work for Water Line A, Activity 170, is planned before trenching of Water Line B, Activity 190. Other similar constraints are shown in the network to illustrate that planning must be done before project scheduling can be accomplished.

The input data required for a computer scheduling analysis is shown in Figure 5-6. The first part of the input data defines information related to each activity. The second part defines the order in which the activities are performed, that is, the sequencing or interfacing of the activities. The project title is shown above the activity list and project start date is shown at the end of the sequence list.

Figure 5-7 shows the activity schedule report for the project that is typically available from a CPM computer program. Both calendar and work days are shown. Start dates represent beginning of the day while finish dates represent end of the day. The free and total floats are shown for each activity. The letter "C" at the left of an activity denotes it is a critical activity, that is, it has zero total and free float.

SCHEDULE CODING SYSTEM

One of the advantages of CPM scheduling by computer methods is the ability to sort specific activities from the complete list of activities for the project. For example, the project manager may only want information about sewer activities, the time required for trenching equipment, or the assignment of the surveying crew. The sorting of these activities can easily be accomplished by a coding system.

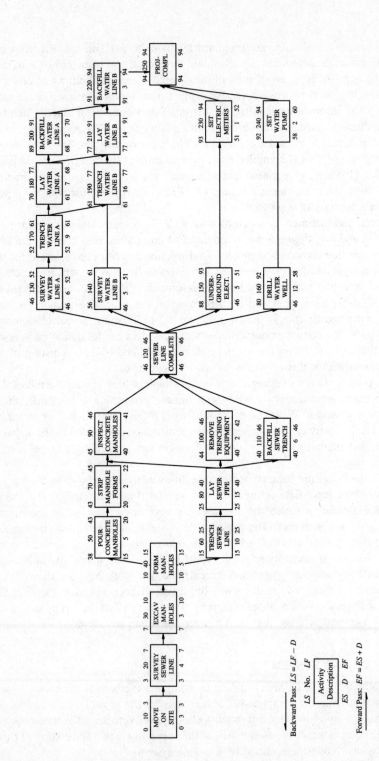

Backward Pass: $LS = LF - D$

$$LS \quad No. \quad LF$$

	Activity	
	Description	

$$ES \quad D \quad EF$$

Forward Pass: $EF = ES + D$

FIGURE 5-5
CPM Diagram for Construction Phase of Sewer and Water Line Project.

FIGURE 5-6
Computer Input Data File for Sewer and Water Project.

```
***********************
**   INPUT DETAILS   **
***********************
```

PROJECT: SEWER & WATER LINE

ACTIVITY LIST:

NUMBER	CODE	DESCRIPTION	DURATION	COST	ASSIGNED START
10	5000	MOVE ON SITE	3	1400.	
20	1100	SURVEY SEWER LINES	4	2700.	
30	1200	EXCAVATE FOR MANHOLES	3	3500.	
40	1200	INSTALL MANHOLE FORMWORK	5	6000.	
50	1200	PLACE CONCRETE MANHOLES	5	4700.	
60	1300	TRENCH SEWER LINE	10	12600.	
70	1200	STRIP MANHOLE FORMWORK	2	2100.	
80	1400	LAY SEWER PIPE	15	11250.	
90	1200	INSPECT MANHOLES	1	800.	
100	1300	REMOVE TRENCHING EQUIPMENT	2	1400.	
110	1500	BACKFILL SEWER TRENCH	6	3600.	
120	5000	SEWER LINE COMPLETE	0	0.	
130	2110	SURVEY WATER LINE A	6	4000.	
140	2120	SURVEY WATER LINE B	5	3400.	
150	3000	UNDERGROUND ELECTRICAL	5	2500.	
160	4000	DRILL WATER WELL	12	7000.	
170	2310	TRENCH WATER LINE A	9	8800.	
180	2410	LAY PIPE FOR WATER LINE A	7	16800.	
190	2320	TRENCH WATER LINE B	16	15600.	
200	2510	BACKFILL WATER LINE A	2	900.	
210	2420	LAY PIPE FOR WATER LINE B	14	33600.	
220	2520	BACKFILL WATER LINE B	3	2850.	
230	3000	INSTALL WATER METERS	1	600.	
240	4000	SET WATER PUMP	2	1400.	
250	5000	PROJECT COMPLETE	0	0.	

SEQUENCE OF ACTIVITIES:

FROM	TO
10	20
20	30
30	40
40	50
40	60
50	70
60	80
70	90
80	90
80	110
80	100
90	120
100	120
110	120
120	130
120	160
120	150
120	140
130	170
140	190
150	230
160	240
170	180
170	190
180	200
180	210
190	210
200	220
210	220
220	250
230	250
240	250

PROJECT START DATE: 5/26/93

81

FIGURE 5-7
Computer Generated Activity Schedule for Sewer and Water Lines Project.

```
****************************
**   ACTIVITY SCHEDULE   **
****************************
```

PROJECT: SEWER & WATER LINES
SCHEDULE FOR ALL ACTIVITIES

ACTIVITY NUMBER	DESCRIPTION	DURA-TION	EARLY START	EARLY FINISH	LATE START	LATE FINISH	TOTAL FLOAT	FREE FLOAT
C 10	MOVE ON SITE	3	26MAY93 / 1	28MAY93 / 3	26MAY93 / 1	28MAY93 / 3	0	0
C 20	SURVEY SEWER LINES	4	31MAY93 / 4	3JUN93 / 7	31MAY93 / 4	3JUN93 / 7	0	0
C 30	EXCAVATE FOR MANHOLES	3	4JUN93 / 8	8JUN93 / 10	4JUN93 / 8	8JUN93 / 10	0	0
C 40	INSTALL MANHOLE FORMWORK	5	9JUN93 / 11	15JUN93 / 15	9JUN93 / 11	15JUN93 / 15	0	0
50	PLACE CONCRETE MANHOLES	5	16JUN93 / 16	22JUN93 / 20	19JUL93 / 39	23JUL93 / 43	23	0
C 60	TRENCH SEWER LINE	10	16JUN93 / 16	29JUN93 / 25	16JUN93 / 16	29JUN93 / 25	0	0
70	STRIP MANHOLE FORMWORK	2	23JUN93 / 21	24JUN93 / 22	26JUL93 / 44	27JUL93 / 45	23	18
C 80	LAY SEWER PIPE	15	30JUN93 / 26	20JUL93 / 40	30JUN93 / 26	20JUL93 / 40	0	0
90	INSPECT MANHOLES	1	21JUL93 / 41	21JUL93 / 41	28JUL93 / 46	28JUL93 / 46	5	5
100	REMOVE TRENCHING MACHINE	2	21JUL93 / 41	22JUL93 / 42	27JUL93 / 45	28JUL93 / 46	4	4
C 110	BACKFILL SEWER TRENCH	6	21JUL93 / 41	28JUL93 / 46	21JUL93 / 41	28JUL93 / 46	0	0
C EVENT 120	SEWER LINE COMPLETE	0	29JUL93 / 47	29JUL93 / 47	29JUL93 / 47	29JUL93 / 47	0	0
C 130	SURVEY WATER LINE A	6	29JUL93 / 47	5AUG93 / 52	29JUL93 / 47	5AUG93 / 52	0	0
140	SURVEY WATER LINE B	5	29JUL93 / 47	4AUG93 / 51	12AUG93 / 57	18AUG93 / 61	10	10
150	UNDERGROUND ELECTRICAL	5	29JUL93 / 47	4AUG93 / 51	27SEP93 / 89	1OCT93 / 93	42	0
160	DRILL WATER WELL	12	29JUL93 / 47	13AUG93 / 58	15SEP93 / 81	30SEP93 / 92	34	0
230	INSTALL WATER METERS	1	5AUG93 / 52	5AUG93 / 52	4OCT93 / 94	4OCT93 / 94	42	42
C 170	TRENCH WATER LINE A	9	6AUG93 / 53	18AUG93 / 61	6AUG93 / 53	18AUG93 / 61	0	0
240	SET WATER PUMP	2	16AUG93 / 59	17AUG93 / 60	1OCT93 / 93	4OCT93 / 94	34	34
180	LAY PIPE FOR WATER LINE A	7	19AUG93 / 62	27AUG93 / 68	1SEP93 / 71	9SEP93 / 77	9	9
C 190	TRENCH WATER LINE B	16	19AUG93 / 62	9SEP93 / 77	19AUG93 / 62	9SEP93 / 77	0	0
200	BACKFILL WATER LINE A	2	30AUG93 / 69	31AUG93 / 70	28SEP93 / 90	29SEP93 / 91	21	21
C 210	LAY PIPE FOR WATER LINE B	14	10SEP93 / 78	29SEP93 / 91	10SEP93 / 78	29SEP93 / 91	0	0
C 220	BACKFILL WATER LINE B	3	30SEP93 / 92	4OCT93 / 94	30SEP93 / 92	4OCT93 / 94	0	0
C EVENT 250	PROJECT COMPLETE	0	4OCT93 / 94	4OCT93 / 94	4OCT93 / 94	4OCT93 / 94	0	0

```
*************************************    END OF SCHEDULE    *************************************
```

TABLE 5-4
CODING SYSTEM FOR SEWER AND WATER LINE PROJECT

Code Number X X X X

Code Digit 1	Code Digit 2	Code Digit 3	Code Digit 4
0 – Unassigned	0 – Unassigned	0 – Unassigned	0 – Unassigned
1 – Sewer Line	1 – Surveying	1 – Line A	1 – Unassigned
2 – Water Lines	2 – Manholes	2 – Line B	2 – Unassigned
3 – Water Meter	3 – Trenching	3 – Unassigned	3 – Unassigned
4 – Water Pump	4 – Laying Pipe	4 – Unassigned	4 – Unassigned
5 – Milestones	5 – Backfill	5 – Unassigned	5 – Unassigned
6 – Unassigned	6 – Unassigned	6 – Unassigned	6 – Unassigned
7 – Unassigned	7 – Unassigned	7 – Unassigned	7 – Unassigned
8 – Unassigned	8 – Unassigned	8 – Unassigned	8 – Unassigned
9 – Unassigned	9 – Unassigned	9 – Unassigned	9 – Unassigned

Table 5-4 is a simple 4-digit coding system to illustrate sorting capabilities for the sewer and water project that is shown in Figure 5-5. All activities related to the sewer line are represented by the number "1" in the first digit. Water line activities are represented by the number "2." The second code digit represents the type of work, such as, surveying, forming manholes, trenching, laying pipe, backfilling, etc. Thus, a 4-digit code is assigned to each activity in the project. For example, the code for activity number 180 is 2410. This code represents the activity pertains to water line, laying pipe, and line A. The 4-digit code number for each activity in the sewer and water project is shown in the activity list of Figure 5-6.

The coding system provides numerous options for selection of activities by the project manager. For example, all sewer line activities can be sorted from the complete list of project activities by selecting those activities that have a "1" in the first digit. A schedule report for these activities is shown in Figure 5-8. A project manager may also print a bar chart for these activities as shown in Figure 5-9. A coding system provides a means of obtaining many other reports. For example, a sort of all activities related to trenching and laying pipe can be obtained by selecting activities that have a second code digit number that is greater than "2" and less than "5," reference Table 5-4.

COST DISTRIBUTION

The distribution of costs, with respect to time, must be known to successfully manage a project. In the preceding sections the scheduled early and late starts, and finishes, were calculated based on the duration and sequencing of activities. A cost analysis can also be performed by assigning the cost that is anticipated to complete each activity. The cost of an activity may be distributed over the duration of the activity, however,

FIGURE 5-8
Computer Printout of Sewer Line Activities Only (Sort of Activities List by Code Digit #1 Equal to One).

```
******************************
**   ACTIVITY  SCHEDULE   **
******************************
```

PROJECT: SEWER & WATER LINES
SCHEDULE FOR SEWER LINE ACTIVITIES ONLY   ** PAGE 1 **
                                                                              ACTIVITY SCHEDULE
****

ACTIVITY NUMBER	DESCRIPTION	DURA-TION	EARLY START	EARLY FINISH	LATE START	LATE FINISH	TOTAL FLOAT	FREE FLOAT
C 20	SURVEY SEWER LINES	4	31MAY93 4	3JUN93 7	31MAY93 4	3JUN93 7	0	0
C 30	EXCAVATE FOR MANHOLES	3	4JUN93 8	8JUN93 10	4JUN93 8	8JUN93 10	0	0
C 40	INSTALL MANHOLE FORMWORK	5	9JUN93 11	15JUN93 15	9JUN93 11	15JUN93 15	0	0
50	PLACE CONCRETE MANHOLES	5	16JUN93 16	22JUN93 20	19JUL93 39	23JUL93 43	23	0
C 60	TRENCH SEWER LINE	10	16JUN93 16	29JUN93 25	16JUN93 16	29JUN93 25	0	0
70	STRIP MANHOLE FORMWORK	2	23JUN93 21	24JUN93 22	26JUL93 44	27JUL93 45	23	18
C 80	LAY SEWER PIPE	15	30JUN93 26	20JUL93 40	30JUN93 26	20JUL93 40	0	0
90	INSPECT MANHOLES	1	21JUL93 41	21JUL93 41	28JUL93 46	28JUL93 46	5	5
100	REMOVE TRENCH EQUIP	2	21JUL93 41	22JUL93 42	27JUL93 45	28JUL93 46	4	4
C 110	BACKFILL SEWER TRENCH	6	21JUL93 41	28JUL93 46	21JUL93 41	28JUL93 46	0	0

```
*******************************************  END OF SCHEDULE  *******************************************
```

the activity may be performed over a range of time, starting from the early to late start and ending with the early to late finish.

Because activities can occur over a range of time, a cost analysis must be performed based on activities starting on an early start, late start, and target schedule. The target schedule is the mid-point between the early start and late start. Table 5-5 illustrates the early-start cost analysis calculations for the sewer and water line project shown in Figure 5-5. For each day in the project, the cost per day of each activity that is in progress is summed to obtain the total cost of the project for that day. Cumulative project costs are divided by the total project cost of $147,500 to obtain the percentage-cost for each day. The percentage-time for each day is calculated by dividing the number of the working days by the total project duration of 94 days. Similar calculations can be performed for activities starting on a late start schedule and target schedule.

Although the calculations for a cost analysis are simple, many are required, as illustrated by the small sewer and water line project that has only 25 activities and a 94 day project duration. A small microcomputer can perform all the calculations for cost analysis of a project with several hundred activities in less than two seconds.

```
                              ********************
                              **   BAR  CHART   **
                              ********************

PROJECT: SEWER & WATER LINES                                              **PAGE 1. 1 **
BAR CHART FOR ALL SEWER LINE ACTIVITIES ONLY                                  BAR CHART

                                              1        10       20       30       40       50       60
ACTIVITY  DESCRIPTION                DURATION  26MAY93  8JUN93   22JUN93  6JUL93   20JUL93  3AUG93   17AUG93
                                              +........+........+........+........+........+........+
C   20    SURVEY SEWER LINES             4     *XXX     .        .        .        .        .        .
C   30    EXCAVATE FOR MANHOLES          3     .  *XX   .        .        .        .        .        .
C   40    INSTALL MANHOLE FORMWORK       5     .     *XXXX       .        .        .        .        .
C   50    PLACE CONCRETE MANHOLES        5     .        .  XXXX------------*        .        .        .
C   60    TRENCH SEWER LINE             10     .        . *XXXXXXXXX       .        .        .        .
C   70    STRIP MANHOLE FORMWORK         2     .        .        . XX-----------------*    .        .
C   80    LAY SEWER PIPE                15     .        .        . *XXXXXXXXXXXXXX   .        .        .
C   90    INSPECT MANHOLES               1     .        .        .        . X-------*        .        .
C  100    REMOVE TRENCHING EQUIPMENT     2     .        .        .        .  XX----*         .        .
C  110    BACKFILL SEWER TRENCH          6     .        .        .        . *XXXXX  .        .        .
                                              +........+........+........+........+........+........+
                            WORK DAYS          1        10       20       30       40       50       60
                       CALENDAR DATES          26MAY93  8JUN93   22JUN93  6JUL93   20JUL93  3AUG93   17AUG93
```

FIGURE 5-9

Computer Generated Bar Chart for Sewer Line Activities Only.

TABLE 5-5
CALCULATIONS FOR PROJECT COSTS PER DAY ON AN EARLY START BASIS
TOTAL PROJECT DURATION = 94 WORKING DAYS
TOTAL PROJECT COST = $147,500.00

Day	%-Time	Activities in Progress			Project Cost/Day	Cumulative Project Cost	%-Cost
1	1.06%	Act. 10	$1,400/3	= $466.67/Day	$466.67	$466.67	0.32%
2	2.12%	" "	"	= "	"	$933.33	0.63%
3	3.19%	" "	"	= "	"	$1,400.00	0.95%
4	4.25%	Act. 20	$2,700/4	= $675.00/Day	$675.00	$2,075.00	1.41%
5	5.32%	" "	"	= "	"	$2,750.00	1.86%
6	6.38%	" "	"	= "	"	$3,425.00	2.32%
7	7.45%	" "	"	= "	"	$4,100.00	2.78%
8	8.51%	Act. 30	$3,500/3	= $1,167.67/Day	$1,167.67	$5,267.67	3.57%
9	9.57%	" "	"	= "	"	$6,433.33	4.36%
10	10.63%	" "	"	= "	"	$7,600.00	5.15%
11	11.70%	Act. 40	$6,000/5	= $1,200.00/Day	$1,200.00	$8,800.00	5.97%
12	12.77%	" "	"	= "	"	$10,000.00	6.78%
13	13.83%	" "	"	= "	"	$11,200.00	7.59%
14	14.89%	" "	"	= "	"	$12,400.00	8.41%
15	15.96%	" "	"	= "	"	$13,600.00	9.22%
16	17.02%	Act. 50	$4,700/5	= $940.00/Day			
		Act. 60	$12,600/10	= $1,260.00/Day	$2,200.00	$15,800.00	10.71%
17	18.09%	" "	"	= "	"	$18,000.00	12.20%
18	21.70%	" "	"	= "	"	$20,200.00	13.69%
19	20.21%	" "	"	= "	"	$22,400.00	15.19%
20	21.28%	" "	"	= "	"	$24,600.00	16.68%
21	22.34%	Act. 60	$12,600/10	= $1,260.00/Day			
		Act. 70	$2,100/2	= $1,050.00/Day	$2,310.00	$25,910.00	18.24%
⋮	⋮					⋮	⋮
94	100.0%					$147,500.00	100.0%

Figure 5-10 is a computer printout of the daily distribution of costs for the calculations illustrated in Table 5-5. A similar analysis can be performed for other resources, such as labor and equipment. For example, a daily distribution of labor-hours, similar to Figure 5-10, can be used to detect periods of time when the need for labor is high or low. The project manager and his or her team can detect this problem early and appropriately adjust the project plan, or acquire additional personnel if needed and available.

A tabular format of the distribution of costs on an early start, late start, and target basis is presented in Figure 5-11. The target scheduled costs are average values between the early and late start schedules. The right hand two columns of Figure 5-11 show the percentage-cost and percentage-time values for the target schedule. As shown in the figure there is a non-linear relationship between the time and cost for a project.

The cumulative cost graph for a project is commonly called the *S-curve*, because it resembles the shape of the letter "S." The early, late, and target cumulative distribution of costs can be superimposed onto one graph to form the envelope of time over which

FIGURE 5-10
Computer Printout of Daily Distribution of Costs for Sewer and Water Lines Project.

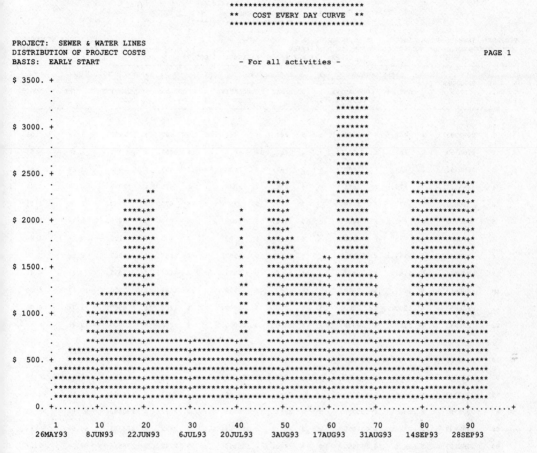

```
                                 ********************************
                                 **    COST EVERY DAY CURVE    **
                                 ********************************

PROJECT:  SEWER & WATER LINES
DISTRIBUTION OF PROJECT COSTS                                                      PAGE 1
BASIS:  EARLY START                    - For all activities -

$ 3500. +
       .
       .                                           *******
       .                                           *******
       .                                           *******
$ 3000. +                                          *******
       .                                           *******
       .                                           *******
       .                                           *******
       .                                           *******
$ 2500. +                                          *******
       .                            ***+*          *******            **+**********+*
       .              **            ***+*          *******            **+**********+*
       .         ****+**            ***+*          *******            **+**********+*
       .         ****+**       *    ***+*          *******            **+**********+*
$ 2000. +         ****+**       *    ***+*          *******            **+**********+*
       .         ****+**       *    ***+*          *******            **+**********+*
       .         ****+**       *    ***+**         *******            **+**********+*
       .         ****+**       *    ***+**         *******            **+**********+*
       .         ****+**       *    ***+**   *+    *******            **+**********+*
$ 1500. +         ****+**       *    ***+**********+  *******          **+**********+*
       .         ****+**       *    ***+**********+  *********+        **+**********+*
       .         ****+**       **   ***+**********+  *********+        **+**********+*
       .     ********+*****     **   ***+**********+  *********+        **+**********+*
       .  **.**********+*****    **   ***+**********+  *********+        **+**********+*
$ 1000. +  **+**********+*****    **   ***+**********+  *********+        **+**********+*
       .  **.**********+*****    **   ***+**********+**********+*********************+****
       .  **+**********+*****    **   ***+**********+**********+*********************+****
       .  **+*********+***********+**********+**   ***+**********+**********+*********************+****
       . *******+**********+**********+**********+**********+**********+**********+*********************+****
$  500. + *******+**********+**********+**********+**********+**********+**********+*********************+****
       . *******+**********+**********+**********+**********+**********+**********+*********************+****
       . *******+**********+**********+**********+**********+**********+**********+*********************+****
       . *******+**********+**********+**********+**********+**********+**********+*********************+****
       . *******+**********+**********+**********+**********+**********+**********+*********************+****
    0. +.........+.........+.........+.........+.........+.........+.........+.........+.........+.........+

        1        10        20        30        40        50        60        70        80        90
     26MAY93   8JUN93   22JUN93    6JUL93   20JUL93   3AUG93   17AUG93   31AUG93   14SEP93   28SEP93
```

costs may be distributed for the project, reference Figure 5-12. This graph links two of the basic elements of a project, time and cost. The third element, accomplished work, must also be linked to time and cost. Chapter 6 discusses linking accomplished work to the S-curve.

The type of reports presented in this section are typical examples of the reports that can be obtained from the many computer software programs that are available. The only input data that a project manager must prepare, to obtain the described analyses, is shown in Figure 5-6.

QUESTIONS FOR CHAPTER 5—PROJECT SCHEDULING

1 One of the obvious purposes of project planning and scheduling is to complete a project on time. Identify other benefits that can be derived from good project planning. Also describe typical problems that can be prevented by good planning and scheduling.

FIGURE 5-11
Computer Printout of Daily Costs for All Activities of Sewer and Water Lines Project.

```
                              *******************************
                              **   DAILY COST SCHEDULE   **
                              *******************************

PROJECT:  SEWER & WATER LINES                                              DAILY COST SCHEDULE
DAILY DISTRIBUTION OF PROJECT COSTS FOR ALL ACTIVITIES                      - For all activities -
                     START : 26 MAY 93      FINISH :  4 OCT 93
```

WORK DAY	CALENDAR DATE	EARLY START COST/DAY	CUMULATIVE COST	LATE START COST/DAY	CUMULATIVE COST	TARGET SCHEDULE COST/DAY	CUMULATIVE COST	%TIME	%COST
1	26MAY93	$ 467.	$ 467.	$ 467.	$ 467.	$ 467.	$ 467.	1.1%	.3%
2	27MAY93	$ 467.	$ 933.	$ 467.	$ 933.	$ 467.	$ 933.	2.1%	.6%
3	28MAY93	$ 467.	$ 1400.	$ 467.	$ 1400.	$ 467.	$ 1400.	3.2%	.9%
4	31MAY93	$ 675.	$ 2075.	$ 675.	$ 2075.	$ 675.	$ 2075.	4.3%	1.4%
5	1JUN93	$ 675.	$ 2750.	$ 675.	$ 2750.	$ 675.	$ 2750.	5.3%	1.9%
6	2JUN93	$ 675.	$ 3425.	$ 675.	$ 3425.	$ 675.	$ 3425.	6.4%	2.3%
7	3JUN93	$ 675.	$ 4100.	$ 675.	$ 4100.	$ 675.	$ 4100.	7.4%	2.8%
8	4JUN93	$ 1167.	$ 5267.	$ 1167.	$ 5267.	$ 1167.	$ 5267.	8.5%	3.6%
9	7JUN93	$ 1167.	$ 6433.	$ 1167.	$ 6433.	$ 1167.	$ 6433.	9.6%	4.4%
10	8JUN93	$ 1167.	$ 7600.	$ 1167.	$ 7600.	$ 1167.	$ 7600.	10.6%	5.2%
11	9JUN93	$ 1200.	$ 8800.	$ 1200.	$ 8800.	$ 1200.	$ 8800.	11.7%	6.0%
12	10JUN93	$ 1200.	$ 10000.	$ 1200.	$ 10000.	$ 1200.	$ 10000.	12.8%	6.8%
.	.	.	.	.	.	.	.	.	.
84	20SEP93	$ 2400.	$ 127850.	$ 2983.	$ 117783.	$ 2692.	$ 122817.	89.4%	83.3%
85	21SEP93	$ 2400.	$ 130250.	$ 2983.	$ 120767.	$ 2692.	$ 125508.	90.4%	85.1%
86	22SEP93	$ 2400.	$ 132650.	$ 2983.	$ 123750.	$ 2692.	$ 128200.	91.5%	86.9%
87	23SEP93	$ 2400.	$ 135050.	$ 2983.	$ 126733.	$ 2692.	$ 130892.	92.6%	88.7%
88	24SEP93	$ 2400.	$ 137450.	$ 2983.	$ 129717.	$ 2692.	$ 133583.	93.6%	90.6%
89	27SEP93	$ 2400.	$ 139850.	$ 3483.	$ 133200.	$ 2942.	$ 136525.	94.7%	92.6%
90	28SEP93	$ 2400.	$ 142250.	$ 3933.	$ 137133.	$ 3167.	$ 139692.	95.7%	94.7%
91	29SEP93	$ 2400.	$ 144650.	$ 3933.	$ 141067.	$ 3167.	$ 142858.	96.8%	96.9%
92	30SEP93	$ 950.	$ 145600.	$ 2033.	$ 143100.	$ 1492.	$ 144350.	97.9%	97.9%
93	1OCT93	$ 950.	$ 146550.	$ 2150.	$ 145250.	$ 1550.	$ 145900.	98.9%	98.9%
94	4OCT93	$ 950.	$ 147500.	$ 2250.	$ 147500.	$ 1600.	$ 147500.	100.0%	100.0%

```
*********************************** END OF DAILY COST SCHEDULE ***********************************
```

2 Describe advantages and disadvantages of each of the two basic techniques of project scheduling: bar charts and CPM networks. Include situations most appropriate for each of the two techniques.
3 Provide a brief summary of the responsibilities of the owner, designer, and contractor related to project planning and scheduling. Describe how the schedule of each party should

FIGURE 5-12
S-Curve for Sewer and Water Project.

CUMULATIVE COST CURVE

PROJECT: SEWER AND WATER PROJECT
CUMULATIVE COST CURVE FOR PROJECT

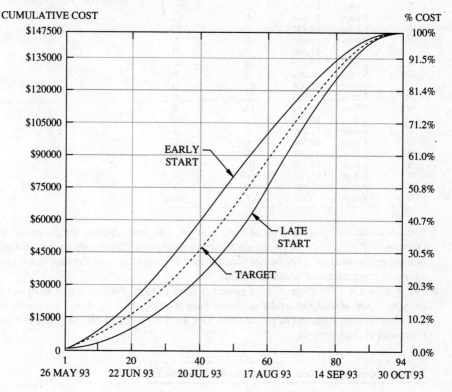

be related, including the advantages and disadvantages of maintaining one common schedule for a project.

4 A project manager is usually assigned the responsibility of either managing a single large project or many small projects at a time. Describe the different approaches to planning and scheduling that must be used by these two types of project managers.

5 Describe the purpose and use of a coding system for activities in a CPM project schedule. Include factors that should be considered in the development of the coding system and describe how the coding system can relate to the work breakdown structure, organizational breakdown structure, and the cost breakdown structure.

6 A list of activities that are required to complete a project is shown below. Draw a CPM precedence diagram for the project and calculate the project schedule. Provide the schedule in a tabular form, showing early/late starts and finishes as well as the total and free float for each activity. Denote the critical path on the network.

Activity	Duration	Cost	Preceded By	Followed By
A	2 days	$500	None	B,C,D
B	3 days	$900	A	E
C	4 days	$1,600	A	F
D	5 days	$500	A	G
E	7 days	$1,400	B	H
F	7 days	$1,500	C	I,L
G	8 days	$2,400	D	J,K
H	4 days	$800	E	L
I	2 days	$1,000	F	N
J	12 days	$3,600	G	M,O
K	5 days	$2,000	G	P
L	6 days	$1,200	F,H	Q
M	2 days	$900	J	N
N	2 days	$700	I,M	S
O	6 days	$1,800	J	R,T
P	4 days	$1,200	K	T
Q	4 days	$2,000	L	U
R	4 days	$1,600	O	S
S	2 days	$1,400	N,R	V
T	9 days	$1,800	O,P	V
U	2 days	$1,200	Q	V
V	3 days	$300	S,T,U	None

7 Perform a cost analysis based on an early start and late start schedule for the project in Question 6. Plot the S-curve for the early and late start costs. Show costs on the left-hand ordinate and percent costs on the right-hand. Along the abscissa, show the time in working days and in percentage of project duration.

8 The data for the CPM diagram for a project is shown below. Perform a cost analysis for the project and present the results in tabular form showing the daily distribution costs on an early start, late start, and target schedule. Plot the three S-curves on one graph to show the results of your analysis.

Activity	Duration	Cost	Preceded By	Followed By
A	2 days	$1,200	None	B,C,D
B	3 days	$3,300	A	E
C	8 days	$12,000	A	F
D	6 days	$18,000	A	F,G,H
E	8 days	$8,000	B	J
F	9 days	$27,000	C,D	K
G	12 days	$7,200	D	K,L,M
H	5 days	$5,000	D	I
I	3 days	$12,000	H	M
J	2 days	$1,600	E	N,R
K	5 days	$6,000	F,G	R
L	1 days	$1,500	G	O
M	2 days	$4,000	G,I	P,R
N	2 days	$8,000	J	Q
O	2 days	$1,200	L	R
P	4 days	$5,200	M	S
Q	2 days	$6,000	N	T
R	7 days	$7,000	J,K,M,O	V
S	2 days	$2,800	P	U
T	1 days	$5,000	Q	V
U	3 days	$3,000	S	V
V	5 days	$10,000	R,T,U	None

REFERENCES

1 Antill, J. M. and Woodhead, R. W., *Critical Path Methods in Construction Practice*, 3rd ed., Wiley, New York, 1982.
2 Armstrong-Writhe, A. T., *Critical Path Method*, Longman Group Ltd., London, 1969.
3 Burman, P. J., *Precedence Networks for Project Planning and Control*, McGraw-Hill, Inc., London, 1972.
4 Callahan, M. T., Quackenbush, D. G., and Rowings, J. E., *Construction Project Scheduling*, McGraw-Hill, Inc., New York, 1992.
5 Harris, R. B., *Precedence and Arrow Networking Techniques for Construction*, Wiley, New York, 1978.
6 Moder, J. J., Phillips, C. J., and Davis, E. D., *Project Management with CPM, PERT, and Precedence Diagraming*, 3rd ed., Van Nostrand Reinhold Company, New York, 1983.
7 O'Brien, J. J., *CPM in Construction Management*, 2nd ed., McGraw-Hill, Inc., New York, 1971.
8 Paulson, B. C., Jr., "Man-Computer Concepts for Planning and Scheduling," *Journal of Construction Division*, ASCE, New York, Vol. 100, No. 3, September, 1974.
9 Priluck, H. M., Hourihan, P. R., *Practical CPM for Construction*, Robert S. Means, Co., Duxbury, MA, 1968.
10 Spencer, G. R. and Rahbar, F. F., *Automation of the Scheduling Analysis Process*, Transactions of the American Association of Cost Engineers, San Diego, CA, October, 1989.
11 Stevens, J. D., *Techniques for Construction Network Scheduling*, McGraw-Hill, Inc., New York, 1990.
12 Wiest, J. D., and Levy, F. K., *A Management Guide to PERT/CPM*, Prentice-Hall, Englewood Cliffs, NJ, 1969.
13 Willis, E. M., *Scheduling Construction Projects*, Wiley, New York, 1986.

CHAPTER 6

TRACKING WORK

CONTROL SYSTEMS

Effective project management requires planning, measuring, evaluating, forecasting, and controlling all aspects of a project: quality and quantity of work, costs, and schedules. An all encompassing project plan must be defined before starting a project, otherwise there is no basis for control. Project tracking can not be accomplished without a well-defined work plan, budget, and schedule as discussed in the previous chapters of this book.

The project plan must be developed with input from people who will be performing the work, and it must be communicated to all participants. The tasks, costs, and schedules of the project plan establish the benchmarks and check-points that are necessary for comparing actual accomplishments to planned accomplishments, so the progress of a project can be measured, evaluated, and controlled.

At the end of any reporting period (N), a project is expected to have achieved an amount of work (X) with a level of quality (Q) at a predicted cost (C). The objective of project control is to measure the actual values of these variables and determine if the project is meeting the targets of the work plan, and to make any necessary adjustments to meet project objectives. Project control is difficult because it involves a quantitative and qualitative evaluation of a project that is in a continuous state of change.

To be effective, a project control system must be simple to administer and easily understood by all participants in a project. Control systems tend to fall into two categories; they are either so complex that no one can interpret the results that are obtained, or they are too limited because they apply to only costs or schedules rather than integrating costs, schedules, and work accomplished. A control system must be developed so information can be routinely collected, verified, evaluated, and communicated to all participants in a project; so it will serve as a tool for project improvement rather than reporting flaws that irritate people.

Since the introduction of small personal computers in the early 1980s, the automation of the concept of an integrated project control system has become widely discussed. Many papers have been written that describe different, but similar, approaches to integrated project control systems. Common among the approaches is development of a well-defined Work Breakdown Structure (WBS) as a starting point in the system. The smallest unit in the WBS is the work package, which defines the work in sufficient detail so it can be measured, budgeted, scheduled, and controlled.

The Critical Path Method (CPM) is used to develop the overall project schedule from the WBS by integrating and sequencing the work in accordance with the work packages. A coding system is designed that identifies each component of the WBS, so information from the WBS can be related to the project control system. To control costs the WBS is linked to the Cost Breakdown Structure (CBS) by the code of accounts. Likewise, the WBS is linked to the Organizational Breakdown Structure (OBS) to coordinate personnel to keep the project on schedule. A coding system allows the sorting of information to produce a variety of reports that are subsets of the entire project.

This general concept of project control was developed by the Department of Energy for federal and energy projects. Since that time, several modifications have been suggested to simplify the process of transferring information from the WBS to the CPM, linking the WBS and OBS to the coding system, and measurement of work accomplished.

LINKING THE WBS AND CPM

The work packages of the WBS provide the information necessary to develop a CPM logic network diagram. With a well-defined detailed WBS a single work package often becomes one activity on the diagram. However, sometimes it is necessary to combine several work packages into a single activity or to develop a single work package into several activities. The process of developing the CPM diagram requires good judgement with extensive involvement of key participants in the project. Although the level of detail should be kept to a minimum, all activities that may influence the project completion date must be included in the diagram.

A CPM diagram for project scheduling and control can be classified as one of three types: design, construction, or engineering/procurement/construction (EPC). For each, the WBS defines the project framework for planning, scheduling, and control of the work. The level of detail of the CPM diagram depends upon the completeness of the WBS.

The products of design are production drawings and specifications. As discussed in Chapter 5, a bar chart is frequently preferred for scheduling individual design activities. However, for effective scheduling control of the whole project, a composite of the individual bar charts must be integrated into a CPM diagram that shows the interrelationship and sequencing of related work. Thus, a CPM diagram for design is often a summary level schedule. CII publication 6-1, *Project Control for Engineering*, provides a good description of the current industry practice of scheduling and control of design.

CPM logic diagrams have been successfully used for scheduling and control of construction for many years. A detailed WBS can be developed as a cooperative effort of the estimating, project control, and field operations management personnel. The estimate must be prepared so that costs, durations, and resources can be assigned to work packages in the WBS. The work packages then become activities on the CPM diagram. The purchase and delivery of long lead-time material must also be included in the diagram. In addition, the work performed by subcontractors on the job must be integrated with other work to form a complete integrated CPM diagram. For large projects, a separate CPM diagram can be prepared for each individual area of the project, then a master CPM diagram can be developed that links the individual area diagrams.

The CPM diagram for an EPC project must interface the design work packages with the procurement and construction activities. It is often best to first develop separate individual working schedules for design, procurement, and construction. Then link the individual schedules into a summary EPC schedule that integrates the total system. It is imperative to sequence all related activities that may influence the completion date of the project.

To illustrate the linking of the WBS to the CPM, the WBS shown in Figure 6-1 is used to develop the CPM diagram in Figure 6-2. This EPC project is an expansion of the design project presented in Chapter 5, to now include the procurement and construction activities. It is a service facility for maintenance operations and consists of site-work, on-site utilities, an employee's office building, and a maintenance building. To handle this project, the contracting strategy is to use in-house personnel to design the on-site utilities, site-work, and the maintenance building. A separate contract is assigned for the design of the employee's building. The maintenance building is denoted as Building A and the office building as Building B on the WBS and CPM.

The contracting strategy for construction is to assign one contract to a heavy construction contractor to build all on-site utilities and site-work activities. Two building contractors will be used, one for the office building and the other for the industrial maintenance building. The construction activities are limited on the EPC schedule but will be expanded into more detail by each construction contractor as a part of their contractual requirements.

As shown in Figure 6-2, the appropriate design activities are directly linked to the procurement activities for materials and equipment. For example, the design of the overhead crane for Building A is followed by procurement and then construction. Likewise, design of the elevator for Building B is linked to its respective procurement and construction activities.

CODING SYSTEM FOR PROJECT REPORTS

A coding system can be developed that identifies each component of a project to allow the sorting of information in order to produce a variety of reports for project monitoring

FIGURE 6-1
WBS for EPC of Service Facility Project.

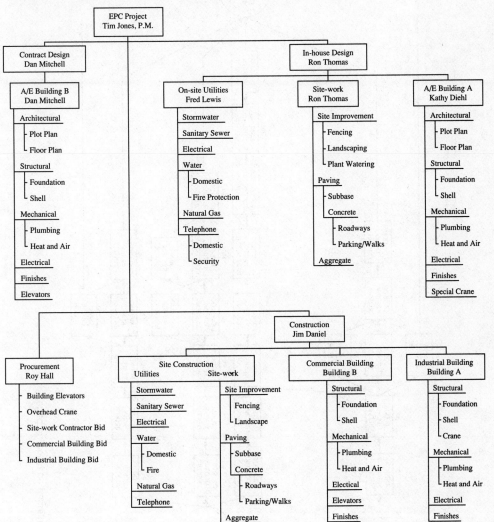

and control. A code number can be assigned to each work item that identifies a variety of information, such as, phase of project, type of work, responsible person, or facility of which the work item is a part. Table 6-1 is an illustrative example of a simple 4-digit coding system for the project shown in Figure 6-2.

Table 6-1 can be used to assign a code number that is unique to each activity in the CPM diagram of Figure 6-2 to link the WBS to the OBS and the CPM. For example, Activity 95 (Design of Foundations and Structure for Building A), is assigned the code

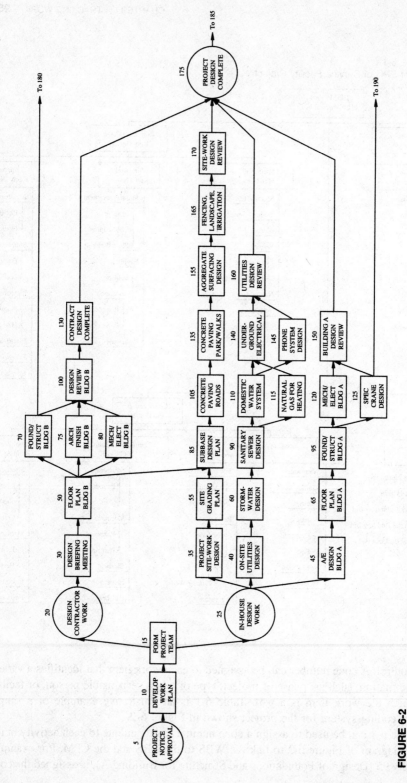

FIGURE 6-2
CPM Diagram for EPC Project (continued on following page).

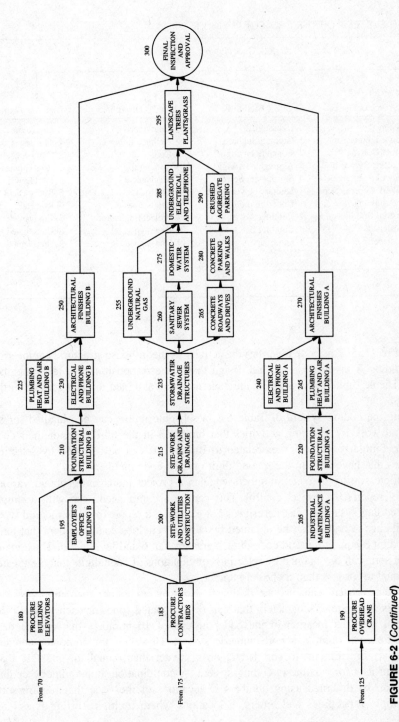

FIGURE 6-2 (*Continued*)
CPM Diagram for EPC Project (continued from previous page).

TABLE 6-1
CODING SYSTEM FOR THE PROJECT IN FIGURE 6-2

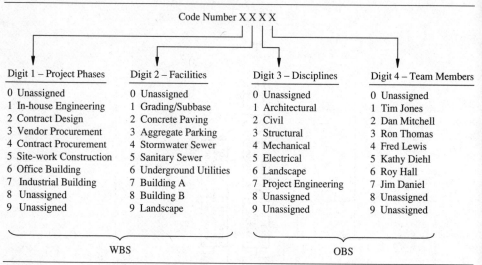

Code Number X X X X

Digit 1 – Project Phases	Digit 2 – Facilities	Digit 3 – Disciplines	Digit 4 – Team Members
0 Unassigned	0 Unassigned	0 Unassigned	0 Unassigned
1 In-house Engineering	1 Grading/Subbase	1 Architectural	1 Tim Jones
2 Contract Design	2 Concrete Paving	2 Civil	2 Dan Mitchell
3 Vendor Procurement	3 Aggregate Parking	3 Structural	3 Ron Thomas
4 Contract Procurement	4 Stormwater Sewer	4 Mechanical	4 Fred Lewis
5 Site-work Construction	5 Sanitary Sewer	5 Electrical	5 Kathy Diehl
6 Office Building	6 Underground Utilities	6 Landscape	6 Roy Hall
7 Industrial Building	7 Building A	7 Project Engineering	7 Jim Daniel
8 Unassigned	8 Building B	8 Unassigned	8 Unassigned
9 Unassigned	9 Landscape	9 Unassigned	9 Unassigned

WBS   OBS

number of 1735. This code identifies the activity as the in-house structural engineering for Building A involving structural design that is the responsibility of team member Kathy Diehl. Table 6-2 is a list of the code numbers assigned to each activity in the project.

Using the coding system of Table 6-1, a schedule report can be obtained for all structural work by selecting activities that have a 3 in the third digit of their code number. Similarly, all activities related to Building B can be obtained by selecting activities that have an 8 in the second digit of their code number.

Multiple sorting of codes numbers enables a project manager to obtain various levels of reports for project control. This can be accomplished even with a simple 4-digit coding system as just described. For example, a report for all structural work for Buildings A and B can be obtained by sorting activities code numbers that have a code digit 3 equal to 3, and code digit 2 greater than 6 and less than 9. Thus, many types of sorts can be obtained by selecting combinations of code digits that are greater than, equal to, or less than a chosen number.

A coding system can also be designed using letters, rather than numbers. Using letters there are 27 characters that can be designated (one for each letter in the alphabet), for each location in the code, instead of 10 numbers that can be designated for each digit in a pure numeric system. However, for computer applications it is more difficult to sort letters on a greater than, equal to, and less than basis, than it is for a numeric coding system. A combination alpha-numeric coding system can be designed using numbers in locations of the code that require sorting multiple capabilities and letters in locations where multiple sorting is not required.

TABLE 6-2
EPC PROJECT ACTIVITY LIST
EXAMPLE EPC MAINTENANCE FACILITY PROJECT

NO.	CODE	ACTIVITY DESCRIPTION	DURATION	COST	TEAM MEMBER
5	0071	PROJECT NOTICE APPROVAL	3	500.	TIM JONES
10	0071	DEVELOP WORK PLAN	7	12000.	TIM JONES
15	0071	FORM PROJECT TEAM	5	850.	TIM JONES
20	2872	DESIGN CONTRACTOR'S WORK	2	3000.	DAN MITCHELL
25	1073	IN-HOUSE DESIGN WORK	3	1500.	RON THOMAS
30	2872	DESIGN BRIEFING MEETING	1	1200.	DAN MITCHELL
35	1073	PROJECT SITE-WORK DESIGN	1	1400.	RON THOMAS
40	1624	ON-SITE UTILITIES DESIGN	1	1200.	FRED LEWIS
45	1715	A/E DESIGN BUILDING A	1	1500.	KATHY DIEHL
50	2812	FLOOR PLAN BUILDING B	10	9900.	DAN MITCHELL
55	1123	SITE GRADING PLAN	12	14000.	RON THOMAS
60	1424	STORMWATER DESIGN	10	2000.	FRED LEWIS
65	1715	FLOOR PLAN BUILDING A	15	26000.	KATHY DIEHL
70	2832	FOUND/STRUCT BUILDING B	45	31200.	DAN MITCHELL
75	2812	ARCH FINISHES BUILDING B	30	49500.	DAN MITCHELL
80	2842	MECH/ELECT BUILDING B	45	37300.	DAN MITCHELL
85	1123	SUBBASE DESIGN PLAN	5	4000.	RON THOMAS
90	1524	SANITARY SEWER DESIGN	10	12000.	FRED LEWIS
95	1735	FOUND/STRUCT BUILDING A	30	92700.	KATHY DIEHL
100	2871	DESIGN REVIEW BUILDING B	10	8000.	TIM JONES
105	1223	CONCRETE PAVING ROADS	20	12000.	RON THOMAS
110	1624	DOMESTIC WATER SYSTEM	7	9000.	FRED LEWIS
115	1624	NATURAL GAS SYSTEM	8	6000.	FRED LEWIS
120	1745	MECH/ELECT BUILDING A	30	22200.	KATHY DIEHL
125	1735	SPECIAL OVERLOAD CRANE	11	10800.	KATHY DIEHL
130	2872	CONTRACT DESIGN COMPLETE	1	1000.	DAN MITCHELL
135	1223	CONCRETE PAVING PARKING/WALKS	10	7000.	RON THOMAS
140	1654	UNDERGROUND ELECTRICAL	14	12000.	FRED LEWIS
145	1654	UNDERGROUND TELEPHONE SYSTEM	4	3000.	FRED LEWIS
150	1771	BUILDING A DESIGN REVIEW	3	5000.	TIM JONES
155	1323	AGGREGATE SURFACING DESIGN	8	6000.	RON THOMAS
160	1677	UTILITIES DESIGN REVIEW	1	1100.	TIM JONES
165	1963	FENCING/LANDSCAPE/IRRIGATION	14	28000.	RON THOMAS
170	1071	SITE-WORK DESIGN REVIEW	5	7000.	TIM JONES
175	0071	PROJECT DESIGN COMPLETE	1	1000.	TIM JONES
180	3876	PROCURE BUILDING ELEVATORS	25	95000.	ROY HALL
185	4076	PROCURE CONTRACTOR'S BIDS	20	7000.	ROY HALL
190	3776	PROCURE OVERHEAD CRANE	40	55000.	ROY HALL
195	6887	EMPLOYEE'S OFFICE BUILDING B	3	1000.	JIM DANIEL
200	5087	SITE-WORK/UTILITIES CONSTRUCTION	4	1500.	JIM DANIEL
205	7787	INDUSTRIAL/MAINTENANCE BLDG A	2	1400.	JIM DANIEL
210	6882	FOUND/STRUCT BUILDING B	45	195000.	DAN MITCHELL
215	5083	SITE-WORK/GRADING/DRAINAGE	18	85000.	RON THOMAS
220	7785	FOUND/STRUCT BUILDING A	110	390000.	KATHY DIEHL
225	6882	PLUMBING, HEAT, & AIR BLDG B	75	285000.	DAN MITCHELL
230	6882	ELECTRICAL/PHONE BUILDING B	60	215000.	DAN MITCHELL
235	5484	STORMWATER/DRAINAGE STRUCTURES	15	22000.	FRED LEWIS
240	7785	ELECTRICAL/PHONE BUILDING A	65	167000.	KATHY DIEHL
245	7785	PLUMBING, HEAT, & AIR BLDG A	85	192000.	KATHY DIEHL
250	6882	ARCH FINISHES BUILDING B	50	260000.	DAN MITCHELL
255	5684	UNDERGROUND NATURAL GAS	5	10500.	FRED LEWIS
260	5584	SANITARY SEWER SYSTEM	21	33200.	FRED LEWIS
265	5283	CONCRETE PAVING ROADS & DRIVES	60	185000.	RON THOMAS
270	7785	ARCH FINISHES BUILDING A	30	175000.	KATHY DIEHL
275	5684	DOMESTIC WATER SYSTEM	7	13200.	FRED LEWIS
280	5283	CONCRETE PARKING & WALKWAYS	15	35000.	RON THOMAS
285	5684	UNDERGROUND ELECT & PHONE	14	47000.	FRED LEWIS
290	5383	CRUSHED AGGREGATE PARKING	40	76000.	RON THOMAS
295	5983	LANDSCAPE TREES/PLANTS/GRASS	20	62000.	RON THOMAS
300	9977	FINAL INSPECTION & APPROVAL	3	3500.	TIM JONES

CONTROL SCHEDULES FOR TIME AND COST

The CPM network diagram shows the sequencing of activities that represent the work packages identified by the WBS. The expected time and cost that is required to perform each activity can be obtained from the work packages of the WBS in order to establish the parameters for control of cost and time. For each activity of the EPC project shown in Figure 6-2, Table 6-2 provides the cost and duration along with the team member who is responsible for the activity. These costs and durations are directly related to the WBS and their expenditure is directly related to the work that is produced. To measure the progress of the project, the actual costs and durations are compared to these control costs and durations.

The total cost for the project includes the direct costs (from the previous paragraph) plus indirect costs, contingency reserve, and profit. A cost breakdown structure (CBS) for the project includes all of these costs. However, only the direct costs that are tied to the WBS are used for project control purposes to manage the accomplishment of work. Indirect costs include support personnel, equipment, and supplies that are not be directly chargeable to the project. The cost of insurance, bonds, general office overhead, etc., are also excluded from the project control system for monitoring costs and managing work because these items are fixed at the beginning of the project and they are independent of the work accomplished. The management of these costs is generally a function of the accounting department, because the project manager and his or her team usually do not have control of these costs. These costs are typically distributed over a specified period of time and will expand or contract with the schedule.

A good description of the relationship between engineering cost breakdown structures (CBS) and work breakdown structures (WBS) is provided in CII publication 6-1, *Project Control for Engineering*. Figure 6-3 is an example from the publication that illustrates a total engineering budget matrix. The CBS includes all elements in the budget matrix that have been given a dollar amount. The total dollar value of all of the elements is the total engineering budget. The WBS for the project consists of budget items from the CBS for tasks that produce deliverables; design calculations, drawings, and specifications.

For the example of Figure 6-3, the functions that are chosen for work control are shaded in the matrix, and are: design and drawings, specifications, procurement support, and field support. The detailed WBS would be expanded from these budget items into areas, systems, and subsystems that define the total project. For example, the deliverable to be produced by the electrical group would be a drawing list that included all drawings for electrical work. The number of work-hours (WH) for each drawing and the number of WH of calculations that are required to produce the drawings would represent the budget.

The schedule for the work is the total time to produce the final drawings, including the overlap of design calculations and design drafting. As discussed in Chapter 5 most engineers prefer a bar chart for scheduling individual design tasks. However, for project control the individual bar charts must be developed into activities on the CPM diagram for the total project schedule. The start and finish of each activity of

Engineering Budget Matrix

ACTIVITY OR COST ELEMENT / FUNCTION	DESIGN AND DRAWINGS	SPECS	PROCUREMENT SUPPORT	FIELD SUPPORT	SUPERVISION AND CONTROL	TRAVEL	SUPPLIES AND SERVICES
MANAGEMENT					WH & $		
PROCUREMENT			WH & $	WH & $		$	$
DISCIPLINES — CIVIL	WH & $	WH & $	WH & $	WH & $	WH & $		
ELECTRICAL	WH & $	WH & $	WH & $	WH & $	WH & $		
ETC.	WH & $	WH & $	WH & $	WH & $	WH & $		

FIGURE 6-3

Engineering Cost Breakdown Structure and Work Breakdown Structure.
Source: Construction Industry Institute, Publication No. 6-1.

the CPM engineering design schedule is a composite of all tasks of the work package. The following illustrates the evaluation of overlapping tasks of the work package to determine the duration of an activity on the CPM diagram.

Tasks of Work Package	Duration
Project Engineering	7 days
Electrical Engineering	19 days
CADD Operator	8 days
Total Budgeted Days =	34 days

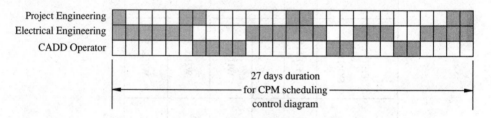

Project Engineering
Electrical Engineering
CADD Operator

27 days duration
for CPM scheduling
control diagram

CII publication 6-4, *Contractor Planning for Fixed-Price Construction*, provides a good description of the relationship of the CBS and WBS for construction. Figure 6-4 is an example from the publication that shows the WBS is the direct cost portion of the CBS. The WBS includes work that is budgeted, scheduled, and controlled. The estimate should be prepared in the same organizational format as the WBS. The quantity takeoff from the plans and specifications is used as the basis for direct labor, material, and equipment costs. The cost estimate should also consider the method of construction and the sequencing of work for development of the project schedule.

The general superintendent who will be responsible for the project on the construction jobsite must be involved in developing the detailed construction schedule. However, during the early stages of project development, it is often necessary to develop a construction schedule before the construction contractor has been identified. For this type of situation, the initial CPM diagram for construction must be developed without excessive constraints in the sequencing of activities. The CPM schedule should show the sequencing of major areas of the project and identify the general flow of work. Then, prior to construction, a detailed CPM diagram can be developed by the construction personnel who will actually perform the work.

A construction contractor usually performs some work with direct-hire (force account) personnel and contracts portions of the work to one or more subcontractors. Since many subcontractors do not have an elaborate project control system, the assignment of work to a subcontractor should be a work package that has a scope of work, budget, and schedule that is defined in sufficient detail so their responsibilities and duties are clearly understood. The subcontract work package must be compatible with the WBS, otherwise there is no basis for control.

Milestone dates that are required for the start and completion of each subcontractor's work should be clearly defined, including any hold in work that may be necessary in order to schedule the work of other subcontractors. Each subcontractor is an independent company and not an employee of the general contractor. However, each

FIGURE 6-4
WBS vs. CBS.
Source: Construction Industry Institute, Publication No. 6-4.

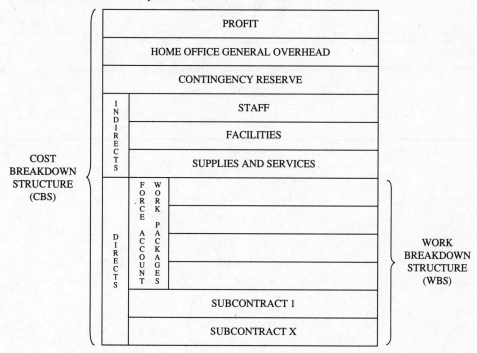

subcontractor's work must be included in the total project schedule since the work of any one contractor usually affects the work of other contractors on the job, which can impact the completion date of the project.

The unsuccessful procurement of material is a common source of delays during construction. A procurement plan must be included in the project schedule to guide the purchase of contractor furnished materials. Although the contractor generally obtains most of the material as a part of his or her construction contract, many projects require the procurement of special material and equipment that is unique to the project. Also, the owner may procure equipment or bulk materials that are to be installed by the construction contractor. The project schedule should identify and sequence all activities that can impact the delivery of special material and equipment.

The previous sections presented the list of activities, costs, durations, and coding system for the EPC project that is shown in Figure 6-2. The preparation of this data provides the base for a project monitoring and control system. For example, to evaluate the engineering design phase of the project an S-curve, see Figure 6-5, can be produced that shows the distribution of costs for all design work. This curve is obtained using the coding system of Table 6-1, by selecting all activities in which the first digit of their code is less than 3.

FIGURE 6-5
S-Curve for All Design Work.

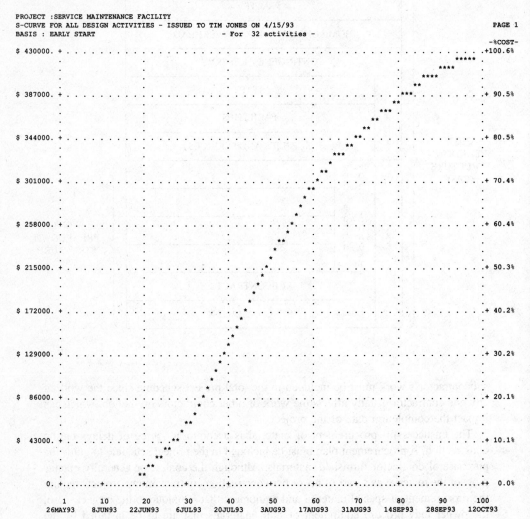

```
                        ******************************
                        **  CUMULATIVE COST CURVE   **
                        ******************************

PROJECT :SERVICE MAINTENANCE FACILITY
S-CURVE FOR ALL DESIGN ACTIVITIES - ISSUED TO TIM JONES ON 4/15/93                    PAGE 1
BASIS : EARLY START                       - For  32 activities -
                                                                                      -%COST-
$ 430000. + . . . . . . . . . . . . . . . . . . . . . . . . . . . . . . . . . . .+100.6%
           .             .             .             .             .         *****
           .             .             .             .             .        ****
           .             .             .             .             .    ****
$ 387000. + . . . . . . . . . . . . . . . . . . . . . . . . . . **. . . .+ 90.5%
           .             .             .             .        ***.
           .             .             .             .       ***
           .             .             .             .      **
$ 344000. + . . . . . . . . . . . . . . . . . . . . **. . . . . . . . . .+ 80.5%
           .             .             .             .    **
           .             .             .           ***
           .             .             .          **
$ 301000. + . . . . . . . . . . . . . . . . .*. . . . . . . . . . . . . .+ 70.4%
           .             .             .    **
           .             .             .   *
           .             .             .  *
$ 258000. + . . . . . . . . . . . . . . . . . . . . . . . . . . . . . . .+ 60.4%
           .             .           **
           .             .          *
           .             .         *
$ 215000. + . . . . . . . . . . . .*. . . . . . . . . . . . . . . . . . .+ 50.3%
           .             .        *
           .             .       *
           .             .      *
$ 172000. + . . . . . . . . . .*. . . . . . . . . . . . . . . . . . . . .+ 40.2%
           .             .   *
           .             .  *
           .             . *
$ 129000. + . . . . . . . .*. . . . . . . . . . . . . . . . . . . . . . .+ 30.2%
           .            *
           .           *
           .          *
$  86000. + . . . . . .*. . . . . . . . . . . . . . . . . . . . . . . . .+ 20.1%
           .          *
           .        **
           .       *
$  43000. + . . . .**. . . . . . . . . . . . . . . . . . . . . . . . . . .+ 10.1%
           .     **
           .    **
           .   **
        0. + . .**. . . . + . . . . + . . . . + . . . . + . . . + . . . + . . . + . . . + . . . ++ 0.0%
           1        10        20        30        40        50        60        70        80        90       100
        26MAY93   8JUN93   22JUN93    6JUL93   20JUL93    3AUG93   17AUG93  31AUG93  14SEP93  28SEP93  12OCT93
```

Additional reports can be computer generated as discussed in Chapter 5. For example, Figure 6-6 shows the graph of daily cost for all in-house engineering design. It can be obtained by selecting all activities that have a 1 in the first digit of their code number. A similar curve can be obtained for work-hours which would show the personnel requirements needed to perform the work.

Table 6-3 is a partial listing of the project control schedule for all activities in the project. Only the first and last portion of the total schedule is shown to illustrate the

FIGURE 6-6
Distribution of Daily Costs for All In-House Design Work.

```
                              ****************************
                              **  COST EVERY DAY CURVE  **
                              ****************************
PROJECT: SERVICE MAINTENANCE FACILITY
DISTRIBUTION OF COSTS FOR ALL DESIGN WORK - ISSUED TO TIM JONES ON 4/15/93          PAGE 1
BASIS : EARLY START                      - For  32 activities -
$ 10000. +
        .
        .
        .
$  9000. +
        .                           +******
        .                           +******
        .                           +****** **+*
$  8000. +                    **    +****** **+*
        .                    *****+****** **+*      **
        .                    *****+******* **+* *********
        .                    *****+***********+*********
        .            +*      *****+***********+*********
$  7000. +            +*      *****+***********+*********
        .            +*********+***********+*********
        .            +*********+***********+*********
        .            +***********+***********+*********    *
        .            *+***********+***********+*********    *
$  6000. +            *+***********+***********+*********+**
        .            *+***********+***********+*********+**
        .            *+***********+***********+*********+**
        .            *+***********+***********+*********+**
        .            *+***********+***********+*********+****
$  5000. +      *     *+***********+***********+*********+****
        .      *     *+***********+***********+*********+****
        .      *     *+***********+***********+*********+****
        .      *     *+***********+***********+*********+****
        .      *     *+***********+***********+*********+****               *
$  4000. +      *+***********+***********+***********+*********+****          *
        .      *+***********+***********+***********+***********+***  *
        .      *+***********+***********+***********+***********+***  *        *
        .      *+***********+***********+***********+***********+*** *****+****
        .      *+***********+***********+***********+***********+***********+****
$  3000. +      *+***********+***********+***********+***********+***********+****
        .      *+***********+***********+***********+***********+***********+****
        .      *+***********+***********+***********+***********+***********+********
        .      *+***********+***********+***********+***********+***********+********
        .      *+***********+***********+***********+***********+***********+********
$  2000. +   ** *+***********+***********+***********+***********+***********+****
        .   ** *+***********+***********+***********+***********+***********+****
        . ****+***********+***********+***********+***********+***********+*********** ***
        . ****+***********+***********+***********+***********+***********+*********** ***
        . ****+***********+***********+***********+***********+***********+*********** ***
$  1000. +   ****+***********+***********+***********+***********+***********+*********** ****
        . ****+***********+***********+***********+***********+***********+*********** ****
        . ****+***********+***********+***********+***********+***********+***********+*******
        . ****+***********+***********+***********+***********+***********+***********+*******
        . ****+***********+***********+***********+***********+***********+***********+*******
     0. +........+.........+.........+.........+.........+.........+.........+.........+.........+.........+
        1       10        20        30        40        50        60        70        80        90       100
      26MAY93  8JUN93   22JUN93   6JUL93   20JUL93   3AUG93   17AUG93   31AUG93   14SEP93   28SEP93  12OCT93
```

type of information that can be obtained for all of the 93 activities in the total project. Critical activities are those activities that have zero float time and are denoted by the letter (C) at the left of the activity number. Major milestone events are also noted on the schedule. This schedule is a summary-level schedule report that integrates engineering, procurement, and construction.

```
                    ******************************
                    **  ACTIVITY  SCHEDULE   **
                    ******************************
```

PROJECT: SERVICE MAINTENANCE FACILITY
SCHEDULE FOR ALL ACTIVITIES - ISSUED TO TIM JONES ON 4/15/93   ** PAGE 1 **
                                                                                ACTIVITY SCHEDULE

ACTIVITY NUMBER		DESCRIPTION	DURA-TION	EARLY START	EARLY FINISH	LATE START	LATE FINISH	TOTAL FLOAT	FREE FLOAT
C	5	PROJECT NOTICE APPROVAL	3	26MAY93 1	28MAY93 3	26MAY93 1	28MAY93 3	0	0
C	10	DEVELOP WORK PLAN	7	31MAY93 4	8JUN93 10	31MAY93 4	8JUN93 10	0	0
C	15	FORM PROJECT TEAM	5	9JUN93 11	15JUN93 15	9JUN93 11	15JUN93 15	0	0
	20	DESIGN CONTRACTOR'S WORK	2	16JUN93 16	17JUN93 17	25JUN93 23	28JUN93 24	7	0
C	25	IN-HOUSE DESIGN WORK	3	16JUN93 16	18JUN93 18	16JUN93 16	18JUN93 18	0	0
	30	DESIGN BRIEFING MEETING	1	18JUN93 18	18JUN93 18	29JUN93 25	29JUN93 25	7	0
	35	PROJECT SITE-WORK DESIGN	1	21JUN93 19	21JUN93 19	25JUN93 23	25JUN93 23	4	0
	40	ON-SITE UTILITIES DESIGN	1	21JUN93 19	21JUN93 19	9AUG93 54	9AUG93 54	35	0
C	45	A/E DESIGN BUILDING A	1	21JUN93 19	21JUN93 19	21JUN93 19	21JUN93 19	0	0
	50	FLOOR PLAN BUILDING B	10	21JUN93 19	2JUL93 28	30JUN93 26	13JUL93 35	7	0
	55	SITE GRADING PLAN	12	22JUN93 20	7JUL93 31	28JUN93 24	13JUL93 35	4	0
	60	STORM-WATER DESIGN	10	22JUN93 20	5JUL93 29	10AUG93 55	23AUG93 64	35	0
C	65	FLOOR PLAN BUILDING A	15	22JUN93 20	12JUL93 34	22JUN93 20	12JUL93 34	0	0
	70	FOUND/STRUCT BUILDING B	45	5JUL93 29	3SEP93 73	22JUL93 42	22SEP93 86	13	0
	.	.	.	.	.	.	.	.	.
	.	.	.	.	.	.	.	.	.
	.	.	.	.	.	.	.	.	.
	225	PLUMBING, HEAT, & AIR BLDG B	75	13JAN94 167	27APR94 241	30MAR94 221	12JUL94 295	54	0
	230	ELECTRICAL/PHONE BUILDING B	60	13JAN94 167	6APR94 226	20APR94 236	12JUL94 295	69	15
	275	DOMESTIC WATER SYSTEM	7	27JAN94 177	4FEB94 183	26JUL94 305	3AUG94 311	128	0
	285	UNDERGROUND ELECT & PHONE	14	7FEB94 184	24FEB94 197	4AUG94 312	23AUG94 325	128	73
	280	CONCRETE PARKING & WALKWAYS	15	23MAR94 216	12APR94 230	8JUN94 271	28JUN94 285	55	0
	240	ELECTRICAL/PHONE BUILDING A	65	13APR94 231	12JUL94 295	11MAY94 251	9AUG94 315	20	20
C	245	PLUMBING, HEAT, & AIR BLDG A	85	13APR94 231	9AUG94 315	13APR94 231	9AUG94 315	0	0
	290	CRUSHED AGGREGATE PARKING	40	13APR94 231	7JUN94 270	29JUN94 286	23AUG94 325	55	0
	250	ARCH FINISHES BUILDING B	50	28APR94 242	6JUL94 291	13JUL94 296	20SEP94 345	54	54
	295	LANDSCAPE TREES/PLANTS/GRASS	20	8JUN94 271	5JUL94 290	24AUG94 326	20SEP94 345	55	55
C	270	ARCH FINISHES BUILDING A	30	10AUG94 316	20SEP94 345	10AUG94 316	20SEP94 345	0	0
C	300	FINAL INSPECTION & APPROVAL	3	21SEP94 346	23SEP94 348	21SEP94 346	23SEP94 348	0	0

```
*********************************  END OF SCHEDULE  *********************************
```

TABLE 6-3
SCHEDULE FOR ALL ACTIVITIES

Table 6-4 is a monthly cost schedule for the entire project. The distribution of costs are shown on an early start, late start, and target basis. The percentage-time and percentage-cost distribution are shown in the two rightmost columns. There is a non-linear distribution between costs and time. For example, at the end of the 6th month, which represents 32.5% of the time of completion, only 17.8% of the costs are anticipated to be expended. However, at the end of the 11th month, 63.8% of the time, 53.9% of the costs are expected to be expended.

RELATIONSHIPS BETWEEN TIME AND WORK

Measurement of design work is difficult because design is a creative process that involves ideas, calculations, evaluation of alternatives, and other tasks that are not physically measurable quantities. Considerable time and cost can be expended in performing these tasks before end results such as: drawings, specifications, reports, etc., which are measurable quantities of work, are ever seen.

The measurement of design is further complicated because of the diversity of the work. For example, all of the design calculations may be complete, half of the drawings may be produced, and yet only one fourth of the specifications may be written. For this situation it is difficult to determine how much work has been accomplished because the work that is produced does not have a common unit of measure. Because of this, a percentage of completion is commonly used as a unit of measure of design work. The criteria for determining the percent complete for measuring work must be developed and confirmed in writing with the project team members prior to commencing design. This provides a common basis for the monthly evaluation of progress.

A weighting multiplier can be assigned to design tasks to define the magnitude of effort that is required to achieve each task. The sum of the weighting factors is 1.0, which represents 100% of the total design effort. The determination of each weight should be a joint effort between the project manager and the designer who is responsible for performing the work. This should be done before starting work.

A significant amount of overlap work is necessary during the design process. For example, initial drafting normally starts before the design calculations are finished. Likewise, final calculations are often not complete before the final production drawings are started. The project manager and his or her team members can jointly define the overlap of related work to show the timing of tasks throughout the duration of a project. Table 6-5 is an illustrative example that lists work items, weight multiplier, and estimated timing for each task required in a design effort. Further division of weight multipliers within each category may also be necessary.

The information in Table 6-5 is provided for illustrative purposes only. Because each project is unique, it is necessary to define the weight multipliers that are appropriate for each individual project. The timing of design work depends upon the availability of personnel. This information can be compiled from a summary of the individual design work packages.

To manage the overall design effort a work/time curve can be developed from the information in Table 6-5, see Figure 6-7. The upper portion of Figure 6-7 is a series of

```
*********************************
**  MONTHLY COST SCHEDULE  **
*********************************
```

PROJECT: SERVICE MAINTENANCE FACILITY
SCHEDULE FOR ALL ACTIVITIES - ISSUED TO TIM JONES ON 4/15/93
                START : 26 MAY 93   FINISH : 23 SEP 94

MONTHLY COST SCHEDULE
- For all activities -

I NO.	MONTH YEAR	I	EARLY START		I	LATE START		I	TARGET SCHEDULE				I
			COST/MON	CUMULATIVE COST		COST/MON	CUMULATIVE COST		COST/MON	CUMULATIVE COST	%TIME	%COST	
1	MAY 93		$ 2214.	$ 2214.		$ 2214.	$ 2214.		$ 2214.	$ 2214.	1.1%	.1%	
2	JUN 93		$ 50556.	$ 52770.		$ 36359.	$ 38573.		$ 43457.	$ 45672.	7.5%	1.5%	
3	JUL 93		$ 168792.	$ 221562.		$ 95992.	$ 134566.		$ 132392.	$ 178064.	13.8%	5.8%	
4	AUG 93		$ 139053.	$ 360614.		$ 136051.	$ 270616.		$ 137552.	$ 315615.	20.1%	10.3%	
5	SEP 93		$ 166931.	$ 527545.		$ 160525.	$ 431141.		$ 163728.	$ 479343.	26.4%	15.7%	
6	OCT 93		$ 65805.	$ 593350.		$ 60334.	$ 491475.		$ 63069.	$ 542413.	32.5%	17.8%	
7	NOV 93		$ 183637.	$ 776987.		$ 65957.	$ 557432.		$ 124797.	$ 667210.	38.8%	21.9%	
8	DEC 93		$ 247116.	$ 1024103.		$ 111945.	$ 669377.		$ 179531.	$ 846740.	45.4%	27.7%	
9	JAN 94		$ 308169.	$ 1332272.		$ 168332.	$ 837710.		$ 238251.	$ 1084991.	51.4%	35.5%	
10	FEB 94		$ 334785.	$ 1667058.		$ 238998.	$ 1076708.		$ 286892.	$ 1371883.	57.2%	44.9%	
11	MAR 94		$ 317029.	$ 1984086.		$ 233279.	$ 1309986.		$ 275154.	$ 1647036.	63.8%	53.9%	
12	APR 94		$ 231428.	$ 2215515.		$ 230945.	$ 1540931.		$ 231187.	$ 1878223.	69.8%	61.5%	
13	MAY 94		$ 262417.	$ 2477932.		$ 318499.	$ 1859431.		$ 290458.	$ 2168681.	76.1%	71.0%	
14	JUN 94		$ 282817.	$ 2760749.		$ 329191.	$ 2188622.		$ 306004.	$ 2474685.	82.5%	81.1%	
15	JUL 94		$ 98089.	$ 2858838.		$ 306575.	$ 2495196.		$ 202332.	$ 2677017.	88.5%	87.7%	
16	AUG 94		$ 109145.	$ 2967983.		$ 356587.	$ 2851783.		$ 232866.	$ 2909883.	95.1%	95.3%	
17	SEP 94		$ 85167.	$ 3053150.		$ 201367.	$ 3053150.		$ 143267.	$ 3053150.	100.0%	100.0%	

END OF MONTHLY COST SCHEDULE

```
*********************************
```

TABLE 6-4
MONTHLY COST DISTRIBUTION FOR ALL ACTIVITIES IN THE PROJECT

TABLE 6-5
ILLUSTRATIVE WEIGHT MULTIPLIERS FOR DESIGN
WORK

Design Work	Weight Multiplier	Project Timing
Review backup material	0.05	0% - 10%
Design calculations	0.10	10% - 25%
Initial drafting	0.25	15% - 45%
Final calculations	0.20	35% - 60%
Production drawings	0.30	50% - 90%
Drawing approval	0.10	90% - 100%
	1.00	

graphs that represent each design task individually, arranged in the order of occurrence. The slope of each graph is the ratio of the weight multiplier to the time required for the work to be performed. The lower portion of Figure 6-7 is the work/time curve for the entire design effort and is obtained by a composite, superposition of the individual graphs. This curve represents the planned accomplishment of work and serves as a basis of control for comparison to actual work accomplished. It can be superimposed onto the time/cost S-curve that was discussed in the preceding section. This forms the overall integrated cost/schedule/work curve which is discussed later in subsequent sections of this chapter.

Construction involves many different types of work that have different units of measurement, such as, cubic yards, square feet, pounds, each, etc. Thus, it is convenient to use percentage as a unit of measure for management and control of overall construction.

The procedure used for the measurement of design can also be applied to construction. For example, a project may consist of three major facilities: site-work, a concrete office building, and a pre-engineered metal building. A weight multiplier can be applied to each of the three major facilities, along with their planned sequence of occurrence, reference Table 6-6.

TABLE 6-6
ILLUSTRATIVE WEIGHT MULTIPLIER FOR
CONSTRUCTION

Facility	Weight Multiplier	Project Timing
Site-work	0.25	0% - 35%
Concrete building	0.40	15% - 75%
Metal building	0.35	65% - 100%
	1.00	

FIGURE 6-7
Work/Time Relationship for All Design Work.

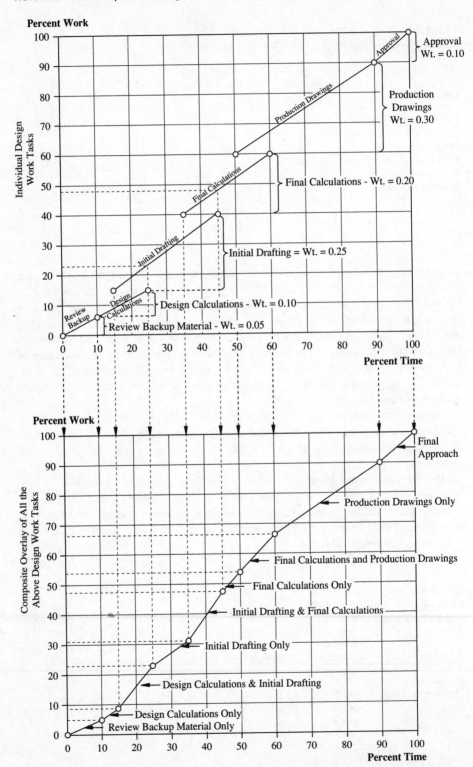

Table 6-6 only lists three major parts of the project. A more accurate definition of the planned work can be achieved by dividing each of the major facilities into smaller components. For example, site-work can be divided into grading, drainage, paving, landscaping, etc. Likewise, each of the two buildings can be divided into smaller components. Regardless of the level of detail of the project, the sum of all of the weight multipliers would be equal to 1.0 to represent 100% of the project. The weight and timing of each major facility is established by key participants of the project team, before starting construction, to serve as a basis of control during construction.

Figure 6-8 shows a composite of the planned accomplishment of work. The upper portion of Figure 6-8 is a graphical display of the overlap and sequence of each of the three major facilities. The lower portion is the integrated work/time curve for the entire project and is obtained by a composite superposition of the three individual graphs of each major facility.

This procedure is a top level summary of all facilities in the total project. This same procedure can be used for each facility, or parts of each facility, depending upon the complexity of the project and the level of control that is desired by the project manager.

At the lowest level it may be possible to use a unit of measure for work that can be physically measured at the job site, rather than using a percentage. For example, "wire pulling" can be easily measured in linear feet, or "concrete piers" can be measured in cubic yards. However, some precautions must be taken when physical quantities are used to measure work in place of a percentage. To illustrate, the construction of concrete piers involves drilling, setting steel, and placement of concrete. For a project that has 18 piers, a progress report may show all piers drilled, steel set in 9 piers, and concrete placed in 3 piers. If cubic yards is the only measure of control, only 3 of the 18 piers would be reported as complete, which would not include the drilling and steel work that is accomplished. For this situation, a weight multiplier system must be developed to account for each task that is required to construct the piers. As previously discussed the sum of all weights must equal 1.0 to represent 100% of the work.

INTEGRATED COST/SCHEDULE/WORK

Experienced project managers are familiar with the problems of using only partial information, such as only costs or time to track the status of a project. To illustrate, half of a project budget may be expended by the mid-point of the scheduled duration, but only 20% of the work may be accomplished. A monitoring of only time and cost would indicate the project is going well, however, upon completion of the project there would likely be a cost overrun and a delay in schedule because the measurement of work was not included in the project control system. Thus, a project manager must develop an integrated cost/schedule/work system which provides meaningful feedback during the project rather than afterwards. The status of the project can then be determined and corrective actions be taken when corrections can be made at the least cost.

The preceding sections presented the relationships of cost/time and work/time for project control. However, evaluating these relationships separately does not provide an accurate status of a project. A cost/schedule/work graph can be prepared that shows

FIGURE 6-8
Work/Time Relationship for Construction of the Entire Project.

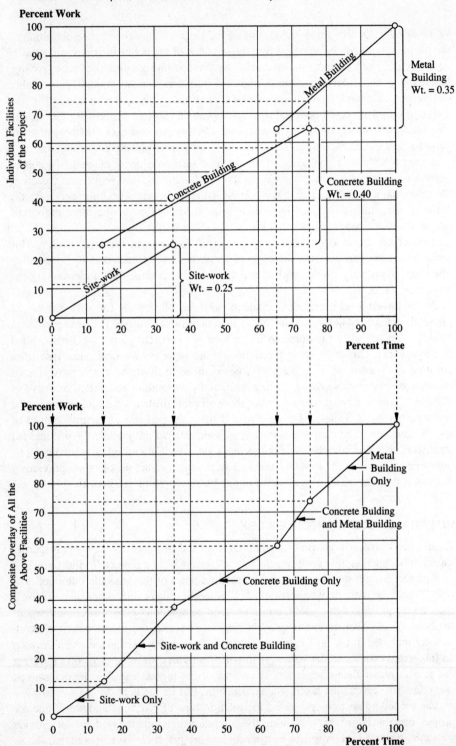

the integrated relationship of the three basic components of a project: scope (work), budget (cost), and schedule (time). Figure 6-9 is a graph that links costs on the lefthand ordinate, time on the abscissa, and work on the righthand ordinate. The upper curve is simply the cost/time S-curve that has been discussed in previous sections of this book. The lower work/time curve shows the relationship between work and time throughout the duration of the project. Thus, the graph is simply a composite overlay of the information previously presented.

The unit for costs is dollars and the unit for schedule is days, which are easily determined units of measure for any type of project. The unit of measure for work is represented as a percentage which provides a common base for all parts of the project. As previously discussed, a project may have three types of buildings: concrete, steel, and wood frame. An appropriate unit of measure for work would be cubic yards for the concrete building, pounds of steel for the steel building, and board feet of lumber for the wood frame building. However, since it is not possible to add cubic yards to pounds or board feet, percent is a dimensionless unit of measure which can conveniently be used to represent work.

Although percentage provides a common unit of measure for work, a multiplier is necessary to define the distribution of work for each part of the project. For example,

FIGURE 6-9
Integrated Cost/Schedule/Work Graph.

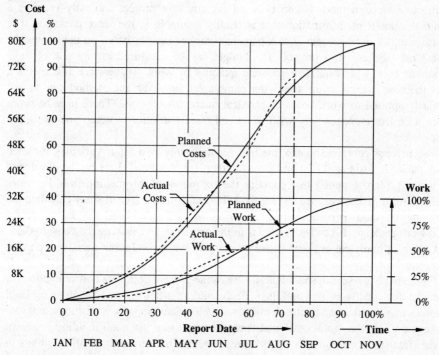

the project with three buildings of the previous paragraph may use a multiplier of 45% for the concrete structure, 35% for the steel structure, and 20% for the wood structure which when combined, represents 100% for the total project. Factors that may be considered for determining the multiplier include work-hours, costs, and/or the time to complete the work. The multiplier that is selected involves both a quantitative and qualitative evaluation of the project, based on good judgement, and should be determined as a joint effort by key participants of the project team.

The actual cost and work accomplished can be superimposed onto the curves to compare with the planned cost and work in order to determine the status of the project; see Figure 6.10a. For this example the actual accomplished work curve is below the planned work curve which shows a schedule slippage. For the same reporting period there is a cost overrun as noted on the upper curve of the graph. Thus, there is a schedule slippage and cost overrun for the reporting period. Other scenarios are possible as illustrated in Figures 6-10b–6.10d.

An integrated cost/schedule/work graph provides a good summary level report on the status of the overall project. Lower level graphs, that is, for the concrete building only, can be prepared to evaluate the status of a part of the total project. Thus, multiple graphs can be developed, depending on the complexity of the project and the level of control desired by the project manager.

PERCENT COMPLETE MATRIX METHOD

A very simple technique for determining the overall status of a project is the percent complete matrix method. It can be used for any size project and only requires a minimal amount of information that is readily available in the work packages. The overall status can be measured as a percent complete matrix, based on the budget for each work package in a project. The budget can be measured as any one of three variables: cost, work-hours, or physical quantity of work. To describe this method, only the cost is used in the following paragraphs; however, the method can be just as easily applied to work-hours or physical quantities of work. There may be times when a project manager may wish to use all three measures to determine the status of a project.

The percent complete matrix method requires only two input variables for each work package: estimated cost and percent complete. A spread sheet can be developed on a small microcomputer that contains the six pieces of information from the work package for a given area, see Figure 6-11. Formulas in the spread sheet calculate the "percent unit" and "percent project" based on the "estimated cost" that is entered for each work package. Likewise, formulas in the spread sheet calculate the "cost to date" and "percent complete project" based on entry of the second input variable, "percent complete."

Figure 6-12 is a spread sheet that illustrates the percent complete matrix method for a project that consists of five buildings. Each building is defined by four summary level components: foundation/structural, mechanical/electrical, finishes/furnishings, and special equipment. The "total cost" and "percent of project" for each building is shown in the righthand two columns of the spread sheet. The total cost of all buildings in

FIGURE 6-10a
Over Costs and Behind Schedule.

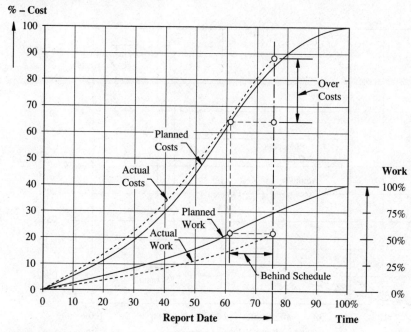

FIGURE 6-10b
Under Costs and Behind Schedule.

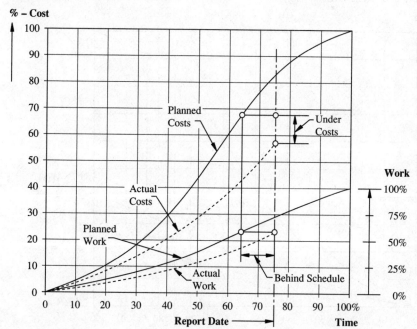

FIGURE 6-10c
Under Costs and Ahead of Schedule.

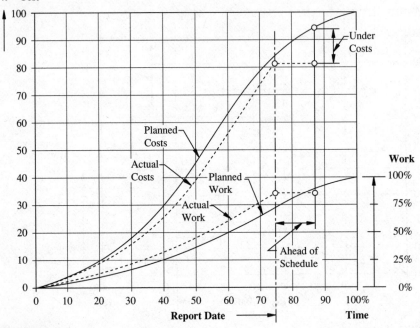

FIGURE 6-10d
Over Costs and Ahead of Schedule.

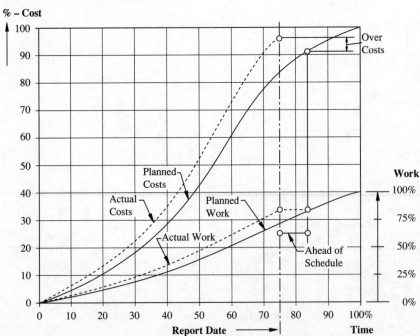

FIGURE 6-11
Work Package Information and Spread Sheet Formulas for %-Complete Matrix.

Work Package	
Estimated Cost*	Percent Unit
Percent Complete*	Percent Project
Cost to Date	% - Complete Project
Spread Sheet Formulas	
Input From Estimate*	Estimated Cost/Total Unit Cost
Variable Input by User*	Estimated Cost/Total Project Cost
Percent Complete × Estimated Cost	Cost to Date/Total Project Cost

*Required Input Data by User

the project represents to total project budget, $240,000. Formulas in the spread sheet calculate the "total cost" of each component in the project. For example, $81,000 represents the budget costs for all structural work.

The summary level components of each building contain the six pieces of information from the work package discussed in Figure 6-11. For example, the work packages for Building A structural is $15,000, which represents 30% of Building A and 6% of the total $240,000 project budget. Upon entry in the spread sheet of 70% complete for Building A, the formulas automatically calculate the $10,500 "cost to date" and the 4%, which represents the percent complete for the total project. The only entry required to obtain the project status is the cell of "%-complete," the entry highlighted by an underline in the spread sheet illustrated in Figure 6-12.

As entries are made for each work package in the matrix, the total values for each component in the project are calculated at the bottom of the spread sheet. For example, all of the "cost to date" values in the vertical column under the heading of structural work sums to $24,550, which represents 10% of the total project. Similarly, formulas in the spread sheet sum all of the total costs values of each component in the bottom horizontal row to calculate the total project cost to date of $30,750, which represents 13% complete for the entire project. This percentage can be used for the evaluation of the integrated cost/time/work graphs that were discussed in the preceding section.

PROGRESS MEASUREMENT OF DESIGN

CII publication 6-1, *Project Control for Engineering*, provides a good description of progress measurement systems for engineering design. The following paragraphs are excerpts from the publication.

The percentage completion of a single activity can usually be determined by one of four systems: Units Completed, Incremental Milestone, Start/Finish Percentages,

FIGURE 6-12
Percent Complete Matrix for Project.

FACILITY	FOUNDATION/STRUCTURAL — ESTIMATED COST / PERCENT COMPLETE / COST TO DATE	FOUNDATION/STRUCTURAL — PERCENT UNIT / PERCENT PROJECT / %-COMPLETE TOTAL	MECHANICAL/ELECTRICAL — ESTIMATED COST / PERCENT COMPLETE / COST TO DATE	MECHANICAL/ELECTRICAL — PERCENT UNIT / PERCENT PROJECT / %-COMPLETE TOTAL	FINISHES/FURNISHINGS — ESTIMATED COST / PERCENT COMPLETE / COST TO DATE	FINISHES/FURNISHINGS — PERCENT UNIT / PERCENT PROJECT / %-COMPLETE TOTAL	SPECIAL/EQUIPMENT — ESTIMATED COST / PERCENT COMPLETE / COST TO DATE	SPECIAL/EQUIPMENT — PERCENT UNIT / PERCENT PROJECT / %-COMPLETE TOTAL	TOTAL COST	PERCENT TOTAL
BUILDING A	$15000. / 70.% / $10500.	30.% / 6.% / 4.%	$ 8000. / 35.% / $2800.	16.% / 3.% / 1.%	$10000. / 0.% / 0.	20.% / 4.% / 0.%	$17000. / 0.% / 0.	34.% / 7.% / 0.%	$ 50000.	21.%
BUILDING B	$25000. / 10.% / $ 2500.	28.% / 10.% / 1.%	$ 9000. / 0.% / 0.	10.% / 4.% / 0.%	$23000. / 0.% / 0.	26.% / 10.% / 0.%	$33000. / 0.% / 0.	37.% / 14.% / 0.%	$ 90000.	38.%
BUILDING C	$ 8000. / 100.% / $ 8000.	40.% / 3.% / 3.%	$ 3000. / 80.% / $2400.	15.% / 1.% / 1.%	$ 4000. / 0.% / 0.	20.% / 2.% / 0.%	$ 5000. / 0.% / 0.	25.% / 2.% / 0.%	$ 20000.	8.%
BUILDING D	$ 2000. / 100.% / $ 2000.	20.% / 1.% / 1.%	$ 1000. / 100.% / $ 1000.	1.% / 0.% / 0.%	$ / 0.% / $ 0.	0.% / 0.% / 0.%	$ 7000. / 0.% / $ 0.	70.% / 3.% / 0.%	$ 10000.	4.%
BUILDING E	$31000. / 5.% / $ 1550.	44.% / 13.% / 1.%	$18000. / 0.% / 0.	26.% / 8.% / 0.%	$21000. / 0.% / 0.	30.% / 9.% / 0.%	0. / 0.% / 0.	0.% / 0.% / 0.%	$ 70000.	29.%
SUM EST. & %-PROJ	$81000.	34.%	$39000.	16.%	$58000.	24.%	$62000.	26.%	$240000.	100.%
SUM COST TO DATE & SUM %-COMPLETE	$24550.	10.%	$ 6200.	3.%	0.	0.%	0.	0.%	$ 30750.	13.%

118

or Ratio. The Units Completed method may be suitable for writing specifications, provided that each part of the specifications can be considered as having equal effort of work. The measurement of work can be determined as a percentage that is calculated by dividing the number of specifications completed by the total number of specifications that are to be produced.

The Incremental Milestone method is appropriate for measurement of production drawings or procurement activities that consist of easily recognized milestones. The following percentages are typical examples of measurement of production for development of production drawings and procurement.

Production Drawings

Start drafting	0%
Drawn, not checked	20%
Complete for office check	30%
To owner for approval	70%
First issue	95%
Final issue	100%

Procurement

Bidders list developed	5%
Inquiry documents complete	10%
Bids analyzed	20%
Contract awarded	25%
Vendor drawings submitted	45%
Vendor drawings approved	50%
Equipment shipped	90%
Equipment received	100%

The Start/Finish Percentage method is applicable to those activities that lack readily definable intermediate milestones, or the effort and time required is difficult to estimate. For these tasks a 20% to 50% is given when the activity is started and 100% when finished. A percentage is assigned for starting, to account for the long time between the start and finish when no credit is being given. This method is appropriate for work such as planning, designing, model building, and studies. It can also be used for specification writing.

The Ratio method is applicable to tasks such as project management or project control which are involved throughout the duration of the project. Such tasks have no particular end product and are estimated and budgeted on a bulk allocation basis, rather than on some measure of production. It can also be used on tasks that are appropriate for the start/finish method. The percent complete at any point in time is found by dividing hours (or costs) spent to date by the current estimate of hours (or costs) at completion.

Percent complete may be determined by one of the above described methods. Earned value techniques can be used to summarize overall work status. The earned value of any one item being controlled is:

$$\text{Earned Work-hours} = (\text{Budgeted Work-Hours}) \times (\text{Percent Complete})$$

Budgeted Work-Hours equal original budget
plus approved changes.

Overall percent complete of the project or of a work package can be calculated as:

$$\text{Percent Complete} = \frac{\text{Sum of Earned Work-Hours of Tasks Included}}{\text{Sum of Budgeted Work-Hours of Tasks Included}}$$

Trends can be tracked through various indices, such as the Productivity Index (PI) and the Schedule Performance Index (SPI). The PI provides a comparison of the number of work-hours being spent on work tasks to the hours budgeted and is an indicator of productivity. The equation for PI is given below:

$$PI = \frac{\text{Sum of Earned Work-Hours of Tasks Included}}{\text{Sum of Actual Work-Hours of Tasks Included}}$$

For the above to be a true indicator of productivity, only those tasks for which budgets have been established should be included in summations. If for some reason there is no budget for an item and people are working on that item, the project manager should prepare a change order for out of scope work. All actual work-hours need to be properly reported to establish accurate historical records for subsequent projects of a similar nature.

The SPI relates the amount of work performed to the amount scheduled at a point in time. The equation for SPI is given below.

$$SPI = \frac{\text{Sum of Earned Work-Hours to Date}}{\text{Sum of Scheduled Work-Hours to Date}}$$

Scheduled work-hours in the above equation are summarized from the task schedules.

In both the PI and SPI equations, an index of 1.0 or greater is favorable. Trends can be noted by plotting both "this period" and "cumulative" PI and SPI values on a graph. While SPI for the total project, or for a work package, is somewhat of an indicator of schedule performance, it only compares volume of work performed to volume of work scheduled. There can be an SPI in excess of 1.0 that can still be in danger of not meeting milestones and final completion dates if managers are expending effort on non-critical activities at the expense of critical activities. The SPI does not show that work is being completed in the proper sequence. Thus, as part of schedule control, the schedules of all included tasks in each work package must be regularly examined so that any items behind schedule can be identified and corrective action taken to bring them back on schedule.

MEASUREMENT OF CONSTRUCTION WORK

CII publication 6-5, *Project Control for Construction*, provides a good description of progress measurement systems for construction. The following paragraphs are excerpts from the publication.

A construction project requires completion of numerous tasks, beginning with initial clearing and site-work through the final punchlist and cleanup. Throughout the duration of a project there must be a systematic reporting of the progress of work for each part of the project. The following paragraphs describe six methods for measuring progress during construction; Units Completed, Incremental Milestone, Start/Finish, Supervisor Opinion, Cost Ratio, and Weighted Units. The system that is selected depends upon the nature and complexity of the project, and the desired level of control by the project manager. Each of the six methods may be used on a given project.

The U.S. Departments of Defense and Energy have established what is known as the Cost and Schedule Control Systems Criteria (C/SCSC) for control of selected federal projects. While intended primarily for high-value, cost-reimbursable research and development projects, it may be applied to selected construction projects. Various methods for measuring the status of a project are described in C/SCSC which have become common usage in the construction industry.

The Units Completed method of measuring progress during construction is applicable to tasks that are repetitive and require a uniform effort. Generally, the task is the lowest level of control so only one unit of work is necessary to define the work. To illustrate, the percent complete for installation of wire is determined as a percentage, by dividing the number of feet installed by the total number of feet that is required to be installed.

The Incremental Milestone method is applicable to tasks which include subtasks that must be handled in sequence. For example, the installation of a major vessel in an industrial facility may include the sequential tasks as shown below. Completion of any subtask is considered a milestone, which represents a certain percentage of the total installation. The percentage may be established based upon the estimated work-hours to accomplish the work.

Received and inspected	15%
Setting complete	35%
Alignment complete	50%
Internals installed	75%
Testing complete	90%
Accepted by owner	100%

The Start/Finish method is applicable to tasks which do not have well-defined intermediate milestones, or the time required is difficult to estimate. For example, the alignment of a piece of equipment may take a few hours to a few days, depending upon the situation. The workers may know when the work will start and when it is finished, but never know the percentage completion in between. For this method, an arbitrary percent complete is assigned at the start of the task and a 100% complete is assigned when it is finished. A starting percentage of 20% to 30% might be assigned for tasks that require a long duration, while a 0% may be assigned for tasks with a short duration.

The Supervisor Opinion method is a subjective approach that may be used for minor tasks, such as construction support facilities, where development of a more discrete method can not be used.

The Cost Ratio method is applicable for administrative tasks, such as project management, quality assurance, contract administration, or project control. These tasks involve a long period of time, or are continous throughout the duration of the project. Generally these tasks are estimated and budgeted as lump sum dollars and work-hours, rather than measurable quantities of production work. For this method the percent complete can be calculated by the following equation.

$$\text{Percent Complete} = \frac{\text{Actual cost or work-hours to date}}{\text{Forecast at completion}}$$

The Weighted Units methods is applicable for tasks that involve major efforts of work that occur over a long duration of time. Generally the work requires several overlapping subtasks that each have a different unit of measurement of work. This method is illustrated by the structural steel example shown in Figure 6-13. A common unit of measure for steel is tons. A weight is assigned to each subtask to represent the estimated level of effort. Work-hours is usually a good measure of the required level of effort. As quantities of work are completed for each subtask, these quantities are converted into equivalent tons and percent complete is calculated as shown in Figure 6-13.

As presented in the previous paragraphs, there are many ways of measuring progress of work for each task in a project. After determining the progress of the different work tasks, the next step is to develop a method that combines the different work tasks to determine the overall percent complete for the project. Earned Value is a system that can be used to define overall percent complete for the entire project. Earned Value can be linked to the project budget, which is expressed as work-hours or dollars. For a single account, the Earned Value can be calculated by the following equation.

$$\text{Earned Value} = (\text{Percent complete}) \times (\text{Budget for that account})$$

A budgeted amount is "earned" as a task is completed, up to the total amount in that account. For example, an account may be budgeted at $10,000 and 60 work-hours. If the account is reported as 25% complete, as measured by one of the previously described methods, then the Earned Value is defined as $2,500 and 15 work-hours. Thus, progress in all accounts can be reduced to earned work-hours and dollars, which provides a method for summarizing multiple accounts and calculating overall progress for the total project. The equation for determining the overall project percent complete is given below.

$$\text{Percent Complete} = \frac{(\text{Earned work-hours/dollar all accounts})}{(\text{Budgeted work-hours/dollars all accounts})}$$

FIGURE 6-13
Illustrative Example of Weighted-Units Method for Measurement of Construction Work.
Source: Construction Industry Institute, Publication No. 6-5.

Wt.	Subtask	U/M	Quan Total	Equiv Steel Ton	Quantity To-date	Earned Tons*
0.02	Run foundation bolts	each	200	10.4	200	10.4
0.02	Shim	%	100	10.4	100	10.4
0.05	Shakeout	%	100	26.0	100	26.0
0.06	Columns	each	84	31.2	74	27.5
0.10	Beams	each	859	52.0	0	0.0
0.11	Cross-braces	each	837	57.2	0	0.0
0.20	Girts & sag rods	bay	38	104.0	0	0.0
0.09	Plumb & align	%	100	46.8	5	2.3
0.30	Connections	each	2977	156.0	74	3.9
0.05	Punchlist	%	100	26.0	0	0.0
1.00	STEEL	TON		520.0		80.5

$$*\text{Earned Tons to Date} = \frac{(\text{Quantity to Date})(\text{Relative Weight})(520 \text{ Tons})}{(\text{Total Quantity})}$$

$$\text{Percent Complete} = \frac{80.5 \text{ tons}}{520 \text{ tons}} = 15.5\%$$

The concepts discussed above provide a system for determining the percent complete of a single work task or combination of tasks. This provides the basis for analyzing the results to determine how well work is proceeding, as compared to what was planned. The Earned Value system provides a system for evaluating the performance of the project.

Previous paragraphs have only discussed budgeted and earned work-hours and dollars. Actual work-hours and dollars must also be included in the performance evaluation of the project. The following definitions are provided to describe the procedure used for evaluation of cost and schedule performance.

- Budgeted work-hours or dollars to date represent what is planned to do. The C/SCSC defines this as Budgeted Cost for Work Scheduled (BCWS).
- Earned work-hours or dollars to date represent what was done. The C/SCSC defines this as Budgeted Cost for Work Performed (BCWP).
- Actual work-hours or dollars to date represent what has been paid. The C/SCSC defines this as Actual Cost of Work Performed (ACWP).

Performance against schedule is a comparison of what was planned against what was done, that is, a comparison of budgeted and earned work-hours. If the budgeted work-hours are less than the earned work-hours, it means more was done than planned and the project is ahead of schedule. The opposite would indicate the project is behind schedule.

Performance against budget is measured by comparing what was done to what was paid. This compares earned work-hours to actual work-hours or cost. If more was paid than is done, then the project would have a cost overrun of the budget. The following variance and index equations can be used to calculate these values.

$$\text{Scheduled Variance (SV)} = \text{(Earned work-hours or dollars)}$$
$$- \text{(Budgeted work-hours or dollars)}$$
$$SV = BCWP - BCWS$$

$$\text{Schedule Performance Index (SPI)} = \frac{\text{(Earned Work-hours or dollars to date)}}{\text{(Budgeted work-hours or dollars to date)}}$$
$$= \frac{BCWP}{BCWS}$$

$$\text{Cost Variance (CV)} = \text{(Earned work-hours or dollars)}$$
$$- \text{(Actual work-hours or dollars)}$$
$$CV = BCWP - ACWP$$

$$\text{Cost Performance Index (CPI)} = \frac{\text{(Earned work-hours or dollars to date)}}{\text{(Actual work-hours or dollars to date)}}$$
$$= \frac{BCWP}{ACWP}$$

A positive variance and an index of 1.0 or greater is a favorable performance. Figure 6-14 is a graphical display of the schedule, cost, and time variance at a particular progress reporting period.

A visual display of the schedule status is best presented on a bar chart representation. A sample of an excellent format for summary level reporting to management is shown in Figure 6-15.

TREND ANALYSIS AND FORECASTING

The preceding sections presented methods for measurement of planned and actual costs, schedules, and accomplishment of work. To be effective, a project control system must routinely collect and record the information from the start of the project. At each reporting period the actual status can be compared to the planned status, so that necessary corrective actions can be taken. As the information is accumulated, a trend analysis can be performed to evaluate the productivity and the variances in costs and schedules.

FIGURE 6-14
Cost and Schedule Variance Graph.

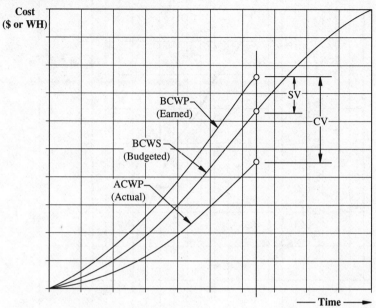

A project manager is always interested in knowing how the actual productivity compares to the productivity that was used in planning the project and estimating the budget. Although there is no industry standard for calculating productivity, the following equation is a common expression of productivity.

$$\text{Productivity Index} = \frac{\text{Estimated Unit Rate}}{\text{Actual Unit Rate}}$$

This equation is valid for calculating productivity for tasks that have measurable units of work. A productivity value of 1.0 or greater is favorable, whereas a value of less than 1.0 is unfavorable. The equation can be used to calculate the productivity of tasks at each reporting period. A productivity profile can then be produced for key crafts by plotting productivity against time as illustrated in Figure 6-16. Percent complete can be used in lieu of time for the abscissa of the graph.

As indicated in Figure 6-16, productivity varies over the life of a project. Minor variations are normal and should be expected due to the nature of project work. Significant variations justify the attention of management to identify the source of the problem and assist in any necessary corrective action. The problem may be due to the skill or morale of the workers, insufficient staff, late delivery of material, unavailable tools or equipment, inadequate instruction, inclement weather conditions, technical difficulties, or poor field supervision. Since the productivity index includes

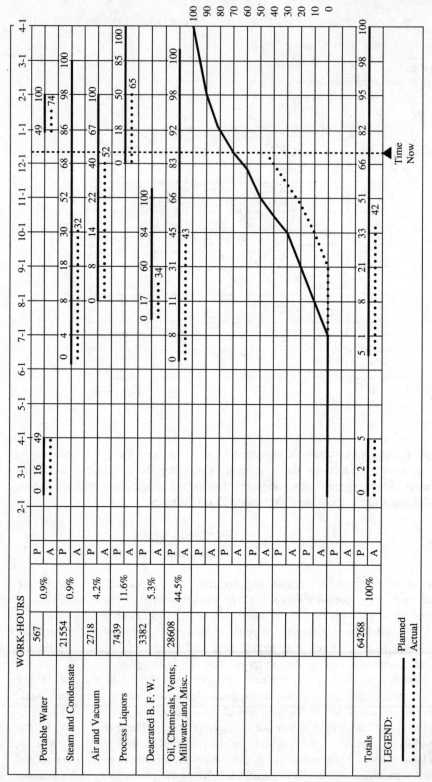

FIGURE 6-15
Illustrative Example of Summary Level Report for Management.
Source: Construction Industry Institute, Publication No. 6-5.

FIGURE 6-16
Craft Productivity Profile.

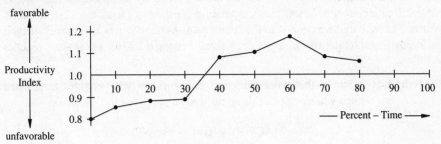

an estimated unit rate, the source of the problem may be due to poor initial estimates. Trends in the productivity index provide an effective tool for project management.

Almost everyone involved in a project is concerned with costs. As presented in previous sections, the work plan includes a distribution of costs that are anticipated throughout the duration of a project. At each reporting period the actual costs to date can be compared to the planned costs for that period in time in order to evaluate the cost variance. The cost variance is the ratio of estimated costs to actual costs as defined below:

$$\text{Cost Variance} = \frac{\text{Estimated Cost}}{\text{Actual Cost}}$$

This equation can be used to calculate the cost variance at each reporting period and plotted against time to show cost trends for a project, see Figure 6-17. A cost variance of 1.0 or higher is favorable, whereas a value of less than 1.0 is unfavorable. Cost variances can be calculated for tasks, groups of tasks, or for the entire project. A similar analysis can be performed for schedule variance.

As a project progresses, the cost variance trend can be used as an indicator to forecast the probable total cost at completion. Likewise, a schedule variance trend can

FIGURE 6-17
Cost Variance.

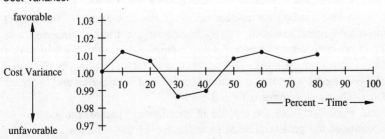

be developed as an indicator to forecast the probable completion date of a project. The cost and schedule forecasting can be accomplished by using one of the various curve fitting techniques. Then, by extrapolating the data to produce a best fit curve, the trend curve may be extended to the future date. Although there is no exact method for forecasting the final cost of a project, CII publication 6-5 identifies two approaches as follows.

Method 1: Assumes that work from this date forward will progress at planned rates whether or not these rates have prevailed to this date.

$$FAC = (ACWP) + (BAC - BCWP)$$

where: FAC = Forecast at Completion ($ or WH)

ACWP = Actual Cost of Work Performed to Date ($ or WH)

BAC = Current Budget at Completion ($ or WH)

BCWP = Budgeted Cost of Work Performed to Date ($ or WH)

Method 2: Assumes that the rate of progress prevailing to date will continue to prevail.

$$FAC = (BAC)/(CPI)$$

where: CPI = Cost Performance Index; ACWP, BAC, and BCWP are defined above

WORK STATUS SYSTEM

The Cost and Schedule Control Systems Criteria (C/SCSC) described in the preceding section is an effective method for managing the cost and schedule of a project. It requires a well-defined, work breakdown structure and a detailed project schedule. It is only effective if the cost and schedule data are reported in a timely manner. For engineering design, the total time to complete a project is short, therefore the project may be substantially complete before cost data is reported. For some project managers, the C/SCSC method appears complicated and difficult to use.

An alternate method that is preferred by some project managers for tracking engineering design work is a work status system that tracks costs and work-hours. Figure 6-18 is a cost status report and Figure 6-19 is a man-hour status report that illustrates the work status system method for project tracking. For this example, the project is divided into three general categories: direct engineering, indirect engineering, and expenses. The direct engineering category is then subdivided into the disciplines that are required to accomplish the work: architectural, civil, electrical, mechanical, and structural. Likewise, major work that is required for indirect engineering and expenses are subdivided as shown in Figures 6-18 and 6-19.

The cost and work-hour data are entered in a computer spreadsheet program to calculate the status of the project. The titles at the top of the columns identify the

EXAMPLE CLIENT
EXAMPLE BOILER REPLACEMENT
Example Project Location
Example Client Project Numbers
Cost Status Report
As of August 31, 1992

Description	A Original Budget Cost	B Approved by Change Order Cost	C Growth Cost	D = A+B+C Budget at Completion Cost	E Cumulative to Last Period Cost	F This Period Cost	G = E+F Cost to Date Cost	H Estimated at Completion Cost	I = G/D Percent Complete %
DIRECT ENGINEERING									
Architectural	$9,799		$2,900	$12,699	$0	$0	$0	$12,699	0.0%
Civil	$4,055		$3,674	$7,729	$217	$1,366	$1,583	$7,729	20.5%
Electrical	$17,203		$2,929	$20,132	$1,327	$529	$1,856	$20,132	9.2%
Mechanical	$44,330		$1,324	$45,654	$7,207	$2,999	$10,206	$45,654	22.4%
Structural	$11,278		$14,086	$25,364	$159	$0	$159	$25,364	0.6%
Subtotal	$86,665	$0	$24,913	$111,578	$8,910	$4,894	$13,804	$111,578	12.4%
INDIRECT ENGINEERING									
Project Manager	$23,412	$12,606		$36,018	$5,794	$1,921	$7,715	$36,018	21.4%
Scheduler	$0	$18,552		$18,552	$3,667	$1,245	$4,912	$18,552	26.5%
Clerical	$0	$3,530		$3,530	$529	$462	$991	$3,530	28.1%
Subtotal	$23,412	$34,688	$0	$58,100	$9,990	$3,628	$13,618	$58,100	23.4%
EXPENSES									
CADD Expense	$9,100			$9,100		$80	$80	$9,100	0.9%
Travel	$1,200			$1,200		$33	$33	$1,200	2.8%
Postage	$300			$300		$0	$0	$300	0.0%
Reproduction	$400			$400		$0	$0	$400	0.0%
Subtotal	$11,000	$0	$0	$11,000	$0	$113	$113	$11,000	1.0%
TOTAL	$121,077	$34,688	$24,913	$180,678	$18,900	$8,635	$27,535	$180,678	15.2%

FIGURE 6-18
Cost Status Report.

EXAMPLE CLIENT
EXAMPLE BOILER REPLACEMENT
Example Project Location
Example Client's Project Numbers
Work-hour Status Report
As of August 31, 1992

Description	A Original Budget Work-hours	B Approved by Change Order Work-hours	C Growth Work-hours	D = A + B + C Budget at Completion Work-hours	E Cumulative to Last Period Work-hours	F This Period Work-hours	G = E + F Hours to Date Work-hours	H Estimate at Completion Work-hours	I = G/D Percent Complete %
DIRECT ENGINEERING									
Architectural	240		104	344	0.0	0.0	0.0	344.0	0.0%
Civil	100		94	194	4.0	35.0	39.0	194.0	20.1%
Electrical	324		70	394	25.0	13.0	38.0	394.0	9.6%
Mechanical	828		42	870	135.0	53.0	188.0	870.0	21.6%
Structural	200		352	552	3.0	0.0	3.0	552.0	0.5%
Subtotal	1,692	0	662	2,354	167	101	268	2,354	11.4%
INDIRECT ENGINEERING									
Project Manager	390	210		600	120.0	32.0	152.0	600.0	25.3%
Scheduler	0	400		400	79.0	26.5	105.5	400.0	26.4%
Clerical	0	150		150	24.0	22.0	46.0	150.0	30.7%
Subtotal	390	760	0	1,150	223	81	304	1,150	26.4%
EXPENSES									
CADD Machine Hours	961			961				961.0	0.0%
Subtotal	961	0	0	961	0	8	0	961	0.0%
TOTAL	3043	760	662	4465	390	189.5	571.5	4465	12.8%

FIGURE 6-19
Work-Hour Status Report.

entries in the spreadsheet. The first column (A) of data represents the original approved project budget, the second column (B) is the approved change orders, and the third column (C) represents the growth in budget that is required to complete the work. Column (D) is the calculated total budget at the completion of the project and is calculated in the spreadsheet as the sum of the data in the first three columns.

Columns (E), (F), and (G) represent the cumulative, current, and to-date expenditure of budget as defined by the titles at the top of the columns. The percent complete for the project is calculated by dividing the "cost to date" by the "budget at completion."

It is necessary to report the costs and work-hours separately because there are different wage rates for each classification of project personnel. In addition, there are different wage rates within each discipline. Therefore, the status of a project can not be accurately determined by reporting only work-hours or only costs. Both must be reported and analyzed.

QUESTIONS FOR CHAPTER 6 - PROJECT TRACKING

1 You are the project manager for a project and have worked with your team members to establish the following criteria for tracking the work of the project. Develop the work/time relationship curve for the project.

Task	Weight Multiplier	Project Timing
Review Backup Material	0.05	0% - 10%
Preliminary Calculations	0.10	10% - 25%
Initial Drafting	0.25	15% - 45%
Final Calculations	0.20	35% - 60%
Production Drawings	0.30	50% - 90%
Drawing Approvals	0.10	90% - 100%

2 The design team for a project has met and determined the grouping of tasks required for the design effort into six categories. The team has also agreed on the following criteria for the weight multipliers to be used to track the design effort. Prepare a graph that shows the relationship between work and time.

Design Work	Weight Multiplier	Project Timing
Initial Configurations	0.15	0% - 10%
Initial Design Calculations	0.10	5% - 15%
Preliminary Layouts	0.05	10% - 25%
Final Calculations	0.25	20% - 50%
CADD Drawings	0.40	45% - 90%
Design Approval	0.05	90% - 100%

3 At 50% into the project duration, the status report for the project in Exercise 2 shows the following information. Prepare a graph that shows the time relationship of the planned work and actual work. Is the project ahead or behind schedule?

Design Work	%-Complete
Initial Configurations	100%
Initial Design Calculations	100%
Preliminary Layouts	80%
Final Calculations	70%
CADD Drawings	10%
Design Approval	0%

4 The following data represents the information that has been jointly compiled by the design team for a project. This data represents the planned cost and the work anticipated during the design phase. Prepare an integrated planned cost/time/work graph for the project.

Anticipated Cost	Planned Work	Expected Time
0%	0%	0%
5%	5%	10%
10%	10%	20%
15%	20%	30%
30%	25%	40%
55%	30%	50%
80%	45%	60%
85%	65%	70%
92%	85%	80%
96%	95%	90%
100%	100%	100%

5 The data shown below represents the planned time, cost, and work at the beginning of the design of a project. Prepare the integrated time/cost/work graph.

Time	Cost	Work
0%	0%	0%
10%	5%	5%
20%	15%	10%
30%	20%	20%
40%	30%	30%
50%	45%	40%
60%	65%	50%
70%	80%	70%
80%	90%	80%
90%	95%	90%
100%	100%	100%

Evaluate the status report for the above project for the following scenarios, assuming the status report is issued at 70% of the project duration. For each scenario, is the project behind or ahead of schedule, and is there a cost overrun or underrun?

A. Reported cost to date is 55% and work accomplished is reported as 40%
B. Reported cost to date is 75% and work accomplished is reported as 50%
C. Reported cost to date is 95% and work accomplished is reported as 70%
D. Reported cost to date is 85% and work accomplished is reported as 80%

---

6 The following weight multipliers have been established for the construction phase of a project. Prepare a graph that shows the relationship between accomplished work and time.

Facility	Weight Multiplier	Project Timing
Site-work	0.10	0% - 15%
Work Frame Building	0.25	10% - 25%
Concrete Building	0.35	15% - 40%
Metal Building	0.20	25% - 80%
Landscape	0.10	75% - 100%

7 Calculate the percent complete value for the project shown below using the Weighted Units methods for measurement of work.

Wt.	Subtask	U/M	Quant. Total	Equivalent Steel Ton	Earned To-date
0.02	Foundation bolts	each	200	10.4	200
0.02	Shims	%	100	10.4	100
0.05	Shakeout	%	100	26.0	100
0.06	Columns	each	84	31.2	80
0.10	Beams	each	859	52.0	60
0.11	Cross-braces	each	837	57.2	20
0.20	Girts & sag rods	bay	38	104.0	10
0.09	Plumb & align	%	100	46.8	5
0.30	Connections	each	2977	156.0	80
0.05	Punchlist	%	100	26.0	0
1.00	STEEL	TON		520.0	

REFERENCES

1 "Cost and Schedule Control Systems Criteria for Contract Performance", DOE/MA-0087, U.S. Department of Energy, Washington, D.C., 1980.
2 Diekmann, J. E. and Thresh, K. B., *Project Control for Design Engineering*, Source Document No. 12, Construction Industry Institute, Austin, TX, May, 1986.
3 Eldin, N. N., "Measurement of Work Progress: Quantitative Technique," *Journal of Construction Engineering and Management*, ASCE, New York, Vol. 115, No. 3, September, 1991.
4 Elmore, R. L. and Sullivan, D. C., "Project Control Through Work Packaging Concepts", *Transactions of the American Association of Cost Engineers*, 1976.
5 Geigrich, D. B. and Schlunt, R. J., *Progress Schedule Tracking System*, PMI Symposium, Project Management Institute, Drexel Hill, PA, 1984.
6 Huot, J.-C., "Integration of Cost and Time with the Work Breakdown Structure," *Transactions of the American Association of Cost Engineers*, Morgantown, WV, 1979.
7 Halpin, D. W., Escalona, A. L., and Szmiurlo, P. M., *Work Packaging for Project Control*, Source Document No. 28, Construction Industry Institute, Austin, TX, August, 1987.
8 Harris, F. W., *Advanced Project Management*, Wiley, New York, 1981.
9 Mueller, F. W., *Integrated Cost and Schedule Control for Construction Projects*, Van Nostrand Reinhold Company, New York, 1986.
10 Neil, J. N., *Construction Cost Estimating for Project Control*, Prentice-Hall, Englewood Cliffs, NJ, 1982.
11 Neil, J. N., *Project Control for Engineering*, Publication No. 6-1, Construction Industry Institute, Austin, TX, July, 1986.
12 Neil, J. N., *Project Control for Construction*, Publication No. 6-5, Construction Industry Institute, Austin, TX, September 1987.
13 Neil, J. N., "A System for Integrated Project Management," *Proceedings Conference on Current Practice of Cost Estimating and Cost Control*, ASCE, New York, 1983.
14 Oberlender, G. D., "Real-Time Project Tracking, Excellence in the Constructed Project," *Proceedings of Construction Congress I*, ASCE, New York, 1989.
15 Rasdorf, W. J. and Abudayyeh, O. Y., "Cost and Schedule Control Integration: Issues and Needs," *Journal of Construction Engineering and Management*, ASCE, New York, Vol. 117 No. 3, September, 1991.
16 Riggs, L. S., *Cost and Schedule Control in Industrial Construction*, Source Document No. 24, Construction Industry Institute, Austin, TX, December, 1986.
17 Stevens, W. M., "Cost Control: Integrated Cost/Schedule Performance," *Journal of Management in Engineering*, ASCE, New York, Vol. 2, No. 2, June, 1986.

CHAPTER 7

DESIGN COORDINATION

PROJECT TEAM MEETINGS

Design is a creative process that involves diverse areas of expertise and numerous decisions that have major impacts on a project. The work of each designer often influences the work of one or more other designers. A difficult task in design coordination is interfacing related work to ensure compatibility of the whole project. Generally, the problem is not finding design people who know how to do the work, it is interfacing the work of all designers. This can only be accomplished through effective communications at regularly scheduled team meetings.

Team meetings should be held weekly throughout the duration of a project. These meetings are necessary to keep the team acting as a unit and to ensure a continuous exchange of information. A typical project involves numerous conflicts. The best way to resolve these conflicts in a timely manner is by input from all those who are affected. This can only be achieved through open discussions and compromise.

The project manager is the leader of all team meetings; however, he or she should not dominate discussions. Often a team member may be assigned the role of leading discussions to resolve a problem that is related to his or her particular area of expertise. Project managers need to use their own judgement and develop the skillful art of knowing when to lead, and when to let others lead.

An agenda should be prepared to direct project team meetings to ensure that important items are addressed and to conclude the meeting in the shortest time. The agenda should include a list, in chronological order, of the items to be discussed, including; work completed, work in progress, work scheduled, and special problems. Each attendee should participate in team meetings. The project manager should prepare and distribute minutes of the meeting to all participants.

WEEKLY/MONTHLY REPORTS

Project management involves a never ending process of the preparation of reports. To be meaningful, reports must be issued on a regular basis and should contain information that is beneficial to the receiver. There is a tendency to include everything in a report, which results in reports that are so bulky that important items may be overlooked.

In general, the project manager should prepare two routine reports, a weekly highlight report and a monthly report for each project. Much of the weekly highlight report can be obtained from the minutes of the weekly team meetings. The report should include: work completed, work in progress, work scheduled, and special problems. Generally, the weekly report is used by the project manager and his or her team to coordinate the work in progress.

The monthly report for a project should contain milestones that have been achieved, a tabulation of costs to date compared to forecast costs, and an overlay of planned and actual time schedules. Trend reports should also be included to show the anticipated project completion date and a forecast of the total cost at completion. Generally, the monthly report is used by upper management and the owner's representative and is a permanent record for the project file.

A format for both the weekly and monthly reports should be developed so all reports will be consistent, to allow comparisons of the project status, and to evaluate the progress of the work and the performance of the team. In addition to communicating the status of a project, the reports serve as a means of individual accountability and recognition of good performance.

DRAWING AND EQUIPMENT INDEX

The final product of design work is a set of contract documents (drawings and specifications) to guide the physical construction of the project. As presented in Chapter 4 the project manager must develop a project work plan before starting design. A part of the work plan includes preparation of work packages by each designer. Included in each work package is a list of anticipated drawings and expected completion dates.

The project manager can develop a drawing index by assembling the list of drawings from all team members. This drawing index is extremely valuable to the project manager because it can be used as a check list of how many drawings to expect, when to expect them, and to assist in scheduling construction. Figure 7-1 illustrates the contents of a drawing index. It is helpful to include the revision number and date for each drawing because a common problem in design coordination is keeping track of the most current issue of a drawing.

The drawing index is in a continuous state of change as design progresses. As work progresses, the number of drawings may increase or decrease, depending upon

FIGURE 7-1
Illustrative Drawing Index.

Drawing Index
for X Y Z Project
Update as of: 10/25/92

Sheet No.	Title	Expected Date	Actual Date	Revision No. 1 2 3 4
C0	**Site-work Drawings**			
C1	" Plot Plan	09/15/92	09/17/92	1 - 10/05/92
C2	" Grading	10/01/92	09/27/92	
C3	" Paving, Sh 1	10/15/92	10/12/92	
C4	" Paving, Sh 2	10/20/92	10/18/92	3 - 10/24/92
A0	**Architectural Drawings**			
A1	" First Floor Plans	10/10/92	10/09/92	
A2	" Second Floor Plans	10/15/92	10/16/92	
A3	" Room Schedules	10/20/92	10/20/92	
A4	" Door/Wall Finishes	10/25/92	10/24/92	
A5	" Window Schedules	11/01/92		
S0	**Structural Drawings**			
S1	" Foundation	10/15/92	10/16/92	
S2	" Floor Slabs	10/25/92	10/28/92	
S3	" Columns & Beams, Sh 1	11/01/92		
S4	" Columns & Beams, Sh 2	11/05/92		
S5	" Roof Framing Plan	11/10/92		
M0	**Mechanical Drawings**			
M1	" Compressor	11/01/92		
M2	" HVAC Ductwork	11/05/92		
E0	**Electrical Drawings**			
E1	" Control Boxes	11/05/92		
E2	" Wiring Diagram, Sh 1	11/10/92		
E3	" Wiring Diagram, Sh 2	11/15/92		
P0	**Plumbing Drawings**			
P1	" Piping	10/10/92	10/14/92	
P2	" Fixtures	10/20/92	10/18/92	

the final design configuration that is selected. Changes in drawings are a necessary part of work and it is the duty of each designer to revise the list as necessary and to keep the project manager informed.

Similar to the drawing index, an equipment index can be developed that lists major equipment to be installed in the project. This equipment index is extremely valuable to the project manager because it can serve as a reference document to track the purchase and delivery of equipment and schedule installation in the field during construction. Figure 7-2 illustrates the contents of an equipment index. Each major piece of equipment is listed along with the drawing number, vendor, purchase order date, and expected delivery date. The project manager can use this index as a reference guide and check list to contact vendors in advance of delivery dates to ensure

FIGURE 7-2
Illustrative Equipment Index.

| | | Equipment Index for X Y Z Project Update as of: 10/25/92 | | | |
Description	Drawing Number	Vendor	Purchase Order No.	Purchase Order Date	Expected Delivery
Transformer	E14	XYZ Company	PO 73925	04/12/92	07/15/92
Switch Assy	E19	ABC Company	PO 83401	04/30/92	08/01/92
Compressor	M12	CIB Company	PO 84294	05/17/92	07/20/92
Pump Assy	M3	BWA Company	PO 17835	06/14/92	08/15/92

the equipment will arrive on schedule. A common source of delay during construction is late delivery of major equipment and material.

DISTRIBUTION OF DOCUMENTS

The design process requires the timely distribution of documents and exchange of information. Generally, there is a sense of urgency among team members to complete work at the earliest possible date. When information is inefficiently distributed, it increases the workload of everyone and leads to delays in work, inefficient productivity, and frustration.

The project manager can develop a distribution of documents key sheet, reference Figure 7-3, that shows the routing of documents among team members and other major participants in the project. This is an effective communication tool because it allows each person to know who is receiving a particular document. Too often, a team member will receive a document, review its contents, and determine that another team member should also be aware of the document. The distribution of document key sheet verifies the recipients, thereby eliminating the necessity of attempting to contact another person who may not be readily available.

There should be a distribution of documents key sheet that is unique to each project. It can be easily prepared on a word processor, duplicated, and bound in a tablet form for use by all team members. It differs from a traditional company routing slip because it has the project title at the top of the sheet along with the names of the team members so it easily identifies which project the document is directed to, and who is receiving the document.

AUTHORITY/RESPONSIBILITY CHECK LIST

A project manager is often responsible for one or more project at a time. Some of the projects may be in the early stage of development while others are in full progress and some in the close out phase. The problem that confronts a project manager who

FIGURE 7-3
Distribution of Documents Key Sheet.

**Distribution of Documents Key Sheet
for X Y Z Project**

Send to	Name	Title	Address	Phone	Date

Comments:

_____

_____

_____

_____

_____

Action: See Me_____   Call Me_____   Review_____

Distributed by:_____   Date:_____

must handle multiple projects generally is not the management of any one project, but it is the difficulty in handling all projects simultaneously. This type of work condition requires some systematic means of knowing the work status of numerous people.

To facilitate and keep track of team members the project manager can develop an authority/responsibility check list for each project, reference Figure 7-4. This list is continuously revised to show the status of completed, active, and pending work of each team member. It is especially useful in preparing agendas for team meetings. It also assists the project manager in organizing his or her own work and preparing reports to upper management and the owner's representative.

The authority/responsibility check list can be prepared as a computer word processing file for each project. The project manager then can easily add, delete, or modify the information as it becomes known. Each update of the file can be saved on the disk under a new file name, with date, so a record can be kept of each update. This provides a thorough documentation of the history of the project which is valuable for future reference in retracing the events in a project. The file of each project can be merged into a single file to provide a composite listing of the information that pertains to all projects for which the project manager is responsible.

A more effective means of managing the authority/responsibility check list can be achieved by using a computer electronic spread sheet. Each piece of information can

FIGURE 7-4
Authority/Responsibility Check List for Project Manager.

Authority/Responsibility Check List
X Y Z Project as of 03/15/92

Task/Work Item	Authority/Responsibility	Status	Date
Soil testing specifications	John Smith, Civil	Issued	02/26/92
Confirmation of wind loads	Tim Jones, Structural	Pending	04/22/92
Approval of shield wire angle	Dan Banks, Owner's Rep.	Approved	03/09/92
Final tower configuration	Tim Jones, Structural	Expected	05/26/92
Steel supplier's bid list	Ron Mitchell, Purchasing	Will Call	04/03/92
Right of way hearings	Joe Thomas, Legal	Pending	06/01/92

be entered into a cell to enable the project manager to produce multiple sorts of the data. For example, a sort can be obtained for all work that is pending by a specific date, or a sort can obtained to list all work of a particular person. The use of a spread sheet enables the project manager to perform any desired sort and is a valuable tool for management of any single project or multiple projects.

CHECK LIST OF DUTIES FOR DESIGN

Table 7-1 provides a comprehensive check list of duties for the design phase of a project that is handled by the construction management (CM) type of contract. For projects other than the CM type of contract, the duties of the CM are distributed between the owner and designer, depending upon the contract arrangement. The architect is the principal design professional for a building type project, whereas the engineer is the principal design professional for a heavy/industrial type project.

TEAM MANAGEMENT

Effective teamwork is a key factor in the successful management of any project. Usually, the project manager is involved in three areas of responsibilities: within the project team, between the team and the client, and between the team and other management of the project manager's organization. In each of these areas, numerous situations often arise that can cause disruptions, conflicts, delays, and misunderstandings that may affect the teams's performance. It is the duty of a project manager to coordinate the team in a manner that minimizes the development of these situations, to be able to identify problems immediately, and to act quickly to resolve them in a satisfactory manner. Table 7-2 is a list of typical problems that can arise related to team management.

A team is a group of individuals, each of whom is usually responsible for performing work on more than one project. As the number of projects increase for which a team member is involved, the risk of losing priorities also increases. The project plan

TABLE 7-1

CHECK LIST OF DUTIES FOR DESIGN PHASE
SOURCE: NSPE/PEC REPORTER, VOL. VII, NO. 2

Design Phase	Owner	CM	Designer*	Contractor
1. Project Team	Head	Member	Member	X
2. Program Information	Provide	Review	Obtain/Approve	X
3. Information Required for Design	Provide	Review	Determine Requirements Obtain, Approve	X
4. Meetings—Project Team	Participate as Required	Organize, Conduct, Record	Participate	X
5. Meetings—Design Team as Required	Participate as Required	Participate Document	Organize, Conduct	X
6. Budget	Provide	Evaluate	Evaluate	X
7. Budget Contingency	Provide	Recommend	Recommend	X
8. Scheduling—Program	Participate, Approve, Comply	Prepare, Monitor, Enforce, Comply	Participate, Approve, Comply	Comply
9. Scheduling—Milestone	Review	Provide	Review, Approve	X
10. Soil Bearings	Review & Pay	Review	Arrange, Review & Recommend	X
11. Drawings—Preliminary	Review, Comment, Approve	Review, Comment, Advise	Provide	X
12. Approvals—Design	Approve	Recommend	Issue Documents	X
13. Drawings—Schematic, Design Development & Working	Review, Comment, Approve	Review, Comment, Advise	Provide	X
14. Specifications— Conceptual	Review, Comment, Approve	Review, Comment, Advise	Provide	X
15. Specifications— Technical	Review, Approve	Review, Comment, Advise	Provide	X
16. Design Alternates	Approve as Required	Recommend	Recommend, Prepare	X
17. Value Engineering & Value Management	Approve as Required	Provide	Assist, Review	X
18. Estimating	Approve as Required	Provide	Assist, Review	X
19. Agency Plan Reviews	Monitor	Monitor	Facilitate	X
20. Permits—Not Assisgned to Contractors in Bid Documents	Pay	Arrange for & Obtain	Assist, Consult with Agencies	X
21. Insurance—All Risk- Builders Risk	Provide	Assist, Recommend	X	X
22. Insurance—Owner's Protective Liability	Provide	Assist, Recommend	X	X
23. Cash Flow Projections	Provide, Utilize	Provide, Update	Assist	X
24. Specifications— Instructions to Bidders	Approve	Provide	Review & Advise	X
25. Specifications— Proposal Section	Approve	Provide	Review & Advise	X
26. Bidding Alternates	Approve as Required	Recommend, Review	Recommend, Review Issue	X

* The referenced NSPE/PEC publication cited "ARCHITECT"; however, the term "DESIGNER" is used here to imply the architect may be the principal design professional for building projects, whereas the engineer may be the principal design professional for heavy/industrial projects.

TABLE 7-2
TYPICAL PROBLEMS IN TEAM MANAGEMENT

1. Differing outlooks, priorities, interests, and judgements of team members
2. Project objectives become unclear to the team members
3. Communication problems
4. Scope changes by the owner
5. Lack of coordination by team members
6. Lack of management support

must include setting priorities at the start of the project. The project manager must ensure that project objectives are known and clearly understood by team members because project objectives can become unclear to the team, particularly during the design phase of a project.

Poor communication is the most common source of problems related to team management. Meetings must be held routinely to keep team members informed so information can be exchanged. Team meetings should serve as forums for getting problems out on the table so then can be resolved, however the project manager must also be accessible to team members who may not feel comfortable airing problems or potential problems in meetings.

Scope changes by the owner can adversely affect the project budget and schedule. Team members must be cautious of expanding the scope of a project in an attempt to please the owner. The scope must be locked in at the beginning of the project and should not be changed without a written agreement between the owner's representative and the project manager. The written agreement must include an appropriate change in the budget and schedule that matches the change in scope.

The project manager is responsible for overall coordination of the entire project team. However, individual coordination between team members is also necessary. The project manager must instill an environment of cooperation that encourages the free exchange of information among team members.

The project manager must have management support from his or her own organization. This can best be achieved by keeping management informed of the status and needs of the project team. Assistance cannot be given unless the need is known. Management should be included as an integral part of project reviews.

To assist the project manager in his or her role of performing team management responsibilities, the project work plan must be kept up to date. It must be formally modified when changes are made in the scope of work, members of the project team, services and tasks to be performed, individual responsibilities, schedule, and budget.

The team must be managed in an open manner. Discussions of roles and relationships, and the rationale behind project decisions, should be done in team meetings rather than private conversations. The project manager must be consistent in making the day-to-day decisions that alter roles and relationships within the team.

The concept of "team" should be instilled in the attitude of all individuals. The project manager must emphasize commitment, clarity, and unity of the team to minimize the number of trivial conflicts. Since each person is unique, there can be differing outlooks, priorities, interests, and judgements. Because of the diversity of individuals, the project manager must deal with the human aspects in his or her role as leader of the project team. Some leadership qualities are inherent in a project manager and others require development through training and experience.

EVALUATION OF DESIGN EFFECTIVENESS

Design is a complex process involving the application of technical knowledge to creative ideas in order to produce a set of specific instructions for construction of the project. It is the focal point of definition of the project and has significant impact on cost and schedule. Thus, it is essential to have the most effective design possible.

Most of the efforts related to measurement and evaluation of productivity and performance of project work has been directed toward the construction phase. The Construction Industry Institute (CII) has sponsored research and published numerous papers on a variety of topics related to project management. *"Evaluation of Design Effectiveness"* is a CII document that provides a thorough description of outputs, or products, of the design process.

The following paragraphs are a summary of excerpts from the CII report *"Evaluation of Design Effectiveness."* The report states this method is not intended to be, nor should it be, used as an evaluation of a designer or the design process. It is instead a measure of design effectiveness and an evaluation of design outputs.

Measurement of design productivity is perhaps more difficult than measuring productivity in the construction phase. Simplistic measurements such as cost per drawing or work-hours per drawing have obvious limitations because of variations in drawing size and content. Also there is increasing realization that the true measures of the effectiveness of the design effort are found in the construction of a project, and use of the project by the owner after construction is complete. Thus, it may be more beneficial to develop a method for evaluating the effectiveness of design rather than the productivity during the design activity itself.

The ability to measure design effectiveness using the following proposed method represents an important step in a broader effort to improve the total design process. Such an effort encompasses the identification of the effect on design effectiveness of various inputs to the design process and of the systems and techniques employed by the designer.

CII researchers have suggested the use of a technique called an "objectives matrix" for productivity evaluation. The same concept can be used to develop an effectiveness measurement for design. An objectives matrix consists of four main components: criteria, weights, performance scale, and performance index.

The criteria define what is to be measured. The weights determine the relative importance of the criteria to each other and to the overall objective of the measurement. The performance scale compares the measured value of the criterion to a standard or selected benchmark value. Using these three components, the performance index is calculated, and the result is used to indicate and track performance.

Use of the objectives matrix is illustrated in Figure 7-5. The seven criteria of design effectiveness are given as column headings, the criteria weights are shown near the

FIGURE 7-5
Design Evaluation Matrix.
Source: Construction Industry Institute, Publication No. 8-1.

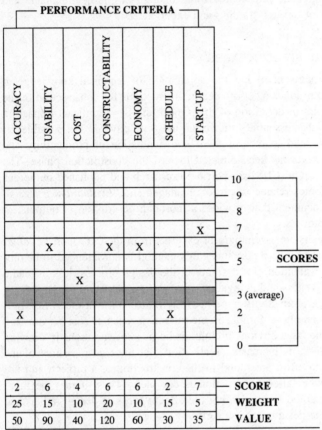

bottom of each column. The performance scale of 0 to 10 is given at the right of the matrix. A score of 10 represents perfection, and a score of 3 is average.

A score for each of the seven criteria is represented by an "X" in the appropriate box, and is entered at the bottom of the matrix. Each criterion's score is multiplied by its weight to obtain its value. The sum of all values constitutes the performance index which is shown at the bottom right of the matrix.

The score for a criterion can be obtained in at least three ways: judgmental, based upon a single quantitative measurement, or based upon a combination of several subcriteria that are represented by a matrix.

Judgmental scoring can be used for some or all criteria. The scoring in Figure 7-5 is representative of judgmental scoring. Although judgmental ratings have the limitation of subjectivity, the objectives matrix approach still allows their appropriate application with multiple criteria of different weights.

For some criteria, quantitative measures can be used instead of judgements to determine scores. For example, the accuracy of the design documents can be evaluated by measuring the amount of drawing revisions per total drawings. The score for performance against the schedule criterion can be determined by using the percent of design document release dates attained. This approach is illustrated in Figure 7-6, in which these two criteria are represented by quantitative measures.

In the example of Figure 7-6 predetermined benchmark values are entered into the boxes representing appropriate scores for each criterion. The benchmark value for a score of 3 is considered normal or average, while that for a level of 0 represents the minimum level of accomplishment realized in recent years. The benchmark value for a level of 10 represents the ultimate expected in the foreseeable future. The score of 3 is used for normal rather than 5 to allow more opportunity for improvement.

The performance value attained is entered at the top of each column. The appropriate score representing that performance is then determined, and is circled in Figure 7-6. If a performance level falls between two scores, the lower score is used. A score is not given until it is attained.

A third approach is to measure each criterion through the use of several subcriteria. The subcriteria themselves can have differing weights and measurements. These can be combined into a single criterion score through the use of a submatrix for that criterion.

Given the many complexities and variables of the total design process, no measurement system can yield absolute quantitative results that are applicable without an interpretation of all the design situations and circumstances. However, the method outlined can be utilized for three purposes: to develop a common understanding between the owner, designer, and contractor concerning the criteria by which design effectiveness on a given project will be measured; to compare design effectiveness of similar projects in a systematic and reasonable quantitative manner, highlighting performance trends; and to identify opportunities to improve the effectiveness of the entire design process as well as the contributions toward the ultimate result made by all participants.

CONSTRUCTABILITY

Traditionally, engineering and construction have been separated early in the project. The adoption of new technology such as three-dimensional computer aided drafting and design (CADD), robotics, and automation in construction has generated increased interest in the constructability of a project. With these new innovations, designs can be configured to enable efficient construction, which places more emphasis on merging engineering and construction to include constructability's input in the design effort.

FIGURE 7-6
Design Matrix Using Quantitative Evaluation.
Source: Construction Industry Institute, Publication No. 8-1.

┌── PERFORMANCE CRITERIA ──┐

ACCURACY DRAWING REVISIONS (%)	USABILITY	COST	CONSTRUCTABILITY	ECONOMY	SCHEDULE DOCUMENT RELEASE (%)	START-UP	
21					83		— PERFORMANCE

							SCORES
4					100		— 10
6					98		— 9
7					96		— 8
9					94	X	— 7
10	X		X	X	92		— 6
12					91		— 5
13		X			89		— 4
15					87		— 3 (average)
(22)					(77)		— 2
28					68		— 1
35					60		— 0

2	6	4	6	6	2	7	— SCORE
25	15	10	20	10	15	5	— WEIGHT
50	90	40	120	60	30	35	— VALUE

INDEX
425

The desired result is to facilitate the exchange of ideas between construction and design before and during design, rather than after design.

The Construction Industry Institute (CII) has sponsored research and published reports related to constructability. CII publication No. 3-3, entitled *"Constructability Concepts File,"* provides a good description of constructability concepts related to conceptual planning, design and procurement, and field operations. The following paragraphs contain excerpts from the report to illustrate the contents of the report.

There are at least five factors that should be considered in constructability deliberations related to design configurations for efficient construction: simplicity, flexibility, sequencing, substitution, and labor skill/availability.

Simplicity is a desirable element of any constructable design. Unwarranted complexity is not the best interest of anyone and markedly increases the probability of an unsatisfactory finished product. Special drawings and instruction may be required to improve the constructability process, particularly for retrofit or rebuild projects.

Flexibility for the field construction forces to select alternative methods or innovative approaches is highly desirable. Designs should specify the desired results and not limit approaches to attain these results. In the fully open and competitive market, it is highly desirable to provide designs that do not limit the construction methods or approaches.

Sequencing of installation is as much a design consideration as it is a procurement and construction consideration. Many times designs have evolved that unnecessarily restrict installation sequences during construction. Design should include careful consideration of layout and spacing of facilities so more than one construction operation can occur at a time.

Substitutions or alternatives warrant attention, but too often are neglected because the attitude prevails that it has always been done a particular way. Improperly considered material applications will impact constructability, resulting in costly modifications. These impacts can be lessened and eliminated when addressed during the design time by constructability programs.

Labor skill/availability are often not considered early enough in a project life cycle. The availability of labor and the skill level of the workers should be fully explored. The absence of either skill levels or availability of the work force can have a costly impact on a project and require consideration during the design phase.

CII research has shown that company or project size is no barrier to constructability and the implementation of a constructability program. The involvement of construction in the design phase results in better projects, lower costs, better productivity, and earlier project completion. A major obstacle to the implementation of effective constructability programs is the concept that designs are merely reviewed by construction to select the design that is easiest to build. CII publication No. 3-2 provides guidelines for implementing a constructability program.

POST DESIGN REVIEW

Evaluation is a continuous process and necessary for improvement of project management. The system used by the project manager's organization to handle work must be flexible enough to respond to differences in individual projects. At the beginning of each project, the project manager must determine what modifications and improvements need to be made in the system, that are appropriate for the project.

After completion of the design for each project, the project manager and his or her team should conduct a complete and candid evaluation of the design effort and the management of the design process. This evaluation should include each member of the project team as well as other key participants that were involved in design.

A check list should be prepared to evaluate all aspects of the project including scope growth, match of quality and scope, owner's expectations and satisfaction, conflicts within the team or other parties, excessive changes in schedules, comparison of final costs with the original budget, and a list of precautions for management of future projects.

After a thorough discussion of the design process, a brief summary report should be prepared by the project manager which should include a list of recommendations to improve the system for future projects.

QUESTIONS FOR CHAPTER 7—DESIGN COORDINATION

1 Describe the purpose of a drawing index and an equipment index in the management of a project. In your response, include the persons responsible for preparing these two documents, and the persons who will use them.
2 Briefly describe the distribution of documents key sheet, for example, what is contained on it, its purpose and use in the management of a project, and how it is different from a traditional routing sheet.
3 Below is the score for each criteria of a design evaluation matrix. Use the weight value in Figure 7-5 and calculate the index.

Criteria	Score
Accuracy	4
Usability	5
Cost	2
Constructability	7
Economy	3
Schedule	4
Start-up	8

4 Describe the authority/responsibility check list and its importance in the management of multiple projects at the same time.
5 A post design review can be an extremely valuable in the design coordination of future projects, because the lessons learned can be identified and shared with others. However, some people are reluctant to perform this task at the end of every project. Why do you think some people are relunctant to a post design review? As a project manager, how would you resolve this problem?

REFERENCES

1 Chalabi, A. F., Beaudin, B. J., and Salazar, G. F., *Input Variables Impacting Design Effectiveness*, Source Document No. 26, Construction Industry Institute, Austin, TX, April, 1987.
2 *Constructability Concepts File*, Publication No. 3-3, Construction Industry Institute, Austin, TX, August, 1987.
3 *Consulting Engineering: A Guide for the Engagement of Engineering Services*, Manual No. 45, American Society of Civil Engineers, New York, 1988.

4 "Effective Management of Engineering Design", *Conference Proceedings*, ASCE, New York, 1981.
5 Eldin, N. N., "Management of Engineering/Design Phase," *Journal of Construction Engineering and Management*, ASCE, New York, Vol. 117. No. 1, March, 1991.
6 *Engineer, Owner, and Construction Related Documents*, Engineers' Joint Contract Documents Committee, ASCE, New York, 1990.
7 Glavinich, T. E., "Microcomputer-Based Project Management for Small Engineering Firms," *Journal of Management in Engineering*, ASCE, Vol. 8, No. 1, New York, June, 1991.
8 O'Connor, J. T., Rusch, S. E., and Schulz, M. J., *Constructability Improvement During Engineering and Procurement*, Source Document No. 5, Construction Industry Institute, Austin, TX, May 1986.
9 Perkins, C., *Guidelines for Implementing A Constructability Program*, Publication No. 3-2, Construction Industry Institute, Austin, TX, July, 1987.
10 "Sampling Responsibility Chart," *PEC Reporter*, Professional Engineers in Construction Practice Division, National Society of Professional Engineers, Vol. VII, No. 2, Alexandria, VA, January, 1985.
11 Stull, J. O. and Tucker, R. L., *Objectives Matrix Values for Evaluation of Design Effectiveness*, Source Document No. 22, Construction Industry Institute, Austin, TX, November, 1986.
12 Tatum, C. B., Vanegas, J. A., and Williams, J. M., *Constructability Improvement During Conceptual Planning*, Source Document No. 4, Construction Industry Institute, Austin, TX, March, 1986.
13 Tucker, R. L. and Scarlett, B. R., *Evaluation of Design Effectiveness*, Publication No. 8-1, and Source Document No. 16, Construction Industry Institute, Austin, TX, November, 1986.
14 Tucker, R. L., *Assessment of Architect/Engineer Project Management Practices and Performance*, Construction Industry Institute, Austin, TX, April, 1990.

CHAPTER 8

CONSTRUCTION PHASE

IMPORTANCE OF CONSTRUCTION

The construction phase is important because the quality of the completed project is highly dependent on the workmanship and management of construction. The quality of construction depends on the completeness and quality of the contract documents that are prepared by the designer and three other factors: laborers who have the skills necessary to produce the work, field supervisors who have the ability to coordinate the numerous activities that are required to construct the project in the field, and the quality of materials that are used for construction of the project. Skilled laborers, and effective management of the skilled laborers, are both required to achieve a quality project.

The construction phase is also important because a majority of the total project budget and schedule is expended during construction. As presented in previous chapters, the design costs for a project generally range from 7% to 12%. Using a 10% medium value, then 90% of the cost of a project is expended during construction. Thus, a 15% variation in design costs may impact the project by only 1.5%, whereas a 15% variation in construction costs may impact the project by 13.5%.

Similar to costs, the time required to build a project is always disproportionally greater than the time required to design it. Most owners have a need for use of their projects at the earliest possible date, therefore any delay from a planned completion date can cause significant problems for both the owner and contractor. Due to the risks that are inherent to construction, and the many tasks that must be performed, the construction contractor must carefully plan, schedule, and manage the project in the most efficient manner.

ASSUMPTIONS FOR CONSTRUCTION PHASE

The objective during the construction phase is to build the project in accordance with the plans and specifications, within budget and on schedule. To achieve this objective there are three assumptions as shown in Table 8-1.

Although the assumptions are reasonable, there are often variations due to the nature of construction work. A project is a single, non-repetitive enterprise. Because each project is unique, its outcome can never be predicted with absolute confidence. To construct a project the owner generally assigns a contract to a contractor who provides all labor, equipment, material, and construction services to fulfill the requirements of the plans and specifications. This requires simultaneously coordinating many tasks and operations, interpreting drawings, and contending with adverse weather conditions.

It is difficult for some individuals to acknowledge the fact that plans and specifications do have errors. The preparation of a design requires many individuals who must perform design calculations, coordinate related work, and produce many sheets of drawings that have elevations, sections, details, and dimensions. Although every designer strives to achieve a flawless set of plans and specifications, this is rarely achieved.

The owner generally accepts and approves the contract documents before commencing construction. However, the plans and specifications don't always represent what the owner wants. The interest of some owners, particularly non-profit organizations or public agencies, is represented by individuals who are members of a board of trustees, board of directors, or a commission. These individuals generally have a background in business enterprises and/or professional occupations with little or no knowledge of project work or interpretation of drawings. Thus, they may approve the selection of a material or configuration of a project without fully understanding what it looks like until it is being installed during construction.

Serious problems can arise for both the owner and contractor if the contractor submits a bid that is less than required to build the project, with a reasonable profit. A contractor that has underbid a project can also cause significant problems for the design organization. A construction company is a business enterprise that must achieve a profit to continue operations. A careful evaluation of each contractor's bid is necessary before award of a construction contract; because if a project is underbid by the construction contractor, the management of the project will be difficult regardless of the ability of the individuals that are involved.

TABLE 8-1
ASSUMPTIONS FOR CONSTRUCTION PHASE

Scope -	The design plans and specifications contain no errors and meet the owner's requirements and appropriate codes and standards.
Budget -	The budget is acceptable, that is, it is what the owner can afford and what the contractor can build it for, with a reasonable profit.
Schedule -	The schedule is reasonable, that is, short enough to finish when the owner needs it and long enough for the contractor to do the work.

Conditions can arise that alter the project budget and schedule, such as changes desired by the owner during construction, modifications of design, or differing site conditions. To reduce the impact of these conditions, there should be a reasonable contingency to allow for these types of variations that can adversely affect the project budget and schedule.

Sufficient time must be allowed for contractors to perform their work. If a reasonable time is not allowed, the productivity of workers and quality of the project will be adversely affected. There are always conditions that arise during construction that can disrupt the continuous flow of work, such as weather, delivery of materials, clarification of questions related to design, inspection, etc. The contractor must plan and anticipate the total requirements of the project and develop a schedule to allow for a reasonable variation of time that is inherent in the construction process.

The project manager must contend with problems as described above. He or she must always be alert to these situations and must continually plan, alter, and coordinate the project to handle the situations as they arise.

CONTRACT PRICING FORMATS

The method that is selected to compensate the construction contractor can have a large impact on a project's cost, schedule, and the level of involvement by the owner and designer. Contract pricing may be divided into two general categories: fixed price and cost reimbursable. For fixed price contracts the contractor may be compensated on a lump sum or unit price basis. Cost reimbursable contracts may include methods of payment by any one or combination of the following: cost plus a percentage or fixed fee, guaranteed maximum price, or incentive.

Many books and articles have been written that discuss the advantages, disadvantages, and conditions that are favorable for the use of the above methods of payment for construction services. The following paragraphs are presented as a summary of what has already been written, to assist the project manager in his or her role of management.

The intent of lump sum contracts is to fix the cost of the project by providing a complete set of plans and specifications that are prepared by the designer prior to construction. However, the contractor is entitled to extra compensation for any changes that may be necessary during construction. For lump sum contracts, changes during construction are a major source of cost overruns. For these types of projects it is necessary to ensure a complete design that is as error free as possible, and to keep any owner changes to a minimum. There should be an adequate review of the contract documents before bidding to detect any discrepancies that may exist, and to confirm the constructability of the project. The project manager should work with the owner during construction to evaluate the full impact of a project change, including the affect on the project's cost and schedule, because a change in one area of the project often affects other areas of the project. There should be a rate schedule for labor and equipment for extra work related to project changes, that is agreed upon before signing the construction contract.

Unit price contracts are awarded because the quantity of work may not be determined with a degree of accuracy to enable a contractor to submit a lump sum bid. A major source of cost overruns for unit price contracts are errors in the estimated pay quantities. Errors in estimated pay quantities can lead to unbalanced bids by contractors which can cause significant increases in the expected cost of the project and expensive legal disputes. There should be a thorough review of all estimated pay quantities of unit price contracts before the request of contractor's bids. After receipt of all the bids, a careful review of each unit cost bid item should be performed to detect any bid unbalancing. In particular there should be a review of large quantity pay items and any unusually large unit cost bid items to detect irregularities.

For some projects it is desirable to start construction before design is complete, for example, projects that are complex in nature, or projects that must be completed due to emergency situations when it is not practical to produce a complete detailed design of the entire project before starting construction. Cost reimbursable projects require extensive monitoring of material deliveries and measurement of work. The owner's organization must establish a field office to review and approve the costs of material, labor, equipment, and other costs associated with the project. This method of contracting can be efficient for owner organizations that need the flexibility of modifying the project as required, during construction, to produce the best end results to meet their needs. However, the owner must have extensive experience with handling projects.

PROSPECTIVE BIDDERS AND BIDDING

The selection of the contractor is important because the successful completion of the project is highly dependent upon the contractor. The owner and/or designer must depend upon the contractor to provide labor, equipment, material, and know-how to build the project in accordance with the plans and specifications. If the contractor has problems, everyone has problems.

The owner generally requires prospective contractors to provide a bid bond before a bid is accepted. Before award of a contract, most owners require the contractor to submit a material and labor payment bond, and a performance bond. All bonds are supplied to the owner from the contractor before commencing construction in the field. Although bonds provide some degree of protection to the owner, they do not guarantee that construction will proceed in a smooth operation. In addition to bond requirements, prospective bidders should be screened by a prequalification process that evaluates their record of experience, financial capability, safety record, and their general character and reputation in the industry.

For competitive bid projects at least three bids should be received to provide a representive comparison of costs. Generally, a higher number of bidders will generate more competition, resulting in lower bids. However, the quality of the bidders is more important than the quantity of bidders. For private projects it is possible to control which companies are allowed to submit a bid. In this type of situation it is better to not allow a company to bid if their capabilities are in question, or they are simply not wanted to build the project.

Careful consideration should be given to the length of time that is allowed for contractors to submit bids. The proposed due date should be adequate for bidders to prepare a thorough bid. If there is uncertainty regarding what length of time that would be adequate, a reputable contractor can be consulted to assist in developing a reasonable time for preparation of bids. If the time is too short, some bidders may decline, or worse the bid may not be properly prepared. If the bid time is too long, there is an unnecessary delay in construction.

Addenda are changes in the bid package during the bidding process to correct errors, clarify requirements of the project, or make changes before awarding a contract to the contractor. Numerous addenda may discourage reputable, prospective bidders or place the bidders in a precarious "beware" status regarding the quality of the plans and specifications, or the possibility of additional changes the owner may make during construction. These conditions can lead to costly change orders which will adversely affect the final cost of a project.

A pre-bid conference should be held to clarify any unique aspects of a project, and assist the bidders in their preparation of a good bid. This is an opportune time to clarify scope, explain special working conditions, and answer questions of contractors. Any item that is clarified at the meeting, that is not in the bid documents, should be confirmed in writing to all parties.

For any project, the party that will administer the contract should prepare a detailed cost estimate from the same set of bid documents that the contractors are using to bid the project. This will assist in the evaluation of contractors' bids because the preparation of an estimate requires a close scrutiny of all aspects of the project. Many problems associated with a project can be detected by thoroughly reviewing the bid documents and going through the process of preparing a detailed cost estimate. There are numerous professional estimating companies that can perform this service if the capability does not exist in the party's organization that will administer the contract.

CHECK LIST FOR BIDDING

Table 8-2 provides a check list of duties for the bidding and award phase of a project that is handled by the construction management (CM) type of contract. For projects other than the CM type of contract, the duties of the CM are distributed between the owner and designer, depending upon the contract arrangement.

KEYS TO A SUCCESSFUL PROJECT

There are several factors that are important in order to achieve a successful project during construction. A good field construction representative must be present to represent the interests of the owner and designer. He or she must know the requirements of the project and be readily available to answer questions and respond to situations as they arise. The field construction representative's authority and responsibility must be clearly defined to all parties including the owner, designer, and contractor. It should be recognized that this individual is an asset available to all the parties involved in the project: the owner, designer, and contractor.

TABLE 8-2
CHECK LIST OF DUTIES FOR BIDDING AND AWARD PHASE
SOURCE: NSPE/PEC REPORTER, VOL. VII, NO. 2

Bidding & Award Phase	Owner	CM	Designer*	Contractor
1. Procedures—Contracting	Approve as Required	Formulate Issue	Advise, Comply	X
2. Bidders List	Approve	Prepare	Assist, Approve	X
3. Bid Documents Estimate	Approve	Prepare	Review, Advise	X
4. Bid Division Descriptions	Review, Approve	Prepare,	Review, Approve	X
5. Proposal Forms	Approve	Prepare	Review, Advise	Complete
6. Specifications—Advertisement for Bids	Approve	Prepare	Review, Advise	Respond
7. Preparation of Bid Documents	Pay Printing & Dist. Cost	Provide Required Forms & Bidders List	Print & Distribute	Receive
8. Meetings—Pre-Bid	Participate as Required	Organize, Conduct	Participate	Participate
9. Addenda	Approve	Recommend, Review	Recommend, Draft & Issue	Acknowledge
10. Bid Openings	Attend as Required	Organize, Conduct	Attend	X
11. Meetings—Post-Bid	Attend as Required	Organize, Conduct	Attend	Attend
12. Letter of Intent to Award	Approve, Sign	Prepare, Issue	Recommend, Approve	Respond
13. Bonds—Performance, Labor & Material	Review, File	Review & Approve	Review & Advise	Provide
14. Insurance—Liability & Property Damage	Specify & Approve	Advise, Monitor & File Certificates	Include Requirements in Bid Documents	Provide
15. Notice to Proceed	Approve, Sign	Prepare, Issue	Recommend, Approve	Respond
16. Award of Contracts	Award	Recommend	Recommend	Receive

* The referenced NSPE/PEC publication cited "ARCHITECT"; however, the term "DESIGNER" is used here to imply the architect may be the principal design professional for building projects, whereas the engineer may be the principal design professional for heavy/industrial projects.

Another important factor is a good, detailed construction schedule that is developed and used by the contractor who is performing the work, not the owner or designer. The owner should only define the start and/or end date of the project. Contractors know their capabilities, resources, and how they plan to coordinate the many activities required to build the project in the field. Thus, they are best qualified to develop a schedule to guide the numerous construction operations.

A good project control system must be developed to monitor, measure, and evaluate the cost, schedule, labor-hours, and quality of work. Chapter 6 provided a detailed discussion of project tracking and control.

The most important key factor in a successful project is good communication. Most experienced project managers readily agree that the source of most problems can be traced to poor communications. People don't intend to do poor work or make mistakes. These types of problems are a result of misunderstanding of what is to be done and when it is to be done because of poor communications. There must be open lines of communications so the right people are available to respond when they are needed.

A project organizational chart normally shows vertical lines of authority. However, strictly following vertical lines of authority is not responsive to dissemination of information in a timely manner. Thus, there is a need for communications that flow horizontally between people who are actually involved in the work.

Figure 8-1 shows a project organizational chart with dotted lines that represent the horizontal communications that are necessary for a project during the construction phase. The horizontal communications between the various organizations are the most difficult to monitor and control because it is primarily verbal and often not documented, which can result in misunderstandings and possible law suits. Therefore, horizontal communications should be restricted to sharing of information, but no decision making. Although these horizontal communications are necessary, it is the responsibility of all individuals to keep their immediate supervisor informed.

RELATIONS WITH CONTRACTORS

Construction contractors have the lead role during the construction phase; however the owner and designer have an important role as well. A cooperative environment of teamwork must be developed so all parties can work together as a unit to achieve the project.

The construction industry is unique compared to other industries. Because each construction project is different: the work force is transient, multiple crafts are involved, projects are planned and worked in short time frames, and there is a tremendous variety of material and equipment that must be installed. Also, much of the work is exposed to weather and construction workers are continually working themselves out of a job. Due to these conditions the management of construction is a challenge, and cooperation of participants is imperative.

In all situations the relations with contractors must be fair, consistent, polite, and firm. A person must conduct his or her affairs in a professional manner to gain the respect of others and to get others to do what must be done. There are times when a person must be assertive, but not obnoxious, and other times when a person must be reserved, but not a push-over. The ability to work with people and to know how to react in each situation must be developed in order to work in a construction environment.

Due to the nature of construction projects there are times when disagreements and conflicts between individuals arise. One must realize that disagreements and conflicts

FIGURE 8-1
Effective Horizontal Communication Channels Necessary During Construction. (Note: Horizontal dashed lines denote exchange of information only and vertical solid lines denote decision making authority.)

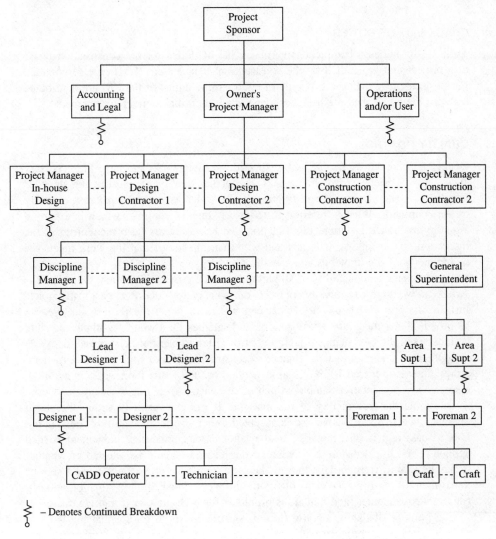

– Denotes Continued Breakdown

are not necessarily all bad because many good ideas have been developed as a result of disagreements. The attitude that should prevail, is that disagreements can be changed to agreements with diplomacy. There are times when it may be desirable to take a neutral position.

Contractors are independent business organizations and are only required to produce the end product of the contract. There are times when a contractor and an owner may not agree, however, achievement of the end product should always remain a priority. Good owner–contractor relationships make the best use of the contractor's expertise, labor, and equipment.

CHECK LIST OF DUTIES

Table 8-3 provides a comprehensive check list of duties for the construction phase of a project that is handled by the construction management (CM) type of contract. For projects other than the CM type of contract, the duties of the CM are distributed between the owner and the designer, depending upon the contract arrangement.

QUALITY CONTROL

Quality is achieved by people who take pride in their work, and have the necessary skills and experience to do the work. The actual quality of construction depends largely upon the control of construction itself, which is the principal responsibility of the contractor. What is referred to today as "quality control," which is a part of a quality assurance program, is a function that has for years been recognized as the inspection and testing of materials and workmanship to see that the work meets the requirements of the drawings and specifications.

Quality is the responsibility of all participants in a project. Too often, the attitude is "what can we do to pass quality control?" or "what can we do to get past inspection?" Instead, the attitude should be, "what can we do to finish the project that we can be proud of that meets the specifications and satisfies the owner?" Without the right attitude, even the best planned quality control program can not be successful.

In the past, the traditional acceptance of construction work by the owner, or owner's representative, involved 100% visual inspection of the construction work. In addition, a so called representative sample, which often consists of a single specimen, is used to determine the true quality of the material. If the test result is within the stated tolerance, the material passes and is accepted, otherwise the material or construction fails to pass and is unacceptable. In the latter case, engineering judgement is then applied to reach a decision as to whether the material should be retested or whether it may be said to substantially comply, because the deviation will not cause a serious impairment to performance. This places the inspector in an difficult situation and can cause delays, disputes, and numerous problems for both the owner and contractor.

The purpose of quality control during construction is to ensure that the work is accomplished in accordance with the requirements specified in the contract. A program of quality control can be administered by the owner, designer, contractor, or an independent consultant. In recent years the trend by many owners is to require prime contractors to take a more active role in the control of project quality by making them manage their own quality control programs. The contractor is required to establish a quality control plan to maintain a job surveillance system of its own, to perform tests and keep records to ensure the work conforms to contract requirements. The owner then monitors the contractor's quality control plan and makes spot-check inspections during the construction process, which constitutes a quality assurance program.

TABLE 8-3

CHECK LIST OF DUTIES DURING CONSTRUCTION PHASE
SOURCE: NSPE/PEC REPORTER, VOL. VII, NO. 2

Construction Phase	Owner	CM	Designer*	Contractor
1. Contracts—Construction	Approve, Execute, Enforce as Required	Prepare Documents Enforce	Review, Approve	Approve, Execute, Conform
2. Meetings—Pre-Construction	Participate as Required	Organize Conduct & Record	Participate	Participate
3. Meetings—Monthly Project	Participate	Organize, Conduct, Record	Participate	Participate
4. Meetings—Monthly Team	Participate	Organize, Conduct, Record	Participate	X
5. Insurance—Workmens Compensation	Specify, Approve	Advise, Monitor, File Certificates	Include Requirement in Bid Documents	Provide
6. Submittals—Shop Drawings & Samples	Approve as Required	Coordinate, Expedite & Review	Specify Submittals Required, Review & Approve	Provide
7. Scheduling—Short Term Construction Activities Plan	Approve as Required, Comply	Prepare, Monitor, Enforce, Comply	Participate, Comply	Participate, Comply
8. Schedule Enforcement	Participate as Required	Provide	Assist	Comply
9. Construction Support Items	Approve as Required & Pay	Recommend & Arrange	Advise	Cooperate
10. Security—Site	Advise, Review, Approve, Pay	Advise & Arrange For	Facilitate	Facilitate
11. Field Layout	Observe	Coordinate, Check Where Practical	Design, Observe	Provide & Be Responsible Use
12. Temporary—Power, Water, Roads, etc.	Approve, Pay	Determine Need, Arrange & Coordinate	Provide Specifications as Required	
13. Meetings—Weekly Construction	Participate as Required	Organize, Conduct, Record	Participate as Necessary	Participate
14. Construction Methods, Procedures	Observe	Observe	Observe	Originate
15. Contractor Coordination	Observe	Provide	Advise	Facilitate
16. Field Reporting	Review	Provide, Review	Provide Review	Cooperate
17. Job-Site Safety	Enforce through CM	Observe, Report	Observe, Report	Responsible
18. Payment Requests	Approve, Respond	Review, Approve Assemble	Review, Approve Endorse,	Submit
19. Waivers of Lien	Review & File	Coordinate, Review & Assemble	Review	Provide
20. Change Orders	Approve, Execute	Request, Review, Approve, Distribute	Request, Prepare, Approve	Execute, Respond
21. Quality Control	Observe	Observe, Evaluate, Report	Observe, Evaluate	Provide & Be Responsible
22. Field Testing	Approve, Pay	Arrange, Coordinate	Recommend, Approve	Cooperate
23. Expediting—Construction	Participate as Required	Originate, Monitor Motivate	Advise, Assist	Responsible
24. Equipment—Owner Purchased	Specify, Purchase, Expedite	Coordinate Scheduling, Installation & Start-up	Incorporate Requirements Into Design	Hook-up
25. Expediting—Owner Purchased Equipment	Provide	Coordinate Scheduling Requirements, Assist	Advise	X
26. Receiving Equipment	Inspect, Approve	Coordinate On-Site Delivery & Storage Requirements	X	Assist
27. Drawings—As-Built	Receive & File	Coordinate, Monitor	Check, Draft	Provide As-Built

* The referenced NSPE/PEC publication cited "ARCHITECT"; however, the term "DESIGNER" is used here to imply the architect may be the principal design professional for building projects, whereas the engineer may be the principal design professional for heavy/industrial projects.

In modern quality assurance programs, traditional specifications are being replaced by statistically based specifications which reflect both the variability in construction materials and the true capabilities of construction processes. Quality requirements are expressed as target values for which contractors are to accomplish, and compliance requirements are specified as plus or minus limits. Statistically based acceptance plans call for random samples, with each sample consisting of a number of specimens taken at random in order to eliminate bias. Acceptance procedures are more detailed and the risks to both the owner and contractor are made known to reduce uncertainty.

Each contractor is expected to have a process control program that will ensure he or she is meeting the acceptance requirements of the owner. Control charts, which are simple line graphs of the target quality level and of the allowable variations from this level, are used as tools in the process control. They provide early detection of trouble before rejections occur, which can result in savings to the contractor by reducing penalties and rework costs. Thus, control charts present the results in a form that enables everyone concerned to observe trends or patterns that may affect quality.

An example of a control chart for a percent passing gradation is given in Figure 8-2. Figure 8-2(a) is referred to as an X-chart and is used to monitor the average

FIGURE 8-2
Control charts for (a) X, and (b) R.)

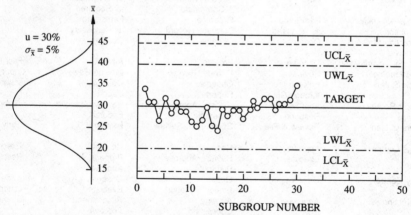

A. $\bar{x}$ CONTROL CHART FOR PERCENT PASSING

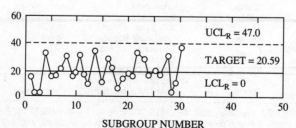

B. R CONTROL CHART FOR PERCENT PASSING

value of the process, that is, whether the process average has remained at a constant level or has shifted. The horizontal axis identifies the number of observations, that is, the number 1 is the first inspection and the number 30 is the last inspection. The vertical axis represents the quality characteristic under consideration, which in this case is the percent passing a given sieve size. Each small circle represents the average value of that sample, or subgroup. The two dashed outer lines are the upper control limit (UCL) and lower control limit (LCL) which are used to judge the significance of a change in the process. It is also possible to place upper and lower warning limits, (UWL) and (LWL). Warning limits are typically placed at two standard deviations from the target value. The second control chart, Figure 8-2(*b*), is called the *R*-chart (range) and is used to detect changes in the process variability.

DISPUTE RESOLUTIONS

Due to the nature of construction projects it is almost certain that contractors, owners, and designers will be involved in disputes. The resolution of a dispute may be by several methods: negotiation, mediation, arbitration, or litigation.

Direct negotiations between parties in the dispute can be held to openly discuss and resolve the conflict to the satisfaction of each party. Usually, no other parties are involved. Mediation allows disputing parties to use an independent, objective person to assist in resolving the dispute. The mediator has no authority to issue a final decision. Arbitration is similar to mediation except the arbitrator has the authority to issue a final binding decision that can not be appealed by the disputing parties. For some disputes there may be a panel of arbitrators to resolve the dispute. Litigation is a resolution of disputes by lawsuits that are resolved in the legal formality of the court system. Generally this technique requires a long period of time and significantly higher legal costs than the other techniques.

The resolution of disputes by negotiations is usually the quickest and most economical technique because factual matters are discussed without the formality of legal formats. Direct negotiations are held on a voluntary informal basis by the parties involved, at a mutually agreed upon time and location. The negotiator for each party must have the authority to act for his or her company. The size of the negotiating teams varies depending upon the complexity of the issue; however the efficiency is usually higher if there are fewer individuals involved. The success of the negotiations depends on the willingness of both parties to negotiate in good-faith, the extent the contract definitively addresses the issues in the dispute, and the amount of preparation prior to negotiation. Direct negotiations can enhance good business relationships between the parties.

In the event that direct negotiations cannot result in a settlement, mediation is often the next most suitable method. Similar to negotiation, mediation is voluntary so there must be a mutual agreement between both parties to have the mediator to serve as a catalyst to explore alternate solutions, to gather facts and clarify discrepancies, and to persuade the parties to adopt flexibility in their stances so a final settlement can be reached. During the process the mediator may have joint or private meetings with the disputing parties. The mediator is mutually agreed upon by both parties in the dispute. The American Arbitration Association (AAA) is a public-service, non-profit organization that has established guidelines and rules for mediation.

Arbitration is the submission of a dispute to a mutually agreed upon impartial third party whose decision is legally binding and enforceable. To use this method an arbitration clause is normally included in the general conditions of a contract so when the contract is signed the parties mutually agree to settle all disputes through arbitration. The Construction Industry Arbitration Rules, established by the AAA, contains 57 articles that have become the most widely recognized arbitration procedures in the construction industry. The procedures follow a 5-step process: agreement to arbitrate, selection of arbitrator, preparation for hearing, hearing of the dispute, and the award. The decision by the arbitrator is usually made within 30 days from the close of the hearing. Thus, decisions are much faster than litigation.

Most parties strive to resolve conflicts before proceeding to litigation because it is the most costly, time consuming, and complex method for the resolution of disputes. Legal counsels, who follow the formalities of the legal judicial system, are used to represent the interest of the parties. The final resolution of the dispute is determined by a court of law. Often, a settlement of the dispute is reached just prior to entering court proceedings.

The American Society of Civil Engineers has produced a booklet entitled "Avoiding and Resolving Disputes During Construction" which presents a method of developing cooperative, problem-solving attitudes on projects, through a basic risk-sharing philosophy between the owner and contractor. It explains special contracting provisions and practices that have been used successfully on hundreds of projects to avoid or to resolve disputes without resorting to litigation. There are three provisions: Dispute Review Boards (DRB), Escrow Bid Documents (EBD), and Geotechnical Design Summary Reports (GDSR) which are described in detail and recommended on all projects subject to potential major disputes.

Formation of a three member DRB at the beginning of construction assists in avoiding disputes and, if necessary, provides timely and equitable recommendations for non-binding resolutions. Escrowing of the contractor's bid documents provides a reliable data base for use in negotiating price adjustments and resolving disputes. Inclusion of the Federal Differing Site Conditions clause and a GDSR in the contract acknowledges the contractor's right to compensation for materially differing site conditions and establishes a concise geotechnical baseline to clearly identify differing site conditions. These provisions are discussed in the booklet, together with guideline specifications for implementation.

JOB-SITE SAFETY

Safety is an important part of project management just as planning, scheduling, estimating, cost control, and other project work. The concern for safety must be shown at all levels and in each phase of the project. Accidents not only affect the worker, but also their families. The economic costs, liability consequences, regulatory requirements, and the image of a company all show the importance of safety related to a project.

Many of the basic principles and approaches that have been previously presented to manage a project can also be applied to safety. The element of safety is a factor that should be considered in each phase of the design and construction of a project. Safety is not included in a project by accident, it must be designed into the project and monitored just as scope, budget, and schedule.

Construction, by the nature of the work, involves many potential hazards to workers and equipment, such as heat, noise, wind, dust, vibrations, and toxic chemicals. The Occupational Safety and Health Administration (OSHA) was enacted by the federal government as a regulatory agency to ensure safety for workers. It applies to all parties involved in a project; designers, owners, workers, and contractors. Although OSHA and other legislation has been enacted for safety, the responsibility rests with management.

The project manager must work closely with his or her team members to include safety in every aspect of the project: planning, design, budget, and construction. Safety should start at the top level of an organization, and by words and actions, be infused in each level of management through to the crews and workers at the job-site.

Although the current practice places final responsibility for construction safety with the contractor, there should be a united teamwork approach to understanding and implementing a safety philosophy that improves construction job-site safety.

Accident costs include medical costs, premiums for compensation benefits, liability, and property loss. These costs have been escalating in recent years. However, there are other significant costs attributed to accidents. These include: the cost of lost time of the injured employee, the cost of work stoppage of other employees due to an accident, and the lost supervisory time. Safety requires everyone's full attention.

Research has shown that safer job-site managers are also the better producers. They are better at keeping down job costs and better at keeping jobs on schedule. These facts contradict two reasons that managers sometimes give as excuses for a poor safety record: accidents are inevitable in a dangerous industry like construction, and our first priority has to be getting the job done. Such managers are misled by myths that can cost the project and the company a great deal of money. Job-site safety management should treat productivity and safety as two related parts of high job performance. A successful job-site manager has been quoted as "You don't have to sacrifice productivity for safety. The safer the crew, the quicker they work. The more safety you have, the more productivity you have."

The prequalification of contractors is usually based on bonding capacity and past experience. The selection of the construction contractor usually is based upon the lowest bid price of all prequalified contractors. Perhaps, a contractor's safety record should also be considered as a necessary part of construction bids so an unsatisfactory safety record could be one possible basis for rejection of a bid.

MANAGEMENT OF CHANGES

Every project requires some changes during construction in order to complete the project. The source of changes may be the owner, designer, or the contractor. An owner may wish to make a change to better achieve his or her intended use of the project after construction is complete. A designer may make a change in the original plans or specifications or the contractor may wish to make a change, because it is not always possible to accurately predict all the events that will arise during the construction process. Thus, changes during construction are almost inevitable.

The mechanism for making changes during construction is the change-order, a written document that describes the modification in the work. All approved change-orders are incorporated into the original bid documents to form the binding contract documents for the project. Although a change-order may increase or decrease the cost and/or schedule of a project, most change-orders add cost to a project and impact the schedule. Thus, every project manager must be cautious in dealing with changes during construction, because a change in the work almost always adversely affects the cost and schedule of the project.

The management of changes is greatly enhanced if the changes can be predicted in advance. There are some factors that can be determined, prior to commencing construction, that are early warning signs of future changes in a project. Research has shown that lump-sum projects which have a large difference between the low bid and next higher bid amount tend to have significant increases in project costs. In the construction industry the term, money-left-on-the-table, is commonly referred to as the difference between the bid amount of the low bidder and the next higher bidder. Thus, a project manager should expend more effort in monitoring and controlling a project if there is high money-left-on-the-table, because it is an indicator of potential cost growth.

One approach to the management of changes during construction is to request a list of anticipated change-orders on a monthly basis. The project manager, or his or her assistant, then works with the party anticipating the change, to evaluate the need and/or value of the change. Sometimes a candid discussion of the merits of a change can result in a decision that the change is not necessary afterall, when the full impact of the change is compared to the true value of the change.

There must be a thorough evaluation of all aspects of a change, because a change in any part of a project often affects other parts of a project. Sometimes the full impact on other parts of a project are not known until some later date, which can adversely affect the cost later in the project. The term "ripple-effect" is commonly used to describe a change that occurs late in the project as a result of a change made earlier in the project.

A project manager should avoid changes during construction unless they are absolutely necessary. If a change is necessary, it should be thoroughly evaluated, clearly defined, agreed on by all parties, and implemented in the most efficient and economical manner.

RESOURCE MANAGEMENT

Many resources are needed to accomplish the construction phase of a project. Resources include people, equipment, materials, and subcontractors. Each resource must be managed in the most efficient manner to keep costs to a minimum during construction.

The crafts that install material and operate equipment are the most important resource on the project. These individuals gain their skills through training and experience. They have the ability to accomplish the work, provided adequate instruction, tools, and materials are available when they are needed. Too often, the skilled workers are criticized for not producing good work on a project. However, it is not a trait of people to intentionally do poor work. The cause of poor work is usually from poor instructions, late delivery of material, unavailable tools, or lack of leadership and supervision. These sources of problems are the responsibility of management on the project. Thus, there must be a well-defined work plan for the project that clearly defines the work that must be accomplished today, and the work that is planned ahead. This plan must be communicated to the teams of crafts on the project.

The type and number of equipment used on a project depends on the nature of the project. For example, construction of a large earthen dam may require a large spread of scrapers, dozers, water wagons, compactors, and motor patrol graders. However, the construction of a strip shopping center may only need a small front end loader, truck, and small portable crane. The selection and utilization of equipment on a project must be an integral part of the total construction plan and schedule, just as there must be a plan for the workers on the project. It is the responsibility of the construction project manager and his or her field superintendent to develop an equipment plan for the project. Adequate consideration should be given to the down-time and maintenance of equipment, because the unavailability of equipment can have a significant impact of the schedule of a project.

A major cost of many construction projects is the acquisition and installation of materials. A materials management system includes the major functions of identifying, acquiring, storing, distributing, and disposing of materials needed in a construction project. The effective utilization of people can be greatly enhanced by ensuring that quality materials are available when and where required. A material plan will vary depending on the project size, location, cash flow requirements, and the procedure for purchasing and inspection. The timing of delivery of material to the job-site is extremely important, because the cause of delays during construction is often late delivery of material, incomplete delivery of material, or delivery of the wrong type of material. Materials requiring a long lead time must be included in the construction project schedule. It is the responsibility of the contractor to ensure that a well-defined materials management system and materials management plan is developed for the project.

For most projects, the owner assigns one contract to a prime contractor, usually called the general contractor, to accomplish the construction phase of a project. In turn, the general contractor assigns contracts to numerous subcontractors, usually called specialty contractors, to perform the construction work that requires special skills or equipment. Thus, much of the work required on many construction projects is performed by numerous subcontractors who work for the general contractor. This multiple contract arrangement requires careful planning, scheduling, and coordinating by the general contractor to integrate the work of all subcontractors on the job. This is necessary because the work of any subcontractor usually affects one or more other subcontractor on the project. The owner may use multiple prime contractors for a large project that extends over a long period of time.

The management of subcontractors should be accomplished using the same management principles presented throughout this book. There must be a well-defined scope of work, cost, and schedule for each subcontractor on the project. In addition, there must be a clear interfacing of the work of all subcontractors on the project. It is the responsibility of the general contractor to effectively manage his or her subcontractors.

QUESTIONS FOR CHAPTER 8—CONSTRUCTION PHASE

1 The pricing format for construction projects can be divided into two general categories: fixed price and cost reimburseable. Describe the conditions that are favorable to each of these two types of pricing formats.

2 Bonding capacity is the criteria that is normally used in evaluating contractors for bidding construction projects. What other criterias would you suggest for evaluating contractors?

3 Describe the important factors that can greatly contribute to a successful project during the construction phase.

4 You are in the bidding phase of a project and have received numerous inquiries about a particular part of the project. You have issued several addendas for clarification, but still continue to receive questions.

(A) What is your assessment of the possible causes for the numerous questions from bidders?

(B) What could you, as project manager, have done that might have prevented the problem?

(C) How would you handle the problem, considering you are now in the bidding phase?

5 You are responsible for a project where you are uncertain of the cost of various parts of the project. The owner has a limited budget, yet needs the project completed at the earliest possible date. What are your recommendations? Discuss the contracting pricing format you would use in preparing the bid documents.

6 You are in the process of evaluating bids for a cost plus contract. Discuss the factors you would consider in your evaluation and how you would attempt to compare the costs of bidders.

7 Much of the day-to-day work on a project is accomplished by informal exchanges of information between team members. Examples are phone calls and informal meetings between two or more individuals. How should a project manager handle informal exchanges that may have an important impact on a project?

8 Describe the difference between a traditional specification and a performance specification for construction work.

9 Name and briefly describe the methods that can be used to resolve disputes related to construction work.

REFERENCES

1 *Avoiding and Resolving Disputes During Construction*, ASCE, New York, 1991.

2 Ahmed, S. A., *Statistical Methods for QA-QC for Highway Construction*, Oklahoma State University Press, Stillwater, OK, 1990.

3 Barrie, D. S. and Paulson, B. C., *Professional Construction Management*, 3rd ed., McGraw-Hill, Inc., New York, 1992.

4 Clough, R. H. and Sears, G. A., *Construction Project Management*, 3rd ed., Wiley, New York, 1992.

5 *Construction Industry Arbitration Rules*, American Arbitration Association, New York, 1991.

6 Grant, E. L. and Leavenworth, R. S., *Statistical Quality Control*, 5th ed., McGraw-Hill, Inc., New York, 1980.

7 Halpin, D. W. and Woodhead, R. W., *Construction Management*, Wiley, New York, 1980.

8 Hester, W. T., Kuprenas, J. A., and Thomas, H. R., "Arbitration: A Look at Its Form and Performance," *Journal of Construction Engineering and Management*, ASCE, New York, Vol. 113, No. 3, September, 1987.

9 Jervis, B. M. and Levin, P., *Construction Law: Principles and Practice*, McGraw-Hill, Inc., New York, 1987.

10 Levitt, R. E. and Samelson, N. M., *Construction Safety Management*, McGraw-Hill, Inc., New York, 1987.

11 Muller, F., "Mediation: An Alternative to Litigation," *Journal of American Water Works Association*, February, 1984.

12 Oglesby, C. H., Parker, H. W., and Howell, G. A., *Productivity Improvement in Construction*, McGraw-Hill, Inc., New York, 1989.

13 Peurifoy, R. L. and Oberlender, G. D., *Estimating Construction Costs*, 4th ed., McGraw-Hill, Inc., New York, 1989.

14 *Quality in the Constructed Project: A Guide for Owners, Designers, and Constructors*, Volume 1, Manual No. 73, ASCE, New York, 1990.

15 Ryan, T. P., *Statistical Methods for Quality Improvement*, Wiley, New York, 1989.

16 "Sampling Responsibility Chart," *PEC Reporter*, Professional Engineers in Construction Practice Division, National Society of Professional Engineers, Vol. VII, No. 2, Alexandria, VA, January, 1985.

17 Stukhart, G., *Construction QA/QC Systems that Work: Case Studies*, ASCE, 1985.

18 Tucker, R. L., *Assessment of Construction Industry Project Management Practices and Performance*, Construction Industry Institute, Austin, TX, April, 1990.

CHAPTER 9

PROJECT CLOSE OUT

SYSTEM TESTING AND START-UP

For heavy industrial plant projects, inspection of construction is performed throughout the project, however, the owner's representative generally requires inspection of vessels before closure and the testing of major equipment upon installation. The term "mechanical completion" is often used to define the stage of project development that these procedures are performed.

It is sometimes difficult to define mechanical completion, therefore, the project manager should develop a plant completion standard with the owner's representative to clarify what constitutes completion. This should be in the construction contract so that all involved in the project know who is to do what for each phase of the project.

The project manager needs to work with the construction contractor to coordinate the interface between the owner's representative, the principal designers, and the contractor. The roles and responsibilities of each must be clearly defined. Also the types of tests and the procedure for testing must be clearly defined in accordance with the contract documents.

A formal plan should be prepared for defining when a vessel can be closed, the lead time notice required for inspection, what is to be monitored, and a sign-off sheet for the owner's representative. This is required to eliminate unnecessary opening and closing of vessels which can require a substantial amount of project time.

The project manager must obtain in writing from the owner's representative the procedure for turning equipment over to the owner. Care and custody is importance because substantial costs are involved. It is important for each party involved to know who is responsible and when they are responsible. The project manager should notify the plant when a certain piece of equipment is complete, tested, and ready for turnover to the owner. Upon acceptance, any additional changes require a work authorization from the owner. This procedure should be handled in a formal manner with signatures required from the responsible representatives.

The project manager needs to coordinate with the contractor and designer to define the procedure for start-up. The process must be formal, but also flexible. The project manager should obtain in writing from the owner's representative what they require from the various members of the project team for support during start-up. The project manager must have the owner's input and should not make assumptions as to their needs.

FINAL INSPECTION

Inspection of construction work is performed throughout the duration of a project. Before completion of the entire project, various equipment, electrical systems, and mechanical systems may be completed and ready for testing and acceptance in accordance with the contract documents. The project manager must work closely with the owner's representative and the design professionals who are responsible for inspection, testing, and final acceptance.

A definition of mechanical completion should be developed and a formal notification provided to the construction contractor that allows adequate lead time for the process. This is necessary so substantial time is not lost which may adversely affect the project completion date. There must be a clear understanding regarding what the owner wants to verify during tests, what tests they want to witness, and the types of testing required. The responsibilities of the three principal contracting parties: the owner, designer, and contractor must be clearly defined. It is the duty of the project manager to effectively coordinate this effort.

The start of project close out begins near the end of a project, when the contractor requests a final inspection of the work. Prior to the request, a punch list is prepared listing all items still requiring completion or correction. To develop this punch list, the field inspection personnel must carefully review their daily inspector's log to note all work items which have been entered that require corrective actions. It is sometimes necessary to recycle through the punch list process several times before the work is satisfactory for acceptance. The final walk-through inspection should include representatives of the owner, contractor, and the key design professionals; the architect, as well as civil, electrical, and mechanical engineers, etc., who have worked on the project. The project manager should schedule and conduct the final walk-through inspection.

Acceptance of the work and final payment to the contractor must be done in accordance with the specifications in the contract documents. Substantial completion of a project is the date when construction is sufficiently complete in accordance with the contract documents so the project can be used for the purposes it was intended. This means that only minor items remain to be finished and that the project is complete enough to be put in use. The contractor may issue a Certificate of Substantial Completion with an attached list of all work remaining to be done to complete the project. Approval of the Certificate of Substantial Completion, with the attached deficiency list, certifies acceptance of the work that is completed. Thus, it is important to ensure the list is complete because the contractor has no further obligations under the contract after the owner signs the certificate. Generally final payment, including the release of all retainage, is withheld for 30 to 40 days after completion of all deficiencies. Before final payment, the contractor is to submit final paperwork: warranties, lien releases, and other documents required under the contract.

GUARANTEE AND WARRANTIES

Generally, the contract requires the contractor to guarantee all material, equipment, and work to be of good quality and free of defects in accordance with the contract documents for a period of one year after completion of construction. The guarantee of the overall project can be extended beyond the normal one year period, however this is not common.

Individual pieces of equipment often have warranties that extend from one to five years after installation. Operating instructions, manuals, spare parts, and warranty certificates must be supplied to the owner. The project manager must ensure that all warranties are compiled and supplied to the owner before final payment to the contractor.

LIEN RELEASES

Material suppliers, subcontractors, or workers who have furnished materials, equipment, or performed work on a project for which payment has not been made may file a lien against the property. The unpaid party has a right to file a lien even though the owner has paid the general contractor the full contract amount. Consequently, the owner may be forced to pay for some of the contract twice if the general contractor fails to pay its subcontractors, material suppliers, or employees.

During construction, the owner can withhold payments (called retainage) from the general contractor to cover open accounts and/or liens. The general conditions of most contracts have a clause that requires the general contractor and all tiers of subcontractors to supply a lien release for all labor and material for which a lien could be filed, or a bond satisfactory to the owner that indemnifies the owner against any lien. The project manager must ensure receipt of all lien releases, or the bond, prior to approval of final payment to the contractor.

RECORD AND AS-BUILT DRAWINGS

Revisions and changes to the original drawings are almost certain for any project. At least one set of the original contract documents that were issued for bidding purposes must be kept in a reproducible form. This is necessary for the resolution of claims and disputes, because inevitably the question will arise: "What did the contractor bid on?" In addition, there must be a thorough documentation of all change orders during construction.

A common contract requirement is that the contractor must keep one as-built copy of all specifications, drawings, addenda, change orders, and shop drawings at the work site. The drawings are marked to show dimensions and details of work that was not performed exactly as it was originally shown. Examples are changes in the location of doors, the routing of electrical wires or air conditioning ducts, or the location of underground piping, utilities, and other hidden work. These documents are marked-up in red pencil to show all the changes to the original contract bid documents and are provided to the owner upon completion of the project.

CHECK LIST OF DUTIES

Table 9-1 provides a brief check list of duties for project close out for the construction management (CM) method of contracting. If the project is not handled by the CM method, the duties of the construction manager are performed by either the owner or the designer.

DISPOSITION OF PROJECT FILES

During a project, the project manager usually maintains two files; a record file and a working file. The record file contains original copies of important information related to agreements, contracts, and other legal matters. The working file is the project manager's file that is used for the day-to-day management of the project, and usually contains copies of documents from the record file plus correspondence, minutes of meetings, telephone logs, reports, etc. Upon completion of a project, a large amount of information pertinent to the project, including the records and files, are accumulated.

Most organizations have a defined procedure for disposition of files. Information from the record file should be organized and indexed for easy access and retrival for future reference. The working file often has duplicate information of the record file,

TABLE 9-1
CHECK LIST OF DUTIES FOR PROJECT CLOSE OUT
SOURCE: NSPE/PEC REPORTER, VOL. VII, NO. 2

Project Close Out	Owner	CM	Designer*	Contractor
1. Certificate of Substantial Completion	Approve	Review, Approve, File	Review, Approve	Originate
2. Clean-up	Observe & Comment	Coordinate, Enforce	Observe	Responsible
3. Punch List	Approve as Required	Expedite & Coordinate Work	Prepare, Evaluate Work	Respond
4. Call Backs (After Construction)	Request	Arrange & Coordinate	Review & Approve Work	Respond

* The referenced NSPE/PEC publication cited "ARCHITECT"; however, the term "DESIGNER" is used here to imply the architect may be the principal design professional for building projects, whereas the engineer may be the principal design professional for heavy/industrial projects.

some of which may have hand written notes that should not be destroyed. Although much of the contents from the file can be discarded, sufficient information should be retained so the project manager can retrace his or her work on the project.

POST PROJECT CRITIQUE

A post project critique should be held at the conclusion of every project, because there are lessons to be learned from every project that can be used to improve the success of future projects. Attendees should include the owner and key participants in the project, including lead designers and construction representatives. The feedback that is gained through a non-accusatory discussion of the problems and solutions encountered during a project is beneficial to all team members in the planning and execution of future projects.

For the meeting to achieve the desired results, it is important that the entire discussion be presented in a positive and professional manner. The good, as well as the bad, aspects of the project need to be discussed. The emphasis should be on how to avoid or lessen the problems on future jobs based on problems encountered on this job; not who was at fault or caused the problem on this project. Minutes of the meeting should be distributed to others who did not attend the post project critique, so they also can benefit from the lessons learned.

It may be desirable to perform a project peer review, which is an independent evaluation of a particular project's design concepts or management procedures. Project peer reviews can address the needs of the owner, designer, or another interested party. The American Consulting Engineer's Council (ACEC) and the American Society of Civil Engineers (ASCE) have produced a document entitled *Project Peer Review: Guidelines*, that describes the process of project peer review.

OWNER FEED-BACK

After a project is completed and in use by the owner, a formal meeting should be held with representatives from the owner's organization to obtain feed-back regarding performance of the project. This is an important activity for evaluation of the quality of a completed project and satisfaction of the owner, because the true measure of the success of a project can only be determined by how well the project is utilized by the owner's organization.

QUESTIONS FOR CHAPTER 9—PROJECT CLOSE OUT

1 As the project manager of a project, describe a plan you would use for system testing and start-up for a project. Reference other publications to support your response.
2 Describe the procedure for development of a punchlist, final inspection, and issuance of a certificate of substantial completion for a project. What precautions should be taken before acceptance of the certificate?
3 Describe the methods of protecting the interests of the owner in the closing phase of a project: warranties, guarantees, and lien releases.

4 Why is it necessary to retain at least one set of original contract documents that were issued for bidding?
5 As the project manager of a project, define the individuals you would select for participation in a post project critique. Give the reasons you would select these individuals.

REFERENCES

1 Corrie. R. K., *Project Evaluation*, ASCE, New York, 1991.
2 Fisk, E. R., *Construction Project Administration*, Wiley, New York, 1978.
3 *Inspection of Building Structure During Construction*, Institution of Structural Engineers, New York, 1983.
4 "Sampling Responsibility Chart," *PEC Reporter*, Professional Engineers in Construction Practice Division, National Society of Professional Engineers, Vol. VII, No. 2, Alexandria, VA, January, 1985.
5 *Project Peer Review: Guidelines*, American Consulting Engineers Council, and the American Society of Civil Engineers, Washington, D.C., 1990.

CHAPTER 10

TIPS FOR MAKING THINGS HAPPEN

HUMAN ASPECTS

The preceding chapters defined the information that must be gathered and managed to successfully bring a project to completion. Although a system must be developed for management and control of a project, it is people who make things happen.

A project management system serves as a guide for overall coordination of the entire project; however, some refinement and modification of the system is sometimes necessary for a particular project. People are the only resource that have the capability to detect problems and make the adjustments that are necessary to successfully manage a project. Thus, a project manager should not depend solely on the system of project management and neglect the importance of the people who are associated with the project.

To summarize, successful *project management* can best be described as *effective communications* between the people who perform the work that is necessary to complete the project. Management of any project requires coordination of the work of individuals who each provide an area of specialization. A successful project manager must be a good planner, delegator, and communicator.

There is a tendency of some project managers to complain that the work is not being accomplished because of factors beyond their control. For example, a project manager may feel that team members are too inexperienced, or that it takes more time to explain what needs to be done than the time it takes to do it themselves, or fear that a mistake by a team member would be too costly. Other typical examples are the feeling that others are too busy and don't have time for additional assignments or that others avoid accepting responsibility. Although these factors are of concern, they and similar factors are a routine part of working with people and can be overcome with good management skills.

Usually project managers have many years of experience of doing the work before their assignment of managing the work. Because they are familiar with what is required, they may prefer doing the work themselves rather than delegating it to others. The result is they become overworked from attempting to both do and manage the work, spend nights and week-ends devoted to their job, and then complain that the work is not accomplished because others are too inexperienced. A project manager must realize that others can only gain experience by doing the work; also that many times others can do the work just as well, if not better, than managers. The problem is acceptance of the fact that others may not do the work exactly the same way the manager would do it. The criteria should not be who can do the job best, but who can do the job satisfactorily. The project manager must balance accuracy and quality of the work for the entire project. The feeling that a person is too inexperienced can be overcome by close communications and training.

The feeling by project managers that it takes more time to explain the job than to do it themselves often results in the project manager doing the work, at nights or on week-ends. Many times a person can do the work quicker than explaining what is needed by others. However, if the work must be repeated on a particular project, or on future projects, it usually is more efficient to explain it to others one time so they are experienced in doing it in the future. Project managers must realize that before telling someone what to do, they must know what needs to be done themselves. A well-defined work plan, as discussed in previous chapters, provides the plan of action to effectively communicate job assignments to team members.

The accomplishment of a project usually involves high costs over an extended period of time with many risks. The fear that a mistake by a person would be too costly is a concern by every project manager. Because of this fear, a project manager may be reluctant to assign the work to others and end up doing the work himself or herself. The problem is the lack of confidence in others and the fear that they don't have sufficient judgement to handle the situation if a problem arises. The excuse that is often given is "If you want it done right, you must do it yourself." However, a good control system will help ensure that work is done right. Fear of taking a chance can prevent finding hidden ability.

Because everyone appears busy, a manager may be reluctant to assign work because of the feeling that others don't have time for additional assignments. This situation often arises when the work to be done requires the expertise that can only be performed by a small number of individuals. A system must be developed to ensure that people who are involved in the project are using their time efficiently. This is best accomplished by developing a well-defined project schedule at the beginning of the project, with participation and input from each person who will be involved. There is always enough time to do what is required.

Another complaint of some project managers is that people avoid accepting responsibility. People will avoid accepting responsibility if they fear unjust criticism if they make a mistake, or feel they will receive inadequate recognition of their work. A manager must develop a project control system that protects a project from major mistakes that are catastrophic, yet tolerates minor mistakes that are inevitable. Some people simply find it easier to ask the manager than to decide themselves because some managers want to make all of the decisions. A project manager must clearly define the work required because people tend to achieve what is expected of them.

ASSIGNMENT OF WORK

Project management involves coordinating the work rather than doing the work, therefore the project manager delegates the work to members of the project team. Assigning work to another person delegates authority and responsibility to that person to accomplish the work and to make decisions that may be necessary. However, delegating authority, responsibility, and decision making does not necessarily relinquish the control of the project manager. A project manager may define different levels of delegation, such as: complete the work and provide the results, propose the work to be performed and inform before proceeding, or perform part of the work and submit for review and approval.

Management involves assignment of work to the right person with a clear explanation of what is expected and when it must be completed. Because miscommunication is a common problem in project management, one must be certain that the other person understands what has been assigned. A project manager must give each person on the team an opportunity to do the job the way he or she wants to do it. Simply stated, "their way is often as good as my way of doing a task."

A project manager should be reasonable in his or her expectations. If an assignment is not reasonably achievable, the person who is assigned to do the task usually will recognize this fact and resist pressure and responsibility. The best way to evaluate the reality of achieving an assigned task is to work with the person to obtain his or her assistance in defining the work that is required to achieve the final end result.

During the course of accomplishing work, many obstacles arise. A project manager must be accessible to explain things that may not be clearly understood and to make any adjustments that may be necessary. In short, the project manager must also be available when he or she is needed. Periodic team meetings are needed to keep the work flowing in a well identified manner so that all concerned can work as a unit.

An effective project manager must lead the project team and reinforce the confidence of individuals. Trust must be shown in their capability, intelligence, and judgement. The leader of any group must occasionally check with members to see what is going on and how they are doing. This builds confidence and respect among the team members, who in turn will strive to accomplish quality work.

A project manager must recognize and reward successful and outstanding performance. People relish this recognition and are entitled to it. Likewise, a manager should hold an employee responsible for unacceptable work, show why the work is unacceptable, where mistakes were made, determine how to improve the work, and identify ways of preventing future problems.

Many project managers are assertive with a tendency to rush in and take over. Although each person must develop their own style of management, he or she must be cautious of over-reacting to situations. With the right attitude and working relationship, problems can be changed to solutions in due time.

MOTIVATION

Each member of a project team provides an expertise that is needed to accomplish a project. Usually individual team members are assigned to the project from various discipline departments by their respective supervisors. Although everyone works for the project, each person may report to a different supervisor. Therefore, the project manager as the leader of a project team is placed in a situation of motivating individuals who actually report to a supervisor other than the project manager. Thus, the project manager must develop effective methods of motivating team members other than the traditional methods of promotion in title or salary.

Experienced managers readily agree that there are all types of people: those who make things happen, those who watch things happen, and in some instances those who don't know what happened. Many managers believe that money is the best motivator of individuals. Obviously few people would work if they were not being paid. Although money may be a motivator to a certain degree, there are other factors that influence the motivation of people. Unless the pay is exceptionally different, there are other factors that must be considered. If money were the only motivator, the project manager would have a problem with motivation because he or she usually is not the person who directly establishes the pay of individual team members. Because most project managers have no control over pay rates, they must motivate by providing individual recognition and, most importantly, by challenging each team member with responsibilities and a chance to grow.

Many books have been written and numerous theories have been proposed related to motivating people. Most people are motivated by needs. Maslow's theory of needs identifies five levels of needs that people strive to achieve: basic survival, safety, social, ego, and self-fulfillment. The theory proposes that an individual strives to satisfy the basic survival needs of food, clothing, and shelter. Upon satisfaction of these needs, a person strives for the next level of need; safety, which may include continued employment, financial security, etc. As each level of need is satisfied, the next higher level of need is sought. A project manager must strive to identify the needs of the people who are involved in the project in order to effectively motivate them. This is difficult to do during day-to-day activities, so it is sometimes desirable to associate with individuals outside the work environment. Many times an awareness of a person's interests and recognition of their needs is a positive step in understanding why they react to situations, and can lead to productive motivation. Good management recognizes the motivational needs of each member of the team and develops methods to improve the performance of people.

Professional people seek job interest, recognition, and achievement. Everyone wants to feel important and to accomplish work. People who feel good about themselves produce good results; therefore a project manager should help people reach their full potential and recognize that everyone is a potential winner. This type of attitude among team members can create motivation for everyone.

DECISION MAKING

Numerous decisions must be made during management of a project which require a significant amount of time and effort of the project manager. While many decisions are routine and can be made rapidly, others are significant and may have a major impact on the quality, cost, or schedule of a project.

Good decisions can not be made unless the primary objectives and goals that are to be accomplished are known and understood. Decision making involves choosing a course of action from various alternatives. It is the duty of the project manager to know and clearly communicate the project objectives to all participants so their efforts can be focused on alternatives that apply to the desired end results. This is important because a significant amount of time and cost can be expended towards evaluation of alternatives that may solve a problem, but not pertain to the central objective to be achieved. The project manager must coordinate the effort of the project team to ensure a focused effort.

Decisions must be made in a timely manner to prevent delays in work which may impact the cost and/or schedule of a project. Most of the project decisions are made internally (within the project manager's organization) which can be managed relatively easy. However, some decisions are made externally (outside the project manager's organization) by owners or regulatory agencies, particularly in the review and approval process. Early in the project, the project manager must identify those activities that require external decisions so the appropriate information will be provided and the person can be identified who will be making the decisions. This must be included in the project schedule to alert the responsible parties so work is not disrupted and the project is not delayed due to lack of a decision at the proper time.

Many organizations have established policies regarding the authority for decision making which a project manager can refer to during management of a project. However, there are many times when others can be consulted who have had similar situations, and who can provide valuable opinions and assistance. Regardless of the situation, there is almost always another person who has had a similar problem.

The project manager should avoid crisis decisions, although many decisions are made under pressure. One must gather all pertinent information, forecast potential outcomes, think, and then use their best judgement to make the decision. It is not possible to anticipate all eventual outcomes, but with careful thought and review, one can eliminate the unlikely events. There is a certain amount of risk in everything we do and sometimes wrong decisions are made by good managers, however, new information may become available or changed circumstances may arise that will require a change in the previous decision.

Decisiveness is required of a project manager to gain the respect of team members. A project manager must avoid procrastination and vacillation and should encourage decision making in team members. Indecision creates tension in most people which causes stress and further indecisiveness. Failure to be decisive can cause many things to go wrong; no one knows what to do, work is not done because of lack of direction, all of which causes a waste in talent, resources, and time.

It is the responsibility of the project manager to ensure that appropriate decisions are made by the right people, at the right time and based on correct information. Once a decision is made it should be communicated to all participants involved in the project so all concerned will know what is to be done. This can be easily accomplished by distributing the minutes of the meeting (or record of the conversation) where the decision was made, with a highlight or flag to denote the decision.

TIME MANAGEMENT

Time is irreplaceable and vital to the personal and business life of everyone. A project manager spends a large amount of time communicating and interacting with others who are involved in the project. Therefore, it is important that time is spent in a productive and effective manner. A project manager must be cautious, because there are always more interesting and worthwhile things to do than time allowed to do them.

An analysis of how time is spent is necessary in order to determine how effective time is used. Occasionally a time log of how major portions of one's time is spent should be maintained. A daily log should be compiled over two or three weeks which shows how much time is spent doing each activity, who was involved, and what was accomplished. Activities can be grouped by categories, such as telephone, meetings, unscheduled visitors, special requests, etc. An analysis of the distribution of time by categories will enable the project manager to determine where his or her time is spent most, so improvements can be made. It is usually easier to reduce a category of high expenditure of time by a small amount than it is to reduce a category of low expenditure of time.

Common time wasters of project managers are unproductive telephone calls and meetings. Although the telephone is necessary for a manager to perform his or her work, it can be quite disruptive. There are times when calls should not be received so other tasks can be done. A secretary, assistant, or answering machine can intercept calls to assist in the management of telephone usage. Meetings are mandatory for project management. The most effective way to conduct a productive meeting is to prepare an agenda that is distributed to all attendees prior to the meeting. An agenda serves as a means of focusing discussions and following an organized coverage of information that should be disseminated. Table 10-1 provides a partial listing of common time wasters.

The project manager must set priorities and develop a system to manage his or her time. Tasks that are the least interesting can be scheduled at the peak of one's energy. There should be a thorough review to evaluate job activities that can be assigned to others and an analysis of work to determine how and what can be combined or eliminated. Emphasis should be placed on long term items, rather than short term items that can often be delegated to others. Most people are more motivated by work that is planned than work that "just happens" at the moment. Priorities should be set and kept to effectively manage time.

TABLE 10-1
COMMON TIME WASTERS

1. Unproductive telephone calls
2. Unproductive meetings
3. Unscheduled visitors
4. Special requests
5. Attempting too much at once
6. Lack of goals and objectives
7. Procrastination on decisions
8. Involvement in routine items that others can handle
9. Inability to set and keep priorities
10. Inability to say no

COMMUNICATIONS

One of the most frequent sources of errors and misunderstandings in the management of a project and working with people is miscommunications. Too often, the "other person" does not hear or interpret the information the way it was intended. Communications may be oral (both speaking and listening) or written (both writing and reading). In each instance it is important that clear, coherent, and efficient communication skills exist to ensure successful work by all participants in a project. The project manager must realize that all people do not interpret the same thing in the same way and that a communication is of no value unless it is both received and understood.

The role of the project manager is analogous to the central server in the local area network of a computer system. He or she is responsible for the continuous and comprehensive flow of information to and from team members, with special attention to communicating information and decisions that may influence the project team's work. These communications include conversations, meetings, minutes, correspondence, reports, and presentations.

Much of the day-to-day work on a project is accomplished by informal exchanges of information among team members. Examples are telephone calls and informal meetings between two or more individuals. Although most of these exchanges are routine, some may impact the work of others or may impact project decisions related to scope, budget, or schedule. Informal exchanges of information that affect the scope, budget, or schedule must be documented into the written record at the next regularly scheduled team meeting.

The project manager should maintain a record of telephone conversations, including the names of parties in the conversation, date, time, place, items discussed, and any pertinent information resulting from the exchange, reference Figure 10-1. Copies of telephone records should be maintained and filed with each project. It is sometimes helpful to maintain a master phone log that records each call for all projects that the project manager is responsible for. Each call can be recorded on one line which contains the date, time, number, person's name, and brief remarks that provide an outline of the conversation, see Figure 10-2. This master log can be cross-referenced

FIGURE 10-1
Individual Telephone Log.

```
┌─────────────────────────────────────────────────────────────────┐
│                                                                   │
│                  Project Title:_____          │
│                                                                   │
│   Name:_____        Date:_____   │
│                                                                   │
│   Title:_____        Time: _____   │
│                                                                   │
│   Firm:_____        Initialed by:_____   │
│                                                                   │
│                                                                   │
│   Items Discussed:_____│
│   _____ │
│   _____ │
│   _____ │
│   _____ │
│   _____ │
│   _____ │
│   _____ │
│   _____ │
│   _____ │
│   _____ │
│   _____ │
│   _____ │
│                                                                   │
│   Conclusions:_____│
│   _____ │
│   _____ │
│   _____ │
│                                                                   │
│   Future Actions: _____ │
│   _____ │
│   _____ │
│   _____ │
│                                                                   │
└─────────────────────────────────────────────────────────────────┘
```

to the individual telephone record which contains the details of each conversation. A master log is helpful in keeping track of the overall work of the project manager.

The project manager must develop and practice good speaking skills. Conversations must be clear, coherent, and to the point without rambling. Thoughts and ideas should be organized in a systematic manner before communicating. This can be accomplished by knowing the objectives of the communication, for example, to give information, to get information, to make decisions, or to persuade someone. Consideration must also be given to timing and location to ensure the other person has your attention, because listening is an important part of communicating. It is often necessary to follow up a conversation to be certain the communication is received and understood. This can be done by obtaining feedback.

FIGURE 10-2
Project Manager's Master Telephone Log.

Date	Time	Number	Name	Company	Project	Remarks

PRESENTATIONS

As the prime contact person for the project, the project manager is the spokesperson who often makes presentations to the owner, agencies, boards, and other interested parties. For an effective presentation, it is important to know the audience and to convey information that is of value and interest to the audience. A presentation is given for the audience, not the individual giving the presentation. It should be prepared from the audiences' point of view and organized in a logical pattern so each part of the presentation will relate to other parts. Examples are problem to solution, unknown to known, cause to effect, or a chronological order.

A flaw of many presentations is an attempt to tell the audience too much, giving a step by step description of everything on the subject. A presentation normally has a limited time and the audience frequently is a busy group. Therefore, the presentation should be more of a summary of important factors of direct interest, leaving detailed information in a report that can be read later. Only a limited number of graphs, tables, or computer printouts can be presented so that they must be carefully choosen.

A presentation should begin with a title, which is a simple statement of the subject, followed by a brief overview of the material that is to be presented. During a presentation, the individual presenting the material must realize that the audience cannot remember every word that is said. To increase clarity and to emphasize key points, the key points can be repeated by selecting alternate words and phrases to bring out the same major ideas. This is necessary for effective speaking, but is not, and should not, be done in writing because a reader can reread material to clarify or understand what is written.

The speaker should define words and acronyms that he or she thinks the audience may not know or understand. This should be done at the time the words are used, not at the beginning or end of the presentation. Defining or clarifying words ensures that the listener hears and understands what is being said. It also ensures that the listener is thinking about the presentation and focusing on the speaker's key points.

Visual aids greatly enhance any presentation, particularly tables of numbers, equations, and technical data. The value of visual aids is that the audience both hears and sees the presentation, which greatly increases their understanding and the amount of information they retain from the presentation. Visual aids also help the speaker keep the presentation flowing in a continuous manner. The small personal computers that are used throughout the industry are now capable of producing slides for presentation purposes from the data generated in graphic form. Current copy machines with enlarging and reducing capabilities can also be used to develop overhead transparencies of printed material, including computer generated reports from laser printers.

Few people are impressed with complicated sentences or an attempt by the speaker to impress the audience. The level of detail that should be presented depends upon how much the audience knows about the subject. Therefore, it is best to know the audience. Simple and direct language should be used that presents the material so it is easily understood. To gain the attention of the audience, the speaker should not make the audience insecure. Apologies and negative comments should be avoided. A positive attitude should prevail, even when controversial subjects are being discussed.

The presentation should be summarized at the end, just as the audience was told the purpose of the presentation at the beginning. Also, adequate time should be allowed for questions and answers at the conclusion of the presentation.

MEETINGS

Numerous meetings are held throughout the duration of a project to exchange information and make decisions. The schedule for the regular team meetings should be defined at the beginning of the project as a part of the project work plan. The project manager chairs team meetings which should be held weekly, preferably on the same day and time. Minutes of the meeting should record items discussed, decisions made, and actions to be taken (including the responsible person and the due date). Occasionally, special meetings may be held to discuss special problems or unforeseen situations. Minutes of these meetings should also be kept in the project files.

Other meetings are held with the owner to report progress or obtain approvals. Special meetings may be held with other interested parties, such as regulatory agencies or the general public. The project manager may not chair these meetings and often is accompanied by lead project team members to assist in discussing the issues related to the project.

Meetings should be conducted in an efficient manner because those in attendance are usually busy people who have other work that must be accomplished. An agenda provides an effective means of organizing a meeting to define and sequence the items that are to be discussed, to prevent discussions from wandering. The time required to conduct a meeting is also significantly reduced when an agenda is used to guide the discussions. An agenda can also prevent an individual from dominating the discussions and give each person an opportunity to participate.

Meetings should be started and finished on time. Starting late penalizes those who arrive on time and rewards those who arrive late. It is preferable to define the start and end time on the agenda. Meetings with constrained times will often cover as much material, if not more, than meetings that have an open-ended time.

Minutes should be prepared for every formal meeting. As previously noted, minutes of the meeting should record items discussed, decisions made, and actions to be taken (including the responsible person and the due date). Copies of the minutes should be distributed to all attendees and a record copy placed in the project file. Minutes provide each attendee with the opportunity to verify the items discussed and decisions made. Minutes also assist the project manager in preparing the agenda for the next meeting.

REPORTS AND LETTERS

Written communications document most of the activities of a project, and often have major impacts related to decisions, costs, schedules, and legal matters. Because of this, all written material should be dated and written in a clear, concise, coherent, and legible manner.

To be effective, one must consider who is going to read the material and the purpose of the writing, such as to obtain information, to give information, to clarify an item, or to submit a proposal for approval. As the leader of the project team the project manager must prepare status reports that describe the progress of a project. Many of these reports contain a significant amount of computer generated graphs and tables with short written narratives. Other typical correspondence is in the form of letters or inter-office memorandums and minutes of meetings.

Although computers with graphic capabilities, word processing software, and laser printers have automated and enhanced written communication capabilities, the project manager must still rely on his or her own writing skills to produce a coherent written document. Cutting, pasting, merging, and spell checkers do not necessarily ensure a coherent document. For example, a spelling check of a document does not verify the correctness of the use of the words of to, too, or two. Likewise deleting or adding lines or paragraphs in one portion of a document can have a major impact on other portions of the document. Even small errors can lead to big problems and misunderstandings. Thus, a project manager must use special precautions to ensure a coherent document.

The arrangement and format of reports vary, depending on the material to be produced. Table 10-2 is a suggested format for a report. Letters should be written with at least three paragraphs: an introductory paragraph, the main body of the letter (one or more paragraphs), and the final closing paragraph, see Table 10-3.

TABLE 10-2
REPORT FORMAT

1. Title Page
      A. Report title, author, location, date

2. Table of Contents
      A. List of subject matter in chronological order with page numbers

3. Front Matter
      A. List of Figures
      B. List of Tables
      C. List of Abbreviations

4. Introduction
      A. Purpose of Report
      B. Scope of Report, including what is contained in the report
         and what is not contained in the report

5. Main Text of Report
      A. Test equipment used
      B. Procedures used
      C. Data obtained
      D. Analysis of data

6. Summary/Conclusions/Recommendations

7. Appendix, for bulk data

8. List of References

TABLE 10-3
LETTER FORMAT

---

1. Introductory Paragraph
  A. State purpose of letter
  B. State how the letter came about

2. Main Body of Letter
  A. One or more paragraphs covering the subject matter
  B. Bulk data should be placed in a separate attachment or enclosure

3. Final Paragraph
  A. Summary and conclusions
  B. Leave open invitation for follow up from reader
  C. Close with final good will sentences, such as, Thank you for
     your consideration in this matter.

QUESTIONS FOR CHAPTER 10—HUMAN ASPECTS

1 List and briefly discuss the reasons that people may give for not accepting responsibility at work. As a project manager, what can you do to prevent the problem of people not accepting responsibility?

2 Many individuals believe that money is the primary motivator of people. Describe several methods, other than money, that a project manager can use for motivating people.

3 Describe methods that a project manager can use to reduce each of the common time wasters that are shown in Table 10-1.

4 The assignment of work is an important part of the work of a project manager. List and briefly explain guidelines that a project manager can use for assigning work.

5 Some people have difficulty in differentiating between big decisions and little problems. Describe guidelines for assisting a project manager in decision making.

6 The project manager is responsible for conducting numerous meetings during the life of a project. List and discuss the factors that a project manager should consider in conducting a meeting.

REFERENCES

1 Blanchard, K. and Johnson, S., *The One Minute Manager*, William Morrow and Company, Inc., New York, 1982.

2 Dinsmore, P. C., Martin, M. D., and Huettel, G. T., *The Project Manager's Work Environment: Coping with Stress*, The Project Management Institute, Drexel Hill, PA, 1981.

3 Herzberg, F., "One More Time: How Do You Motivate Employees?," *Harvard Business Review*, 46, No. 1, January–February, 1968.

4 Hopper, J. R., *Human Factors of Project Organization*, Source Document No. 58, Construction Industry Institute, Austin, TX, September, 1990.

5 Kirchof, N. and Adams, J. R., *Conflict Management for Project Managers*, Project Management Institute, Drexel Hill, PA, 1982.

6 Luthens, F., *Organizational Behavior*, 2nd ed., McGraw-Hill, Inc., New York, 1977.

7 Mitchell, T., R., *People in Organizations*, McGraw-Hill, Inc., New York, 1982.

8 Maslow, A. H., *Motivation and Personality*, Harper & Row Publishing Co., New York, 1954.

9 McGregor, D., *The Human Side of Enterprise*, McGraw-Hill, Inc., New York, 1960.

10 Peters, T. J., *In Search of Excellence*, Harper & Row Publishing Co., New York, 1982.

11 Stuckenbruck, L. C. and Marchall, D., *Team Building for Project Managers*, Project Management Institute, Drexel Hill, PA, 1985.

CHAPTER 11

TOTAL QUALITY
MANAGEMENT

BACKGROUND

In recent years, considerable attention has been given to the Total Quality Management (TQM) concept that emphasizes teamwork at all levels of an organization to improve the quality of a project and achieve maximum customer satisfaction. Much of this attention is due to the successful application of TQM in the manufacturing and electronics industries, particularly in Japan where the TQM concept started in the early 1950s. The TQM philosophy concentrates on process improvement, customer and supplier involvement, teamwork, and training to achieve customer satisfaction, cost effectiveness, and defect-free quality work.

TQM management philosophy focuses on continuously improving the process that makes the product, rather than attempting to inspect or test the product to achieve quality. The approach uses statistics to control the process: where management's role is not to solve all the system problems, but to provide workers with the tools that are necessary for them to effectively address the problems in the system.

Much of the TQM concept is attributed to the teachings of Drs. W. Edward Deming and Joseph M. Juran, who, with other experts from the United States, assisted the Japanese in improving the quality of their products beginning in the early 1950s. At that time the Japanese products were burdened with defects and were considered inferior to products that were manufactured by other countries. Deming made several trips to Japan to conduct seminars on statistical process control, and building quality into the manufacturing process. He emphasized that the majority of the problems encountered in manufacturing are with the process and that statistics can be used to control that process. Juran outlined a managerial approach to quality control and focused on achieving customer satisfaction through a project team approach with project-by-project improvement. He emphasized the importance of training at all levels, from workers to top management. In all instances, the emphasis is placed on continual improvements.

Many articles and books have been written that describe TQM and methods of implementing TQM that refer to the work of Deming and Juran. In 1986, Dr. Deming published a book entitled "Out of the Crisis," which defines 14 points or steps to achieve quality. Table 11-1 is a condensed summary of the 14 points of Deming's management theory.

The National Institute for Engineering Management and Systems (NIEMS) is an organization founded by the National Society of Professional Engineers (NSPE) to focus on engineering issues related to systems management and quality management.

TABLE 11-1
DEMING'S 14 POINTS

1. **Create constancy of purpose for improvement of product and service.** This includes both immediate solutions to today's problems and long range planning for the future.

2. **Adopt the new philosophy.** This charge is not only to the management and workforce of the company, but encompasses the responsibilites of government as well.

3. **Cease dependence on mass inspection to achieve quality.** The problem is not with the defective products found during inspection, but in the system which created them.

4. **End the practice of awarding business on the basis of price tag alone.** Instead, minimize total cost by working with a single supplier.

5. **Improve constantly and forever the system of production and service.** Quality must be built in at the design stage.

6. **Institute training on the job.** Insure everyone understands their job and has the training to do it.

7. **Adopt and institute leadership.** The job of management is not supervision, but leadership.

8. **Drive out fear.** People do their best work when they feel secure. Encourage contributions from everyone to improve the system.

9. **Break down barriers between staff areas.** Instead of optimizing the efforts of individual departments, the effort should be made to develop a team approach for the good of the company.

10. **Eliminate slogans, exhortations, and targets for the work force.** Such devices cultivate resentment when there are flaws in the system hampering optimum performance.

11. **Eliminate numerical quotas for the work force and numerical goals for the management.** Quotas either breed a sense of failure when they are not met or stifle incentive if they are met too easily.

12. **Remove barriers that rob people of pride of workmanship.** Eliminate the annual rating or merit system.

13. **Institute a vigorous program of education and self-improvement for everyone.** Allow people to improve themselves and broaden their knowledge with continuing education.

14. **Take action to accomplish the transformation.** The best made plans for improving the system are worthless unless they are put into action.

The purpose of NIEMS is to apply the concepts of Deming and Juran to engineering to improve the management practices of the industry. Dr. Charles Samson, a past NSPE president, suggested the adoption of the TQM approach by all parties: architects, engineers, owners, vendors, subcontractors, throughout the entire construction process.

The Construction Industry Institute (CII) is a national research organization founded as a result of the Construction Industry Cost Effectiveness task force study of the Business Roundtable. The purpose of CII is to improve the cost effectiveness of the construction industry by identifying research needs, conducting the research, and assisting in implementation of the results.

The CII created a Quality Management Task Force to conduct research in the construction industry to identify attributes of quality management organizations and techniques that have been considered to be effective in the construction industry. The objectives of the task force were to identify the reasons for the effectiveness of the attributes, how they were developed and implemented, and to recommend generic guidelines for implementing improved quality management in the construction industry. CII Source Document No. 51 records the findings of the research done by the task force. The following sections in this chapter contain excerpts from the document.

The CII task force concluded that an integrated approach of TQM and quality assurance/quality control is required to improve the quality of the products and services provided by the construction industry. Construction companies have, with minor modifications, adopted the methods and concepts of TQM that are being used in the United States manufacturing industry and have applied them to their operations.

The development and implementation of a TQM approach must be tailored to the specific needs of an organization. A program cannot simply be adopted from a consultant and implemented. There must be action behind the words and ceremony, and this can only be accomplished by the understanding and involvement of senior management. Management must participate in the implementation process and be fully committed to it if TQM is to succeed.

The use of a small, well-placed, pilot project is an effective method for gaining acceptance of TQM among the employees and management of a company. The TQM process takes about three years before it is accepted throughout a company, and significant results are achieved.

Training for TQM will not succeed unless both the technical and humanistic aspects are addressed. The more technical the processes, the more the emphasis should be placed in the training of interpersonal and communication skills. The topics and examples used in the training effort should be integrated with the actual work processes of the individuals being trained. The employees should apply newly learned skills to their jobs as quickly as possible.

Statistical methods are being effectively applied to engineering and construction processes and are being used to identify and solve problems and to improve processes. For tracking to be utilized effectively, employees and management must first understand the fundamental concepts of TQM and the purpose for controlling and constantly improving their processes.

Owners and contractors are seeking improved relationships with each other and with vendors and subcontractors. Partnership agreements are being formed between owners and contractors. Both owners and contractors are seeking to reduce their numbers of qualified vendors.

The following sections in this chapter are excerpts from Appendix A of CII Source Document No. 51 that describes the basic principles and essential elements of TQM in construction terms, to demonstrate their applicability to the construction industry, and to outline the implementation of the TQM process. The basic principles of TQM are customer satisfaction and continuous improvement. The elements of TQM form the framework that supports the principles of customer satisfaction and continual improvement. The seven elements identified in the CII report are management commitment and leadership, training, teamwork, statistical methods, cost of quality, supplier involvement, and customer service. Although there is no industry standard for implementing TQM, the CII research identified the following four steps that have been used to successfully implement TQM: preparation and planning, implementation of the plan, measuring and verifying the implementation, and evaluating the results and continuing on to the next preparation and planning stage.

CUSTOMER SATISFACTION

Customer satisfaction and continuous improvement are the fundamental goals of TQM and therefore are the principles upon which it is based. All of the efforts undertaken in TQM are directed towards a target of satisfying the customer through continuously improving upon the present methods and procedures that govern the work. The two principles are interdependent and are accomplished through the elements of TQM.

The function of the construction industry is to provide clients with facilities or structures that meet their needs. For a company to remain in business this service must be provided at a competitive cost. TQM is a management philosophy that effectively determines the needs of the client and provides the framework, environment, and culture for meeting them at the lowest possible cost. By ensuring quality at each stage in the construction process, from conception through completion, the quality of the final product will in turn satisfy the customer.

Customers may be either internal or external. External customers are not part of the company producing the product or service, but they are impacted by it. For engineering, the products are the plans and specifications and the customers are the owner and the construction organization responsible for the construction. For construction, the product is the completed facility and the customer is the final user of the facility. These products are intended to satisfy the needs of an external customer.

There are also customers within the design firm and the construction organization. These internal customers receive products and information from other groups or individuals within their organization. Satisfying the needs of these internal customers is an essential part of the process of supplying the external customer with a quality product.

Every party in the process has three roles: supplier, processor, and customer. Juran defines this as the "triple role" concept. These three roles (supplier, processor, and customer) are carried out at every level of the construction process: corporate, division, department, work group, and individual. This concept is illustrated in Figure 11-1,

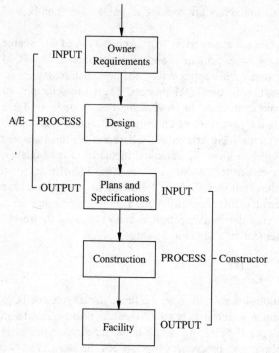

FIGURE 11-1
Juran's Triple Role Applied to
Construction. Source: CII Source
Document No. 51.

where the architect/engineer (A/E) is a customer of the owner, a processor of the
design, and a supplier of plans and specifications to the contractor.

The contractor is a customer of the A/E's plans and specifications, a processor of
the construction, and a supplier of the completed structure to the owner. The success
of this complete process is highly dependent on the effectiveness of the design that is
prepared by the A/E firm. The ability to influence the level of quality in the completed
project declines as the project progresses. This concept emphasizes the importance of
securing customer input, both internal and external, into the planning stages of the
project.

CONTINUAL IMPROVEMENT

To achieve TQM, management has two functions. First, to maintain and incrementally
improve current methods and procedures through process control, and second, to
direct the efforts necessary to achieve major technological advances in engineering
and construction processes through innovation.

The incremental improvement and maintenance functions are achieved through
process improvement and control. In every engineering and construction organization,
there are processes by which all work is accomplished. Each phase of the construction
process, from conceptual design to project close out, is itself a process. Similarly, there
are innumerable processes that together make up the construction process.

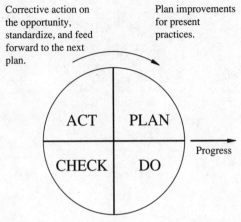

Corrective action on
the opportunity,
standardize, and feed
forward to the next
plan.

Plan improvements
for present
practices.

Verify the results
of the plan.

Implement the plan
on a small scale.

FIGURE 11-2
The PDCA Cycle. Source: CII Source
Document No. 51.

Through the use of flow diagrams every process can be broken down into stages where work flows in, changes state, and moves on to the next stage. Within each stage input changes to output and, through continual improvement, the methods and procedures directing the change of state can be continually improved to better satisfy the customer at the next stage. Those in each stage work closely with both their supplier (preceding stage) and their customer (following stage) to optimize the work process. As a team, those in all the stages work together to achieve a quality level to satisfy the customer.

Deming's Plan-Do-Check-Act (PDCA) cycle, see Figure 11-2, symbolizes a problem analysis process for narrowing the gap between customer needs and present performance. It is a systematic procedure for incrementally improving methods and procedures by focusing on the correction and prevention of defects. This is accomplished by removing the root causes of problems and continuously establishing and revising standards.

The PDCA cycle consists of four processes, occurring over time, that are continuously rotated. This cycle can be applied to all processes and PDCA systems of individual organizations and functions can be integrated and rotated together. The specific steps that are taken within each process are outlined in Figure 11-3.

The eight steps of Figure 11-3 are executed continuously with two intended results. First, to ensure continual incremental improvements in methods and procedures, and second, to ensure that the improvements already made are maintained. This dual purpose concept of the PDCA cycle is illustrated in Figure 11-4.

The second primary function of management under TQM is to support, by research and development, the advancement of engineering and construction technology and management techniques. Through innovation, major shifts in present levels of engineering and construction performance can be achieved. Once established, these new levels of performance must be maintained by the PDCA cycle in order to prevent

PLAN
1. Define the problem and identify the target of improvement

2. Analyze the present situation

3. Identify root causes and their effects

4. Develop plan for corrective action

DO
5. Implement and execute plan

CHECK
6. Confirm results of the executed plan by comparing them with the original planned target

ACT
7. Standardize the necessary steps to prevent the recurrence of the problem

8. Repeat the process by considering remaining problems or improvement opportunities in the next planning stage

FIGURE 11-3
Specific Steps in the PDCA Process.
Source: CII Source Document No. 51.

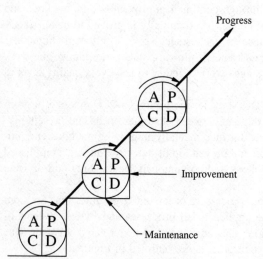

FIGURE 11-4
The Dual Purpose of the PDCA Cycle.
Source: CII Source Document No. 51.

their deterioration. Without any effort toward stabilizing and upgrading the newly established system, its decline will be inevitable. The relationship between incremental improvements, innovation, and maintenance is illustrated in Figure 11-5.

There is a strong relationship between the vitality of an industry and its research and development efforts. To remain competitive, the construction industry needs to make a concerted effort in research and development. Most of the research and devel-

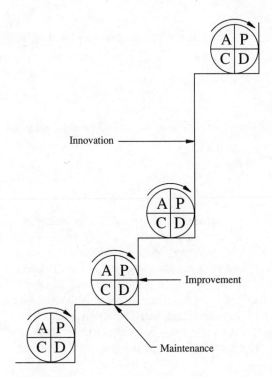

FIGURE 11-5
The Two-Sided Effect of Continual
Improvement. Source: CII Source
Document No. 51.

opment is sponsored by the federal government, as well as materials and equipment manufacturers. In general, private engineering and design firms dedicate virtually none of their revenues to research and development.

MANAGEMENT COMMITMENT

TQM can only be successful under a senior management system that is honestly concerned with the long term well-being of the company. It is a philosophy of doing business that fosters attitudes for improvements that permeate throughout an organization. Top management must embrace these attitudes and incorporate them into the everyday operation of the company. This commitment must be coupled with a thorough understanding of TQM that enables senior management to lead their company in a quality revolution. Supported by this commitment and understanding, senior management can personally establish new goals and directions for the company and then lead the management teams toward the attainment of those goals and directions.

The first step for management is to recognize that there is a problem. The 85-15 rule advocated by both Deming and Juran is that 85 percent of the problems in business today are caused by the system within which people work.

The prominent method of management that is practiced today is management by control and not by participation. For example, top management may set goals to be

FIGURE 11-6
The Deming Chain Reaction. Source: CII Source Document No. 51. Also Reference No. 4.

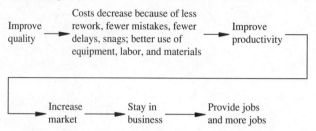

achieved for the next year, then assign subordinates the responsibility of achieving these goals by imposing controls on each of their subordinates.

In construction terms, cost, schedule, and quality goals are established for each project. Project managers in both design and construction are rewarded on the basis of achieving these goals. Although this method has often been successful, there are problems associated with it when the work gets displaced by the controls themselves. If the measurable controls are unattainable or impractical, individuals and groups tend to fabricate conformance. In other situations there may be contradictions between the controls of different departments, which can lead to accusations and adversarial relations.

Management by control encourages an organization to look inward at its own structures, rather than outward at the world in which the customer operates. Once management realizes the presence of negative aspects in its current style of management, it can begin to understand how TQM can benefit the company. Deming illustrates the benefits of TQM with a chain reaction sequence as shown in Figure 11-6.

After management acknowledges that there is a problem, the next step for management is to develop a clear understanding of the underlying principles and elements that constitute TQM. Management can then demonstrate, through action, their commitment to quality.

TRAINING

Using the TQM concept, quality becomes everyone's responsibility, and the training plan must be targeted for every level of the company. There should be customized training plans for management, engineers, technicians, home and field office staff, support personnel, and field labor.

The training effort should include instruction in the basics of TQM: cause and effect analysis, team problem solving, interpersonal communication and interaction, rudimentary statistical methods, and cost of quality measurement. An orientation to the basic concepts and procedures of TQM provide employees with the fundamental knowledge that can be linked to the instruction of the more technical topics. The concepts and procedures of each of the quality experts are necessary in this orientation, but they are not sufficient in themselves. The different approaches are interdependent and should be combined and tailored to fit the organization for which they are intended.

Skills in human interaction, leadership, and initiative are instrumental to the success of any quality improvement effort. The demands on the interpersonal skills that are required increase as the complexity and sophistication of the technical systems increase. These skills should be developed before, or at least in conjunction with, the development of the foundation skills of TQM.

Quality managers can play an important role in the training effort and in transforming the culture of the organization. By leading the training effort, they can provide support to the other parts of the organization and act as a catalyst for change. They should take the lead in demonstrating how TQM, through an obsession with quality, teamwork, and process control, can lead to dramatic improvements in quality and productivity on projects. They should make certain that every individual in the company is aware of the improvement efforts within the company and of changes being made in other companies. They should assist in tracking the TQM implementation effort and ensuring a smooth transition.

Training should not be limited to the technical issues and concepts, it must also address human behavioral issues. The greater the complexity of the technical requirements, the greater the need for communication, leadership, and other interpersonal skills.

For the most part, training should be carried out by the managers and peers of those being trained. Management demonstrates their commitment to the training program through their active participation and support, and uses the training to teach the new organizational vision and values. Assistance from outside consultants should be limited. Training is a job requirement and everyone should be involved in the training effort, from executive management to newly hired personnel.

The training effort should be tailored to the group to which it is being administered. The subject matter should be relevant to the particular job function of the group being trained, with examples and problems that have practical applications. Methods and techniques taught through the training effort should be applied to the job as quickly as possible. Immediate application of the newly acquired skills helps the team to retain the skills, because once a problem is solved in the field the enthusiasm for the new methods will increase.

Follow up training is essential. The retraining of the work teams should be part of the overall training plan and a job requirement for each individual.

TEAMWORK

Quality teams provide companies with the structured environment that is necessary for the successful implementation and continuous application of the TQM process. Quality training is conducted and the continuous improvement process is executed through a well-planned team structure. The ultimate goal of the team approach is to get everyone, including vendors, subcontractors, and customers, involved with the TQM process. Teamwork is an effort led by management to more effectively utilize the vast resource potential of the labor force.

The focal point of the quality team organization is a central advisory committee which is responsible for establishing the team structure and developing the policies and procedures for the implementation process and team formation. The advisory committee oversees and directs the TQM process. Once the quality teams are established, the advisory committee continues to provide direction for maintaining the TQM process. The membership of the committee depends on the needs of the company and is generally determined by the senior management supporting the TQM implementation. The initial training of the advisory committee is generally an orientation to the TQM concepts. They must develop an understanding of the basic TQM concepts and their benefits, learn how to adapt the present management philosophy to TQM concepts, and understand the policies and procedures used by the quality teams and their roles as policy makers.

Supporting the advisory committee is an internal quality consultant, or depending on the size of the organization, a group of quality consultants. The consultant is a resource to the whole organization and is responsible for assisting in establishing the TQM systems, developing training materials, training team leaders, and acts as a liaison between levels of management and employees for the coordination of all activities for the teams.

The consultant must have an extensive knowledge of TQM that has been developed over a long period of time relative to the training effort for the other individuals in the company. Generally, these consultants are industrial engineers or quality managers who have been educated in a university, at another company, or through their own initiative. Depending on the size of the organization, steering teams may be necessary at the department level to assist the advisory committee and the consultant group.

The team meetings are chaired by a team leader who is usually a supervisor or manager. During the team meetings the leader is not in a role of authority, but rather in a role of a discussion moderator that facilitates the problem solving process. To be effective, they must possess certain skills that are quite different from the traditional style of being a boss. The training for the team leaders includes communication skills, group dynamics, statistical methods, presentation skills, problem solving methods, and group leadership skills. The leaders are key persons to the teams just as the quality consultants are key persons to the TQM movement.

The membership of the quality team is voluntary and ranges from 3 to 15 persons, with an average of about 8. The team members work together to continuously study their particular work process, to identify and solve work related problems. The team identifies factors contributing to the problem and prioritizes them in order of importance. Once this is completed the team determines a specific goal for improvement.

After selecting an area for improvement, the team identifies and verifies the causes of the problems and then develops solutions to the most significant root causes of the problem. The solutions are then implemented, their effectiveness is checked, and any necessary modifications are made. Steps are then taken to ensure that any recurrence of the problem is prevented and the result is standardized. Finally, as a follow up measure, the effectiveness of the new standard is continuously tracked and the team begins to look for ways to improve the improvement.

Usually, the teams meet for approximately one hour a week during working hours, to demonstrate management's support and commitment. As time passes, the team meetings should be accepted as a normal part of the job requirements. Initially, the meeting agenda is divided equally between training and the improvement process. The members are trained in planning and controlling projects, brainstorming, flow charting, graphing, statistics, promotional and public relations, presentation techniques, and cost/benefit analysis.

STATISTICAL METHODS

Statistical methods provide essential problem solving tools to the TQM process. They provide teams with the tools to identify and separate the causes of quality problems by communicating them in a precise language that can be understood by all of the team members. They verify, repeat, and reproduce measurements that are based on data, rather than relying on opinions and preferences of individuals or groups. Statistical methods determine the past, present, and to a lesser degree, the future status of a work process.

The most commonly used statistical methods in the TQM problem solving process are know as statistical tools. The following paragraphs are a brief description of some of the tools. Illustrative examples of each tool are shown in Figure 11-7.

Data obtained from work processes can be defined in terms of a distribution about a certain value. The histogram is a type of bar chart that illustrates the distribution pattern of measured or counted data, see Figure 11-7a. The primary function of the histogram is to identify problems by analyzing the shape of the distribution, its central tendency, and the nature of the dispersion.

The cause-and-effect diagram, sometimes called a fishbone diagram, is used to graphically analyze the characteristics of a process, see Figure 11-7b. It is a tool for systematic analysis of effects and the causes that create or contribute to those effects. The effects can be either problems that are to be corrected or the desired results to be achieved when a problem has been solved. It helps to identify the root causes of problems and determine cause and effect relationships.

The purpose of a check sheet is to provide a method of efficiently recording data in a way that makes it easy to obtain and use, see Figure 11-7c. Check sheets are used to determine how often an event occurs over a designated period of time. Data is collected and tabulated on the check sheet during the routine checking of the process. Although the purpose of a check sheet is to track data, not to analyze it, check sheets often help to indicate what the problem is.

Pareto diagrams illustrate the relative importance of problems, conditions, or their causes, see Figure 11-7d. Named for Vilfredo Pareto, a 19th century economist who worked with income and other unequal distributions, a Pareto analysis is designed to identify inequalities. The diagram assists the team in separating the "vital few" from the "trivial many," enabling a person to select the areas that should be addressed first. The basic concept behind a Pareto analysis involves the ranking of data in descending order. The diagram may be used with or without a cumulative curve. The cumulative curve represents the percentage sum of the vertical bars in the Pareto diagram.

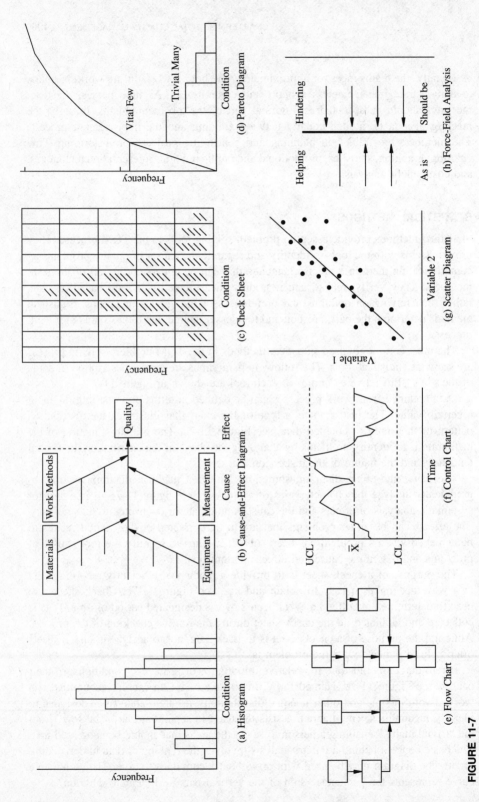

FIGURE 11-7
Examples of Tools for Analysis and Displaying of Data.

200

Flow Charts are used to show the inputs, activities, decision points, and outputs for a given process. Arrows are used to interconnect the activities to be completed and the decisions to be made, see Figure 11-7e. A flow chart can be constructed to show the exchange of information in the design effort to identify areas of potential miscommunication. Flow charts can also be used by groups to methodically identify the steps in the problem-solving process.

Control charts are used to detect abnormal trends that occur outside of the normal limits of variability, see Figure 11-7f. The chart is a basic line graph with the addition of three control lines at the center, top, and bottom levels. The center line is either the average daily value (X) or the daily range (R), the top line is the upper control limit (UCL), and the bottom line is the lower control limit (LCL). The data is plotted as a line graph and the trends and situations are analyzed.

Scatter diagrams are point plots of two variables of corresponding data, see Figure 11-7g. Any relationship between the variables is illustrated by the distribution of the points.

Force-field analysis can be used to identify those forces that both help and hinder an organization or group from where it is, to where it wants to be. Developed by the organizational researcher Kurt Lewin, a force-field analysis is usually performed by a group that is working on a particular problem. A line is drawn down the center of a flip chart to represent the "as-is" situation (what currently exists). At the right-hand edge of the sheet, a second vertical line is drawn parallel to the first representing the situation as it should be, that is, the desired state. Using one or more of the tools for collecting and generating information, the group identifies and lists the helping forces to the left of the center line and the hindering forces to the right of the center line. The forces are often shown as arrows, see Figure 11-7h. Once the analysis is complete the group can use the information to generate potential solutions that will increase the number or strength of helping forces and/or decrease the number or strength of hindering forces.

COST OF QUALITY

The cost of quality is considered by both Crosby and Juran as the primary quality measurement tool. In their approaches it is used to track the effectiveness of the TQM process, to select quality improvement projects, and to provide cost justification to anyone doubting the TQM process. By bringing together the easily assembled costs of review, inspection, testing, scrap, and rework, one can demonstrate an accumulation of expenses to convince management and others of the need for TQM.

Quality costs are broken down into two categories: the cost of prevention and appraisal, and the cost of failure. The breakdown of these costs is show below:

Quality Costs = Control Costs + Failure Costs
Control Costs = Prevention Costs + Appraisal Costs
Failure Costs = Internal Failure Costs + External Failure Costs

In terms of construction, the prevention costs are the costs resulting from quality activities employed to avoid deviations. The appraisal costs consist of costs incurred from quality activities employed to determine whether a product, process or service conforms to established requirements. The failure costs are the costs resulting from not meeting the requirements. Internal failure costs are the costs incurred on the project site due to scrap, rework, failure analysis, re-inspection, supplier error, or price reduction due to nonconformance. External failure costs are costs that are incurred once the project is in the hands of the client. These include costs for adjustments of complaints, repairs, handling and replacement of rejected material, workmanship, correction of errors, and litigation costs.

Cost of quality has received increasing attention in recent years. It is effective in its intended purpose of raising awareness about quality, identifying improvement opportunities, and communicating to management, in terms of dollars, the benefits of TQM. The cost of quality is only one element of the TQM process.

Related to quality, Deming addresses invisible amounts as "unknown and unknowable" and stresses that management must take them into consideration if a company is to remain successful. Examples of "unknown and unknowable" benefits include the return of business of a happy customer and the lost business of an unhappy customer. Also included is the improved productivity of a satisfied employee and the lost productivity of a dissatisfied employee.

SUPPLIER INVOLVEMENT

The concept of continually improving work processes is one of the fundamental principles of TQM. The ability to produce a quality product depends largely on the relationships between the parties involved in the process: the supplier, the processor, and the customer. The quality of any process downstream is dependent upon the quality of the process upstream. This concept applies to both internal and external customers. The quality of the project built by the constructor is directly related to the quality of the plans and specifications of the designer, the quality of the materials and equipment supplied by the vendors, and the quality of the work performed by the subcontractors. Close and long-term relationships with the suppliers to the construction process are required if the contractor is to achieve the best economy and quality.

Traditionally, in the construction industry, contractors, subcontractors, and vendors are all pitted against one another to compete on the basis of low bid contracts. The fourth point of Deming's 14 points stresses that companies should end the practice of awarding business on the basis of a price tag alone.

Successful projects in the future will be decided on the basis of quality (life-time cost of the product and not the initial cost) and supplier responsiveness, which can only be achieved through partnership relationships. These relationships will involve fewer suppliers and they will be based on mutual trust.

The new responsibility of the procurement manager will be to continuously work on improvement issues in their relationships with their suppliers. Some of these improvement issues include improving how purchase orders are placed, and improving the quality of information provided to contractors, subcontractors, and vendors. Other improvement issues include establishing better materials management systems and improving the understanding of the contractor's, subcontractor's, and vendor's internal requirements.

The benefits of these efforts will show in simplified paperwork and the accounting procedures, reduced uncertainty stemming from working with different suppliers from project to project, and improved methods and procedures through team effort with the suppliers.

CUSTOMER SERVICE

TQM is a process that requires universal involvement to be successful. This includes the involvement of the client. As more and more companies adopt the TQM process and demand for improved quality increases, this concept will become increasingly important.

Customer satisfaction is achieved by extending the TQM concept to the customer in the form of joint teams. These joint teams are responsible for establishing joint goals, plans, and controls. The teams provide a mechanism for listening to and communicating with the customer, and for measuring the level of customer satisfaction. The organizational machinery, methods, and tools needed for establishing these joint teams are quite similar to those used for internal customers. The only two roadblocks to establishing joint teams are the state of legal independence between companies and their traditional methods of working together.

IMPLEMENTATION

For many companies TQM is a significant shift away from the standards of management practiced in the past. The task of bringing about that revolutionary change throughout an entire organization is a tremendous undertaking that requires the patient support and leadership of management. Just deciding where to begin can be the most difficult step in the implementation process. Although there are no standard procedures for implementing quality improvement, there are some steps that are common to companies that have successfully implemented TQM. These steps for implementation are similar to the four stages of the PDCA cycle:

1 Preparation and Planning
2 Implementation of the Plan
3 Measuring and Verifying the Implementation
4 Evaluating the Results and Continuing onto the Next Preparation and
  Planning Stage

Senior management should first make itself familiar with the concepts, tools, and methods of TQM. This can be accomplished by visiting companies that have successfully implemented TQM, watching training (video) tapes, attending seminars, and reading books developed by quality experts. Numerous articles have been published on quality management. All of these sources are effective in introducing senior management to TQM and assisting them in developing a new guiding philosophy for the company.

As senior management becomes familiar with TQM it should begin to assemble the quality supporting structure for implementing TQM on some selected pilot projects. The quality support structure consists of an advisory committee comprised of leaders from different areas and levels of the company, a quality consultant group comprised of quality managers versed in TQM, and steering teams at the department level for directing the implementation effort into the departments.

The advisory committee, together with the assistance of the quality management consultants, should then begin formulating the quality approach they want to apply to the company. The formulation of a "customized" quality approach is important to the success of the implementation effort. Management should not simply purchase a "program" and blindly apply it to their company. The concepts from all of the available approaches are valuable, but some companies have difficulty implementing them into their owner operation. They should work to tailor an approach that best suits the culture and requirements of their particular company. This can be accomplished by either adapting a program that is provided by one of the quality experts or by studying all of the different concepts and developing a customized approach that best suits the needs of the company.

As the new approach is formed and the advisory group's understanding of TQM increases, they can begin working on a detailed plan for implementing the TQM process throughout the company. This involves the preparation of a new and carefully worded company mission statement, vision statement, and a quality policy exemplifying the commitment of management to quality. At this time, the advisory group determines the funding arrangements for team training and activities. Annual and mid-term (5–7 years) goals for the TQM process should be developed. Publicizing and promoting the TQM process, and educating every employee about the approach and its progress should be included. Methods and procedures for recognizing team success stories should also be included.

The implementation process should begin with carefully selected pilot projects and, as the momentum of the process increases, the effort should be extended to the rest of the company. Included in the implementation plan should be control points and measures of the implementation effort, to track its effectiveness and make any necessary improvements.

The next step is the announcement to the employees of management's commitment to implementing TQM, the reasons for the decision, and the future benefits. This is followed by the formation of steering teams at the department level for directing quality improvement efforts in each of the departments of the company. The quality consultant group provides assistance to the steering teams to extend the TQM process into the quality teams within the departments.

Training is carried out as the quality teams develop, and is applied to real problems as soon as possible. The team structure is also used to communicate the new company quality policies and goals, throughout the organization, to unify the improvement efforts. As the implementation effort establishes momentum, the success stories from the pilot projects are used to sell TQM to the rest of the company.

The implementation effort is a carefully planned and tightly controlled process. As the process develops, the effectiveness should be compared against measures at the control points that were established at the preparation and planning stage. These measures should be carefully monitored and their conformance to the initial plan should be verified. Any deviations from the established plan should be investigated and removed through the PDCA problem solving process.

REFERENCES

1 Burati, J. L., *Total Quality Management: The Competitive Edge*, Publication No. 10-4, Construction Industry Institute, Austin, TX, April, 1990.
2 Burati, J. L. and Farrington, J. L., *Costs of Quality Deviations in Design and Construction*, Source Document No. 29, Construction Industry Institute, Austin, TX, August, 1987.
3 Crosby, P. B., *Quality is Free*, McGraw-Hill, Inc., New York, 1979.
4 Deming, W. E., *Out of the Crisis*, Massachusetts Institute of Technology Press, Cambridge, MA, 1986.
5 Garvin, D. A., "Quality on the Line," *Harvard Business Review*, Cambridge, MA, October, 1983.
6 Juran, J. M., *Juran on Leadership for Quality*, Macmillan, Inc., New York, 1989.
7 Juran, J. M., *Juran on Planning for Quality*, Macmillan, Inc., New York, 1988.
8 Matthews, M. F. and Burati, J. L., "Quality Management Organizations and Techniques," Source Document No. 51, Construction Industry Institute, Austin, TX, August, 1989.
9 Paulson, B. C., "Competitiveness in Construction," *Impact of International Competitiveness on Construction Technology*, ASCE, New York, May, 1988.
10 Peters, T. J., *Thriving on Chaos*, Harper & Row Publishing Co., New York, 1987.
11 Scherkenbach, W. W., *The Deming Route to Quality and Productivity*, CEE Press Books, Washington, D.C., 1988.
12 Sidwell, A. C., Van Metzinger, W. A., and Tucker, R. L., "Japanese, Korean, and U.S. Construction Industries," Source Document No. 37, Construction Industry Institute, Austin, TX, July, 1988.
13 Tatum, C. B., "Winning with Advanced Construction Technology," *Impact of International Competitiveness on Construction Technology*, ASCE, New York, May, 1988.
14 Tucker, R. L., "The Role of Civil Engineering Research," *Journal of Professional Issues in Engineering*, ASCE, New York, July, 1988.
15 Vorba, L. L. and Oberlender, G. D., "A Methodology for Quality Design," *Project Management Symposium*, Project Management Institute, Drexel Hill, PA, October, 1991.

**Documents, Forms, Commentaries and other publications of
The Engineers Joint Contract Documents Committee:**

**American Consulting Engineers Council
American Society of Civil Engineers
Construction Specification Institute
National Society of Professional Engineers**

Publication	Title
1910-1	Standard Form of Agreement Between Owner and Engineer for Professional Services (1984)
1910-1A	Suggested Listing of Duties, Responsibilities and Limitations of Authority of Resident Project Representative (1984)
1910-2	Standard Form of Letter Agreement Between Owner and Engineer for Professional Services (1985)
1910-8	Standard General Conditions of the Construction Contract (1990)
1910-8A1	Standard Form of Agreement Between Owner and Contractor on the Basis of Stipulated Price (1990)
1910-8A2	Standard Form of Agreement Between Owner and Contractor on the Basis of Cost-Plus (1990)
1910-8B	Change Order (1990)

The Engineers Joint Contract Documents Committee: *(Continued)*

Publication	Title
1910-8D	Certificate of Substantial Completion (1990)
1910-8E	Application for Payment (1990)
1910-8F	Work Change Directive (1990)
1910-9	Commentary on Agreements for Engineering Services and Construction Related Documents by John R. Clark, Esq. (1990)
1910-9A	Commentary on 1990 Editions of Construction Related Documents by John R. Clark, Esq. (1990)
1910-9B	An Update to Indicate Important Changes in EJCDC Standard Agreements for Engineering Services (1986)
1910-9C	Focus on Shop Drawings by John R. Clark, Esq. (1985)
1910-9D	Recommended Competitive Bidding Procedures for Construction Projects by Robert J. Smith, Esq. (1987)
1910-9E	Limitation of Liability in Design Professional Contracts (1986)
1910-9G	Indemnification by Engineers - A Warning (1990)
1910-10	Standard Form of Agreement Between Engineer and Architect for Professional Services (1985)
1910-11	Cross Reference Between EJCDC Standard General Conditions of the Construction Contract (1910-8; 1990) and AIA General Conditions of the Contract for Construction (A201; August 1987) (1990)
1910-12	Guide to the Preparation of Instructions to Bidders (1990)
1910-13	Standard Form of Agreement Between Engineer and Associate Engineer for Professional Services (1985)
1910-14	Standard Form of Agreement Between Engineer and Consultant for Professional Services (1985)
1910-16	Uniform Location of Subject Matter (1981)
1910-17	Guide to the Preparation of Supplementary Conditions (1990)
1910-18	Suggested Bid Form and Commentary for Use (1990)
1910-19	Standard Form of Agreement Between Owner and Engineer for Study and Report Professional Services (1985)
1910-20	Engineer's Letter to Owner Requesting Instructions Concerning Bonds and Insurance Regarding Construction (1990)
1910-21	Owner's Instructions to Engineer Concerning Bonds and Insurance Regarding Construction (1990)
1910-22	Notice of Award (1990)
1910-23	Notice to Proceed (1990)

The Engineers Joint Contract Documents Committee: *(Continued)*

Publication	Title
1910-24	Contract Documents Bibliography (1984)
1910-25	Advice to Engineers Who Intend Using the 1987 Editions of the AIA's Documents (1988)
1910-26A	Standard Form of Procurement Agreement Between Owner and Contractor (1981)
1910-26B	Procurement General Conditions (1981)
1910-26C	Guide to the Preparation of Procurement Supplementary Conditions (1981)
1910-26D	Instructions to Bidders for Procurement Contracts (1981)
1910-26E	Commentary on Procurement Documents by John R. Clark, Esq. (1981)
1910-27A	Standard Form of Agreement Between Owner and Geotechnical Engineer for Professional Services (1989)
1910-27B	Standard Form of Agreement Between Engineer and Geotechnical Engineer for Professional Services (1986)
1910-28A	Construction Performance Bond (1984)
1910-28B	Construction Payment Bond (1984)
1910-28C	Bid Bond (Penal Sum) Form (1990)
1910-28D	Bid Bond (Damages) Form (1990)

AIA List of Documents
The American Institute of Architects

A-Series / Owner-Contractor Documents

Publication	Title
A101	Owner-Contractor Agreement Form–Stipulated Sum (4/87)
A101/CM	Owner-Contractor Agreement Form–Stipulated Sum-Construction Management Edition (6/80)
A107	Abbreviated Owner-Contractor Agreement Form for Small Construction Contracts–Stipulated Sum (4/87)
A111	Owner-Contractor Agreement Form–Cost Plus Fee (4/87)
A117	Abbreviated Owner-Contractor Agreement Form–Cost Plus Fee (4/87)
A171	Owner-Contractor Agreement for Furniture, Furnishings, and Equipment (3/79)
A191	Standard Form of Agreements Between Owner and Design/Builder (1985)
A201	General Conditions of the Contract for Construction (4/87)
A201/CM	General Conditions of the Contract for Construction–Construction Management Edition (6/80)

A-Series / Owner-Contractor Documents *(Continued)*

Publication	Title
A201/SC	General Conditions of the Contract for Construction and Federal Supplementary Conditions of the Contract for Construction (8/77)
A271	General Conditions of the Contract for Furniture, Furnishings, and Equipment (12/77)
A305	Contractor's Qualification Statement (12/86)
A310	Bid Bond (2/70)
A311	Performance Bond and Labor and Material Payment Bond (12/70)
A311/CM	Performance Bond and Labor and Material Payment Bond–Construction Management Edition (6/80)
A312	Performance Bond and Payment Bond (12/84)
A401	Contractor-Subcontractor Agreement Form (4/87)
A491	Standard Form of Agreements Between Design/Builder and Contractor (1985)
A501	Recommended Guide for Bidding Procedures and Contract Awards (6/82)
A511	Guide for Supplementary Conditions
A511/CM	Guide for Supplementary Conditions–Construction Management Edition (3/82)
A521	Uniform Location Subject Matter (1981)
A571	Guide for Interiors Supplemenatry Conditions (3/82)
A701	Instructions to Bidders (4/88)
A771	Instruction to Interiors Bidders (5/80)

B-Series / Owner-Architect Documents

Publication	Title
B141	Standard Form of Agreement Between Owner and Architect (4/87)
B141/CM	Standard Form of Agreement Between Owner and Architect–Construction Management Edition (6/80)
B151	Abbreviated Owner-Architect for Agreement Form (4/87)
B161	Standard Form of Agreement Between Owner and Architect for Designated Services (11/77)

B-Series / Owner-Architect Documents *(Continued)*

Publication	Title
B161/CM	Standard Form of Agreement Between Owner and Architect for Designated Services–Construction Management Edition (12/82)
B162	Scope of Designated Services (11/77)
B171	Standard Form of Agreement for Interior Design Services (3/79)
B177	Abbreviated Interior Design Services Agreement (5/80)
B181	Owner-Architect Agreement for Housing Services (6/78)
B352	Duties, Responsibilities, and Limitations of Authority of the Architects' Project Representative (5/79)
B431	Architects' Qualification Statement (12l79)
B801	Standard Form of Agreement Between Owner and Construction Manager (6/80)
B901	Standard Form of Agreements Between Designer/Builder and Architect (1985)

C-Series / Architect-Consultant Documents

Publication	Title
C141	Standard Form of Agreement Between Architect and Consultant (4/87)
C142	Abbreviated Form of Agreement Between Architect and Consultant (4/87)
C161	Standard Form of Agreement Between Architect and Consultant for Designated Services (6/79)
C431	Standard Form of Agreement Between Architect and Consultant (4/82)
C727	Standard Form of Agreement Between Architect and Consultant for Special Services (4/82)
C801	Joint Venture Agreement (6/79)

AGC List of Documents
The Associated General Contractors of America

Construction Documents
(Engineering Construction)

Publication	Title
200	Standard General Conditions of the Construction Contract (for engineering construction)
201	Contract Documents for Construction of Federally Assisted Water and Sewer Projects
202	Standard Form of Agreement Between Owner and Contractor on the Basis of Stipulated Sum
203	Standard Form of Agreement Between Owner and Contractor on the Basis of Cost-Plus
204	Change Order
205	Certificate of Substantial Completion
206	Application for Payment
207	Work Directive Change
208	Guide to the Preparation of Instruction to Bidders

Construction Documents
(Engineering Construction *(Continued)*)

Publication	Title
209	Guide to the Preparation of Supplementary Conditions
210	Suggested Bid Form and Commentary for Use
211	Engineer's Letter to Owner Requestion Instructions re: Bonds and Insurance During Construction
212	Owner's Instructions to Engineer re: Bonds During Construction
213	Notice to Award
214	Notice to Proceed
221	Standard Questionnairs and Financial Statement for Bidders (for Engineering Construction)
230	Wastewater Treatment Standard Proposal Form
235	Outline for Reports of Site Investigations—Heavy & Utility Construction

Construction Documents
(Building Construction)

Publication	Title
300	Standard Form of Agreement Between Owner and Contractor
301	General Conditions of the Contract for Construction
305	Abbreviated Form of Agreement Between Owner and Contractor
310	Standard Form of Agreement Between Owner and Contractor—Cost-Plus Fee
317	Abbreviated Form of Agreement Between Owner and Contractor
320	Contractor's Qualfication Statement
321	Instructions to Bidders, 1987 Edition
325	Recommended Guide for Competitive Bidding Procedures (and Contract Award for Building Construction)
327	Guide to Supplemental Conditions
330	Change Order
335	Application and Certificate for Payment and Continuation Sheet
340	Certificate of Substantial Completion

Construction Documents
(Building Construction *(Continued)*)

Publication	Title
400	Preliminary Design-Build Agreement
405	Design-Build Guidelines
410	Standard Form of Design-Build Agreement and General Conditions Between Owner and Contractor (guaranteed maximum price)
415	Standard Form of Design-Build Agreement and General Conditions Between Owner and Contractor (lump sum)
420	Standard Form of Agreement Between Contractor and Architect
430	Conditions Between Contractor and Subcontractor for Design-Build
440	Change Order / Contractor Fee Adjustment
450	Standard Design-Build Subcontract Agreement with Subcontractor Not Providing Design
450.1	Standard Design-Build Subcontract Agreement With Subcontractor Providing Design
500	Standard Form of Agreement Between Owner and Construction Manager
501	Standard Form of Agreement Between Owner and Construction Manager (Owner Awards all Trade Contracts)
510	Standard Form of Agreement Between Owner and Construction Manager
520	General Conditions for Trade Contractors Under Construction Management Agreements
525	Change Order / Construction Manager Fee Adjustment
540	Construction Management Guidelines
545	Construction Management Control Process
550	Owner Guidelines for Selection of a Contruction Manager
560	Construction Management Delivery Systems for Hospital Facilities
570	Budget Estimating and Control During the Design Phase
580	Construction Project Planning and Scheduling Guidelines
600	Standard Subcontract Agreement for Building Construction
603	Short Form Subcontract
605	Standard Subbid Proposal
610	Subcontractor's Application for Payment
614	Invitation to Bid Form for Subcontractors

Construction Documents
(Building Construction *(Continued)*)

Publication	Title
615	A Suggested Guide and Checklist for Subcontractors
625	AGC Certificate of Substantial Completion
630	First Budget Estimate Guideline
645	Standard Form of Negotiated Agreement Between Owner and Contractor
650	An Owner's Guide to Building Construction Contracting Methods
655	Guide to Owner's Responsibility for Construction Projects

MASTERFORMAT— MASTER LIST OF SECTION TITLES AND NUMBERS

BIDDING REQUIREMENTS, CONTRACT FORMS*, AND CONDITIONS OF THE CONTRACT*

Document Number **Title**

		00200	**INFORMATION AVAILABLE TO BIDDERS**
00010	**PRE-BID INFORMATION**		
-020	Invitation to Bid	-210	Preliminary Schedules
-030	Advertisement for Bids	-220	Geotechnical Data
-040	Prequalification Forms		*Geotechnical Report*
			Soil Boring Data
		-230	Existing Conditions
00100	**INSTRUCTIONS TO BIDDERS**		*Description of Existing Site*
-120	Supplementary Instructions to Bidders		*Description of Exlsting Buildings*
			Propenty Survey
-130	Pre-Bid Conferences	-240	Project Financial Information

* Documents marked with an asterisk (*) have important legal consequences. Initiation of modificaions without explicit approval and guidance from the owner or the owner's legal counsel is not recommended.

Reprinted courtesy of The Construction Specifications Institute.

00300	**BID FORMS**	
00400	**SUPPLEMENTS TO BID FORMS**	
-410	Bid Security Forms	
-420	Bidders Qualification Forms	
-430	Subcontractor List	
-440	Substitution List	
-450	Equipment Suppliers List	
-460	List of Alternates/Alternatives	
-470	List of Estimated Quantities	
-480	Noncollusion Affidavit	

00500 **AGREEMENT FORMS***

00600 **BONDS AND CERTIFICATES***
-610 Performance Bonds
-620 Payment Bonds
-630 Warranty Bonds
-640 Maintenance Bonds
-650 Certificates of Insurance
-660 Certificates of Compliance

00700 **GENERAL CONDITIONS***

00800 **SUPPLEMENTARY CONDITIONS***
-810 Modifications to General Conditions
-820 Additional Articles
 Equal Employment Opportunity Requirement
 Insurance Requirements
 Non-Segregated Facilities Requirements
 Specific Project Requirements
 Statutory Requirements
 Wage Rate Requirements
-830 Wage Determination Schedule

00900 **ADDENDA**

SPECIFICATIONS— DIVISIONS 1–16

DIVISION 1 — GENERAL REQUIREMENTS

Section Number | **Title**

01010 **SUMMARY OF WORK**
 Work Covered by Contract Documents
 Contracts
 Work Under Other Contracts
 Future Work
 Work Sequence
 Contractor Use of Premises
 Occupancy equirements
 Products Ordered in Advance
 Owner Fumished Products

01020 **ALLOWANCES**
-021 Cash Allowances
 Product Allowances
 Installation Allowances
 Inspection and Testing Allowances
 Contingency Allowances
-024 Quantity Allowances

01025 **MEASUREMENT AND PAYMENT**
 Schedule of Values
 Applications for Payment
 Unit Prices

01030 **ALTERNATES/ ALTERNATIVES**

01035 **MODIFICATION PROCEDURES**
 Change Orders
 Instructions
 Field Orders
 Directives

01040 **COORDINATION**
-041 Project Coordination
-042 Mechanical and Electrical Coordination
-043 Job Site Administration
-045 Cutting and Patching

01600	**MATERIAL AND EQUIPMENT**	
-610	Delivery, Storage, and Handling	
	Packing	
	Shipping	
	Unloading and Acceptance	
	Protection	
-620	Installation Standards	
-630	Product Options and Substitutions	

01650 FACILITY STARTUP COMMISSIONING
-655 Starting of Systems
-660 Testing, Adjusting, and Balancing of Systems
-670 Systems Demonstrations

01700 CONTRACT CLOSEOUT
-710 Final Cleaning
-720 Project Record Documents
-730 Operation and Maintenance
　　Data
　　Operation Manuals
　　Maintenance Instructions
-740 Warranties and Bonds
-750 Spare Parts and Maintenance Materials
-760 Warranty Inspections

01800 MAINTENANCE

DIVISION 2 — SITEWORK

Section Number	Title
02010	**SUBSURFACE INVESTIGATION**
-012	Standard Penetration Tests
	Borings
	Core Drilling
-016	Seismic Investigation
02050	**DEMOLITION**
-060	Building Demolition
-070	Selective Demolition
	Minor Demolition for Remodelling
	Selecbve Structural Demolition
-075	Concrete Removal
-080	Hazardous Material Abatement
02100	**SITE PREPARATION**
-110	Site Clearing
	Clearing and Grubbing
	Large Tract Tree Clearing
-115	Selective Clearing
	Sod Stripping
	Tree and Shrub Removal
	Tree Pruning
-120	Structure Moving
02140	**DEWATERING**
-042	Sand Drains
-044	Well Points
-046	French Drains
-048	Relief Wells
02150	**SHORING AND UNDERPINNING**
-152	Shores
-153	Needle Beams
-154	Grillage
-156	Underpinning
-158	Slabjacking
02160	**EXCAVATION SUPPORT SYSTEMS**
-162	Cribbing and Walers
-164	Soil and Rock Anchors
	Anchor Tieback Systems
-166	Ground Freezing
-167	Reinforced Earth
-168	Slurry Wall Construction

02170   **COFFERDAMS**
-172   Double Wall Cofferdams
-174   Cellular Cofferdams
-176   Piling with Intermediate Lagging
-178   Sheet Piling Cofferdams

02200   **EARTHWORK**
-210   Grading
     Rough Grading
     Finish Grading
-220   Excavating. Backfilling, and Compacting
     Borrow
     Elevator Jack Holes
     Embankment
     Excavating, Backfilling, and Compacting tor Structures
     Excavating, Backfilling, and Compacting for Utilities
     Ecavating, Backfilling, and Compacting for Pavement
     Rock Removal
-230   Base Courses
     Asphalt Base Course
     Caliche Base Course
     Granular Base Course
     Limerock Base Course
     Sand Clay Base Course
     Shell Base Course
     Soil Cement Base Course
     Subsoil Base Course
-240   Soil Stabilization
     Asphalt Soil Stabilization
     Cement Soil Stabilizabon
     Geotextile Soil Stabilization
     Lime Soil Stabilization
     Lime Slurry Soil Stabilizabon
     Pressure Grouting Soil Stabilization
-250   Vibro-Flotation
-270   Slope Protection and Erosion Control
     Gabions
     Membrane Systems
     Retaining Walls
     Riprap
     Sediment Control
     Silt Fences
     Slope Paving
     Stone Slope Protection
     Wire Mats
-280   Soil Treatment
     Rodent Control
     Termite Control
     Vegetation Control
-290   Earth Dams

02300   **TUNNELING**
-305   Tunnel Ventilation and Compression
-310   Tunnel Excavating
-320   Tunnel Lining
     Concrete Tunnel Lining
     Prefabricaed Steel Tunnel Lining
-330   Tunnel Grouting
-340   Tunnel Support Systems
     Rock Bolting
     Steel Rings and Lagging

02350   **PILES AND CAISSONS**
-355   Pile Driving
     Pile Load Tests
     Pile Performance Specifications
-360   Driven Piles
     Composite Piles
     Concrete Displacement Piles
     Concrete Filled Steel Piles
     Precast Concrete Piles
     Prestressed Concrete Piles
     Rolled Steel Sechon Piles
     Sheet Piles
     Wood Piles
     Pressure Injected Foobngs
-370   Bored/Augered Piles
     Auger Cast Grout Piles
     Bored and Belled Concrete Piles
     Bored Friction Concrete Piles
     Cast-in-Place Concrete Piles - Uncased
     Drilled Concrete Piers
-380   Caissons
     Benoto Caissons
     Box Caissons
     Drilled Caissons
     Excavated Caissons
     Open Caissons
     Pneumatic Caissons
-390   Repair of Piles
     Extension and Repair of Concrete Piles
     Repair of Sheet Piles
     Repair of Wood Piles

02450   **RAILROAD WORK**
-452   Railroad Trackwork
-454   Railroad Service Facilities
     Fueling Depots
     Hi-Rail Access
     Yards
-456   Railroad Traffic Control

02480   **MARINE WORK**
-482   Dredging
-484   Seawalls and Bulkheads

-486   Groins and Jetties
-488   Docks and Facilities
     Marine Fenders
-490   Underwater Work

02500   **PAVING AND SURFACING**
-505   Granular Paving
     Crushed Stone Paving
     Cinder Surfacing
-510   Asphaltic Concrete Paving
     Asphaltic Concrete Base Course
     Asphaltic Concrete Surface
     Course
     Asphaltic Concrete Curb and
     Gutter
     Asphaltic Concrete Athletic Paving
-515   Unit Pavers
     Asphaltic Block Pavers
     Brick Pavers
     Concrete Pavers
     Stone Pavers
-520   Portland Cement Concrete
     Paving
     Concrete Curb and Gutter
     Integrally Colored Concrete
     Paving
-525   Prefabricated Curbs
     Granite Curbs
     Precast Concrete Curbs
-540   Synthetic Surfacing
     Synthetic Grass Surfacing
     Resilient Matting
-545   Bituminous Surface Treatment
     Single Bituminous Surface
     Treatment
     Double Bituminous Surface
     Treatment
-575   Pavement Repair
     Pavement Pesurfacing
     Slurry Sealing
-580   Pavement Marking
     Tactile Warning Lines

02600   **UTILITY PIPING MATERIALS**
-605   Utility Structures
     Cleanouts
     Manholes and Covers
     Tunnels
-610   Pipe and Fittings
     Cast Iron Pipe
     Concrete Pipe
     Corrugated Metal Pipe
     Ductile Iron Pipe
     Mineral Fiber Reinforced Cement
     Pipe
     Plastic Pipe

     Pre-Insulated Pipe
     Steel Pipe
     Vitrified Clay Pipe
-640   Valves and Cocks
-645   Hydrants

02660   **WATER DISTRIBUTION**
-665   Water Systems
     Chilled Water Systems
     Cisterns
     Domestic Water Systems
     Fire Water Systems
     Heating Water Systems
     Thrust Restraints
-670   Water Wells
     Test Well Drilling
     Well Drilling and Casing
-675   Disinfection of Water Distribution
     Systems

02680   **FUEL AND STEAM**
     DISTRIBUTION
-685   Gas Distribution Systems
-690   Oil Distribution Systems
     Fuel Tanks
-695   Steam Distribution Systems

02700   **SEWERAGE AND DRAINAGE**
-710   Subdrainage Systems
     Disposal Wells
     Foundation Drainage Systems
     Retaining Wall Underdrains
     Tunnel Drainage Systems
     Underslab Drainage Systems
-720   Storm Sewerage
     Catch Basins, Grates, and Frames
     Culverts
     Curb Inlets
     Drainage Pipe
     French Drains
     Manhole Covers and Frames
     Precast Trench Drains
     Splash Blocks
     Surrace Run-Off Collection
-730   Sanitary Sewerage
     Sewage Collection Lines
     Sewage Force Mains
-735   Combined Wastewater Systems
-740   Septic Systems
     Drainage Fields
     Grease Interceptors
     Leaching Cesspools
     Sand Filters
     Septic Tanks
     Siphon Tanks

02760   **RESTORATION OF UNDERGROUND PIPE**

-762   Inspection of Underground Pipelines

-764   Sealing Underground Pipelines

-766   Relining Underground Pipelines

02770   **PONDS AND RESERVOIRS**

-772   Ponds
   Cooling Water Ponds
   Fire Protection Reservoirs
   Stabilization Ponds
   Storm Water Holding Ponds

-774   Sewage Lagoons

-776   Pond and Reservoir Liners

-778   Pond and Reservoir Covers

02780   **POWER AND COMMUNICATIONS**

-785   Electric Power Transmission
   Overhead Electric Power Transmission
   Underground Electric Power Transmission

-790   Communication Transmission
   Fiber Optics Communications
   Microwave Communications
   Shortwave Communications
   Satellite Antennas

02800   **SITE IMPROVEMENTS**

-810   Irrigation Systems

-820   Fountains

-830   Fences and Gates
   Chain Link Fences and Gates
   Ornamental Metal Fences and Gates
   Tennis Court Windbreakers
   Wire Fences and Gates
   Wood Fences and Gates

-840   Walk, Road, and Parking
   Appurtenances
   Bicycle Racks
   Culvert Pipe Underpasses
   Guardrails
   Parking Barriers
   Parking Bumpers
   Signage
   Traffic Signals

-860   Playfield Equipment and Structures
   Playground Equipment
   Play Structures
   Recreational Facilities

-870   Site and Street Furnishings
   Prefabricated Planters
   Prefabricated Shelters
   Seating
   Tables
   Trash and Litter Receptors
   Tree Grates

-890   Footbridges

02900   **LANDSCAPING**

-910   Shrub and Tree Transplanting

-920   Soil Preparation
   Topsoil

-930   Lawns and Grasses
   Hydro-Mulching
   Plugging
   Seeding
   Sodding
   Sprigging
   Stolonizing

-950   Trees, Plants, and Ground Covers
   Ground Covers
   Plants and Bulbs
   Shrubs
   Trees

-970   Landscape Maintenance
   Fertilizing
   Liming
   Mowing
   Pruning
   Watering

DIVISION 3 — CONCRETE

Section Number   **Title**

03100   CONCRETE FORMWORK
-110   Structural Cast-in-Place Concrete Formwork
    Meal Pan Formwork
    Slip Formwork
-120   Architectural Cast-in-Place Concrete Formwork
-130   Permanent Forms
    Permanent Steel Forms
    Prefabricated Stair Forms

03200   CONCRETE REINFORCEMENT
-210   Reinforcing Steel
-220   Welded Wire Fabric
-230   Stressing Tendons
-240   Fibrous Reinforcing

03250   CONCRETE ACCESSORIES
    Anchors and Inserts
    Expansion and Contraction Joints
    Waterstops

03300   CAST-IN-PLACE CONCRETE
-310   Structural Concrete
    Heavyweight Structural Concrete
    Lightweight Structural Concrete
    Normalweight Structural Concrete
    Shrinkage Compensating Concrete
-330   Architectural Concrete
    Lightweight Architectural Concrete
    Normalweight Architectural Concrete
-340   Low Density Concrete
-345   Concrete Finishing
-350   Concrete Finishes
    Blasted Concrete Finishes
    Colored Concrete Finishes
    Exposed Aggregate Concrete Finishes
    Grooved Sunface Concrete Finishes
    Heavy-Duty Concrete Floor Finishes
    Tooled Concrete Finishes
-360   Specially Placed Concrete
    Shotcrete
-365   Post-Tensioned Concrete

03370   CONCRETE CURING

03400   PRECAST CONCRETE
-410   Structural Precast Concrete - Plant Cast
    Precast Concrete Hollow Core Planks
    Precast Concrete Slabs
    Structural Precast Pretensioned Concrete - Plant Cast
-420   Structural Precast Post-Tensioned Concrete - Plant Cast
-430   Structural Precast Concrete - Site Cast
    Lift-Slab Concrete
    Precast Post-Tensioned Concrete - Site Cast
    Structural Precast Pretensioned Concrete - Site Cast
-450   Architectural Precast Concrete - Plant Cast
    Faced Architectural Precast Concrete - Site Cast
    Glass Fiber Reinforced Precast Concrete - Site Cast
-460   Architectural Precast Concrete - Site Cast
-470   Tilt-Up Precast Concrete
-480   Precast Concrete Specialties

03500   CEMENTITOUS DECKS AND TOPPINGS
-510   Gypsum Concrete
    Gypsum Concrete Floor Underlayment
    Gypsum Concrete Roof Decks
-520   Insulating Concrete Decks
-530   Cementitious Wood Fiber Systems
    Cementitious Wood Fiber Planks
-540   Composite Concrete and Insulation Decks
-550   Concrete Toppings
    Cementitious Floor Underlayment

03600   GROUT
    Catalyzed Metallic Grout
    Epoxy Grout
    Nonmetallic Grout

03700   CONCRETE RESTORATION AND CLEANING
-710   Concrete Cleaning
-720   Concrete Resurfacing
-730   Concrete Rehabilitation

03800   MASS CONCRETE

DIVISION 4 — MASONRY

Section Number	Title

04100 **MORTAR AND MASONRY GROUT**
 Cement and Lime Mortars
 Chemical Resisting Mortars
 Epoxy Mortars
 High Bond Mortar
 Masonry Grouts
 Mortar Coloring Materials
 Premixed Mortars

04150 **MASONRY ACCESSORIES**
 Anchors and Tie Systems
 Manufactured Control Joints
 Joint Reinforcement
 Weep Vents

04200 **UNIT MASONRY**
-210 Clay Unit Masonry
 Brick Unit Masonry
 Clay Tile Unit Masonry
 Structural Clay Tile Unit Masonry
 Terra Cotta Unit Masonry
-220 Concrete Unit Masonry
 Exposed Aggregate Concrete Unit Masonry
 Fluted Concrete Unit Masonry
 Interlocking Concrete Unit Masonry
 Molded Face Concrete Unit Masonry
 Prefaced Concrete Unit Masonry
 Preinsulated Concrete Unit Masonry
 Sound Absorbing Concrete Unit Masonry
 Split Face Concrete Unit Masonry
-230 Reinforced Unit Masonry
 Reinforced Grouted Brick Masonry
 Reinforced Grouted Concrete Unit Masonry
-235 Pre-assembled Masonry Panel Systems
-240 Non Reinforced Masonry Systems
 Single Wythe Masonry Systems
 Multiple Wythe Masonry System
 Veneer Masonry Systems
 Mortarless Concrete Unit Masonry
-270 Glass Unit Masonry
-280 Gypsum Unit Masonry
-290 Adobe Unit Masonry

04400 **STONE**
-410 Rough Stone
-420 Cut Stone
-440 Flagstone
-450 Stone Veneer
-455 Marble
-460 Limestone
-465 Granite
-470 Sandstone
-475 Slate

04500 **MASONRY RESTORATION AND CLEANING**
-510 Masonry Cleaning
-520 Masonry Restoration

04550 **REFRACTORIES**
-555 Flue Liners
-560 Combustion Chambers
-565 Firebrick
-570 Castable Refractories

04600 **CORROSION RESISTANT MASONRY**
-605 Chemical Resistant Brick
-610 Vitrified Clay Liner Plates

04700 **SIMULATED MASONRY**
-710 Simulated Stone
-720 Cast Stone

DIVISION 5 — METALS

Section   Title
Number

05010   **METAL MATERIALS**
Aluminum
Brass
Bronze
Cast Iron
Copper
Ductile Iron
Lead
Stainless Steel
Steel
Zinc

05030   **METAL COATINGS**
Acrylic Coatings
Anodic Coatings
Enamel Coatings
Fluorocarbon Coatings
Galvanic Coatings
Metallic Coatings
Porcelain Enamel Coatings
Powdered Coatings
Urethane Coatings

05050   **METAL FASTENING**
Bolting
Brazing
Chemical Bonding
Riveting
Soldering
Special Fasteners
Welding

05100   **STRUCTURAL METAL FRAMING**
-120   Structural Steel
Architecturally Exposed Structural Steel
Prefabricated Fireproofed Steel Columns
Tubular Steel
-140   Structural Aluminum
Architecturally Exposed Structural Aluminum
-150   Steel Wire Rope
-160   Framing Systems
Geodesic Structures
Space Frames

05200   **METAL JOISTS**
-210   Steel Joists
Longspan Steel Joists
Deep Longspan Steel Joists
Open Web Steel Joists
Steel Joist Girders
-250   Aluminum Joists
-260   Composite Joist System

300   **METAL DECKING**
-310   Steel Deck
Steel Floor Deck
Steel Roof Deck
-320   Raceway Deck Systems
-330   Aluminum Deck
Aluminum Floor Deck
Aluminum Roof Deck

05400   **COLD FORMED METAL FRAMING**
-410   Load-Bearing Metal Stud Systems
-420   Cold Formed Metal Joist Systems
-430   Slotted Channel Framing Systems
-450   Metal Support Systems
Electrical Support Systems
Mechanical Support Systems
Medical Support Systems

05500   **METAL FABRICATIONS**
-510   Metal Stairs
-515   Ladders
-520   Handrails and Railings
Pipe and Tube Railings
-530   Gratings
-535   Floor Plates
-540   Castings
-550   Stair Treads and Nosings

05580   **SHEET METAL FASRICATIONS**
-582   Sheet Metal Enclosures
-584   Heating/Cooling Unit Enclosures

05700   **ORNAMENTAL METAL**
-710   Ornamental Stairs
-715   Prefabricated Spiral Stairs
-720   Ornamental Handrails and Railings
-725   Ornamental Metal Castings
-730   Ornamental Sheet Metal

05800	**EXPANSION CONTROL**
-810	Expansion Joint Cover Assemblies
	Elastomeric Joint Cover Assemblies
	Metal Plate Cover Assemblies
	Strip Seal Floor Joint Covers
-820	Slide Bearings
-830	Bridge Expansion Joint Assemblies
	Bridge Bearings
	Bridge Sole Plates
05900	**HYDRAULIC STRUCTURES**
-910	Penstocks
-915	Bulkheads
-920	Trashracks
-925	Manifolds
-930	Bifurcations

DIVISION 6 — WOOD AND PLASTICS

Section Number	Title
06050	**FASTENERS AND ADHESIVES**
06100	**ROUGH CARPENTRY**
-105	Treated Wood Foundations
-110	Wood Framing
	Assembled Wood Components
-115	Sheathing
-120	Structural Panels
-125	Wood Decking
-128	Mineral Fiber Reinforced-
	Cement Panels
	Cementitious Reinforced Panels
06130	**HEAVY TIMBER CONSTRUCTION**
-132	Mill-Framed Structures
-133	Pole Construction
-135	Timber Trusses
-140	Timber Decking
-145	Timber Bridges and Trestles
06150	**WOOD AND METAL SYSTEMS**
	Wood Chord Metal Joists
06170	**PREFABRICATED STRUCTURAL WOOD**
-180	Glued-Laminated Construction
	Glued-Laminated Decking
	Glued-Laminated Structural Units
-190	Wood Trusses
	Prefabricated Architectural Wood Trusses
	Prefabncated Wood Trusses
-195	Prefabricated Wood Beams and Joists
	Plywood Web Joists
06200	**FINISH CARPENTRY**
-220	Millwork
-240	Laminates
	Plastic Laminates
	Wood Laminates
	Metallic Laminates
-250	Prefinished Wood Paneling
-255	Prefinished Hardboard Paneling
-260	Board Paneling

06300	**WOOD TREATMENT**
-310	Preservative Treatment
-320	Fire Retardant Treatment
-330	Insect Treatment
06400	**ARCHITECTURAL WOODWORK**
-410	Custom Casework
	Plastic Laminate Faced Wood Cabinets
	Shop Finished Wood Cabinets
	Unfinished Wood Cabinets
-420	Panelwork
	Plastic Laminate Faced Paneling
	Stile and Fad Paneling
	Wood Veneer Faced Paneling
-430	Stairwork and Handrails
-440	Wood Ornaments
-450	Standing and Running Trim
-460	Exterior Frames
-470	Screens, Blinds, and Shutters
-480	Custom Wood Turning
06500	**STRUCTURAL PLASTICS**
06600	**PLASTIC FABRICATIONS**
-610	Glass Fiber and Resin Fabrications
-620	Cast Plastic Fabrications
-630	Historic Plastic Reproductions
06650	**SOLID POLYMER FABRICATIONS**

DIVISION 7 — THERMAL AND MOISTURE PROTECTION

Section Number	Title
07100	**WATERPROOFING**
-110	Sheet Membrane Waterproofing
	Bituminous Sheet Membrane Waterproofing
	Elastomeric Sheet Membrane Waterproofing
	Modified Bituminous Sheet Membrane Waterproofing
	Thermoplastic Sheet Membrane Waterproofing
-120	Fluid Applied Waterproofing
-125	Sheet Metal Waterproofing
-130	Bentonite Waterproofing
-140	Metal Oxide Waterproofing
-145	Cementitious Waterproofing
07150	**DAMPPROOFING**
-160	Bituminous Dampproofing
-175	Cementitious Dampproofing
07180	**WATER REPELLENTS**
07190	**VAPOR RETARDERS**
07195	**AIR BARRIERS**
07200	**INSULATION**
-210	Building Insulation
	Batt Insulation
	Building Board Insulation
	Foamed-in-Place Insulation
	Loose Fill Insulation
	Sprayed Insulation
-220	Roof and Deck Insulation
	Asphaltic Perlite Concrete Deck
	Poof Board Insulation
07240	**EXTERIOR INSULATION AND FINISH SYSTEMS**
07250	**FIREPROOFING**
-252	Thermal Barriers for Plastics
-255	Cementitious Fireproofing
-260	Intumescent Mastic Fireproofing

-262	Magnesium Oxychloride Fireproofing	**07500**	**MEMBRANE ROOFING**
-265	Mineral Fiber Fireproofing	-510	Built-Up Bituminous Roofing
			Built-Up Asphalt Roofing
			Built-Up Coal Tar Roofing
07270	**FIRESTOPPING**	-515	Cold Applied Bituminous Roofing
	Fibrous Fire Safing		*Cold Applied Mastic Roof Membrane*
	Fire Penetration Sealants		*Glass Fiber Reinforced Asphalt Emulsion*
	Firestopping Mortars		
	Firestopping Pillows	-520	Prepared Roll Roofing
	Intumescent Firestopping Foams	-525	Modified Bituminous Sheet Roofing
	Silicone Firestopping Foams		
	Mechanical Firestopping Devices for Plastic Pipe	-530	Single Ply Membrane Roofing
		-540	Fluid Applied Roofing
		-545	Coated Foamed Roofing
07300	**SHINGLES AND ROOFING TILES**	-550	Protected Membrane Roofing
		-560	Roof Maintenance and Repairs
-310	Shingles		*Roof Moisture Survey*
	Asphalt Shingles		*Roofing Resaturants*
	Fiberglass Shingles		
	Metal Shingles	**07570**	**TRAFFIC COATINGS**
	Mineral Fiber Cement Shingles	-572	Pedestrian Traffic Coatings
	Porcelain Enamel Shingles	-576	Vehicular Traffic Coatings
	Slate Shingles		
	Wood Shingles		
	Wood Shakes	**07600**	**FLASHING AND SHEET METAL**
-320	Roofing Tiles	-610	Sheet Metal Roofing
	Clay Roofing Tiles	-620	Sheet Metal Flashing and Trim
	Concrete Roofing Tiles	-630	Sheet Metal Roofing Specialties
	Metal Roofing Tiles	-650	Flexible Flashing
	Mineral Fiber Cement Roofing Tiles		*Laminaed Sheet Flashing*
	Plastic Roofing Tiles		*Plasic Sheet Flashing*
			Rubber Shee Flashing
07400	**MANUFACTURED ROOFING AND SIDING**	**07700**	**ROOF SPECIALTIES AND ACCESSORIES**
-410	Manufactured Roof and Wall Panels	-710	Manufactured Roof Specialties
	Manufactured Roof Panels		*Copings*
	Manufactured Wall Panels		*Counterflashing Systems*
-420	Composite Panels		*Gravel Stops and Fasaas*
-440	Faced Panels		*Relief Vents*
	Aggregate Coated Panels		*Reglets*
	Porcelain Enameled Faced Panels		*Roof Erpansion Assemblies*
	Tile Faced Panels	-720	Roof Accessories
-450	Glass Fiber Reinforced Cementitious Panels		*Manufactured Curbs*
			Roof Hatches
-460	Siding		*Gravity Ventilators*
	Aluminum Siding		*Penthouse Ventilators*
	Composition Siding		*Ridge Vents*
	Hardboard Siding		*Smoke Vents*
	Mineral Fiber Cement Siding		
	Plastic Siding		
	Plywood Siding	**07800**	**SKYLIGHTS**
	Steel Siding	-810	Plastic Unit Skylights
	Wood Siding		*Domed Plastic Unit Skylights*
			Pyramid Plastic Unit Skyllghts
07480	**EXTERIOR WALL ASSEMBLIES**		*Vaulted Plastic Unit Skylights*

-820   Metal Framed Skylights
       Domed Metal Framed Skylights
       Motorized Metal Framed Skylights
       Ridge Metal Framed Skylights
       Sloped Metal Framed Skylights
       Vaulted Metal Framed Skylights

07900   **JOINT SEALERS**
-910   Joint Fillers and Gaskets
       Compression Seals

DIVISION 8 — DOORS AND WINDOWS

Section Number	Title

08100	**METAL DOORS AND FRAMES**
-110	Steel Doors and Frames
	Standard Steel Doors and Frames
	Custom Steel Doors and Frames
-120	Aluminum Doors and Frames
-130	Stainless Steel Doors and Frames
-140	Bronze Doors and Frames
08200	**WOOD AND PLASTIC DOORS**
-210	Wood Doors
	Flush Wood Doors
	Prefinished Wood Doors
	Plastic Laminate Faced Doors
	Metal Faced Wood Doors
	Stile and Rail Wood Doors
-220	Plastic Doors
08250	**DOOR OPENING ASSEMBLIES**
-255	Packaged Steel Door Assemblies
-260	Packaged Wood Door Assemblies
-265	Packaged Plastic Door Assemblies
08300	**SPECIAL DOORS**
-305	Access Doors
	Access Panels
-310	Sliding Doors and Grilles
	Sliding Metal Doors
	Sliding Wood Doors
	Sliding Glass Doors
	Sliding Grilles
-315	Pressure Resistant Doors
	Blast Pesistant Doors
	Airtight Doors
	Watertight Doors
-320	Security Doors
-325	Cold Storage Doors
-330	Coiling Doors and Grilles
	Overhead Coiling Doors
	Overhead Coiling Grilles
	Side Coiling Doors
	Side Coiling Grilles
	Coiling Counter Doors
	Coiling Counter Grilles
-350	Folding Doors and Grilles
	Accordion Folding Doors

	Panel Folding Doors
	Accordion Folding Grilles
-355	Chain Closures
-360	Sectional Overhead Doors
-365	Vertical Lift Doors
	Multileaf Vertical Lift Doors
	Telescoping Vertical Lift Doors
-370	Industrial Doors
-375	Hangar Doors
-380	Traffic Doors
	Flexible Traffic Doors
	Rigid Traffic Doors
	Flexible Strip Doors
-385	Sound Control Doors
-390	Storm Doors
-395	Screen Doors

08400	**ENTRANCES AND STOREFRONTS**
-410	Aluminum Entrances and Storefronts
-420	Steel Entrances and Storefronts
-430	Stainless Steel Entrances and Storefronts
-440	Bronze Entrances and Storefronts
-450	All-Glass Entrances
-460	Automatic Entrance Doors
-470	Revolving Entrance Doors
-480	Balanced Entrance Doors
-490	Sliding Storefronts

08500	**METAL WINDOWS**
-510	Steel Windows
-520	Aluminum Windows
-530	Stainless Steel Windows
-540	Bronze Windows

08600	**WOOD AND PLASTIC WINDOWS**
-610	Wood Windows
	Metal Clad Wood Windows
	Plastic Clad Wood Windows
-630	Plastic Windows

08650	**SPECIAL WINDOWS**
-655	Roof Windows
-660	Security Windows and Screens
	Security Windows
	Secunty Screens
-665	Pass Windows
-670	Storm Windows

08700	**HARDWARE**
-710	Door Hardware
	Hanging Hardware
	Latching Hardware
	Controlling Hardware
	Door Trim
	Weatherstripping and Seals
-740	Electro-Mechanical Hardware
	Electrical Locking Systems
	Electro-Magnetic Door Holders
-760	Window Hardware
	Automatic Window Equipment
	Window Operators
	Window Locks
	Window Lifts
-770	Door and Window Accessories

08800	**GLAZING**
-810	Glass
	Float Glass
	Rolled Glass
	Tempered Glass
	Laminated Glass
	Insulating Glass
	Coated Glass
	Mirrored Glass
	Wired Glass
	Decorative Glass
	Bent Glass
-840	Plastic Glazing
	Bullet Pesistant Plastic Glazing
	Decorative Plastic Glazing
	Insulating Plastic Glazing
-850	Glazing Accessories

08900	**GLAZED CURTAIN WALLS**
-910	Glazed Steel Curtain Walls
-920	Glazed Aluminum Curtain Walls
-930	Glazed Stainless Steel Curtain Walls
-940	Glazed Bronze Curtain Walls
-950	Translucent Wall and Skylight Systems
-960	Sloped Glazing Systems
-970	Structural Glass Curtain Walls

DIVISION 9 — FINISHES

Section **Title**
Number

09100 **METAL SUPPORT SYSTEMS**
-110   Non-load Bearing Wall Framing Systems
-120   Ceiling Suspension Systems
-130   Acoustical Suspension Systems

09200 **LATH AND PLASTER**
-205   Furring and Lathing
       Gypsum Lath
       Metal Lath
       Veneer Plaster Base
       Plaster Accessones
-210   Gypsum Plaster
       Acoustical Plaster
       Fireproofing Plaster
-215   Veneer Plaster
-220   Portland Cement Plaster
-225   Adobe Finish
-230   Plaster Fabrications

09250 **GYPSUM BOARD**
-260   Gypsum Board Systems
-270   Gypsum Board Accessories

09300 **TILE**
-310   Ceramic Tile
       Ceramic Mosaics
       Conductive Tile
-320   Thin Brick Tile
-330   Quarry Tile
       Chemical Resistant Ouarry Tile
-340   Paver Tile
-350   Glass Mosaics
-360   Plastic Tile
-370   Metal Tile
-380   Cut Natural Stone Tile

09400 **TERRAZZO**
-410   Portland Cement Terrazzo
-420   Precast Terrazzo
-430   Conductive Terrazzo
-440   Plastic Matrix Terrazzo

09450 **STONE FACING**

09500 **ACOUSTICAL TREATMENT**
-510   Acoustical Ceilings
       Acoustical Panel Ceilings
       Acoustical Tile Ceilings
       Acoustical Metal Pan Ceilings
-520   Acoustical Wall Treatment
-525   Acoustical Space Units
-530   Acoustical Insulation and Barriers

09540 **SPECIAL WALL SURFACES**
       Fiber Reinforced Plastic Coated Panels
       Reintorced Gypsum Units
       Aggregate Coatings

09545 **SPECIAL CEILING SURFACES**
       Linear Metal Ceilings
       Mirror Panel Ceilings
       Textured Metal Ceiling Panels
       Textured Gypsum CeiUng Panels
       Linear Wood Ceilings
       Suspended Decorabve Grids

09550 **WOOD FLOORING**
-560   Wood Strip Flooring
-565   Wood Block Flooring
-570   Wood Parquet Flooring
       Acrylic Impregnated Wood Parquet Flooring
       Vinyl Bonded Wood Parquet Flooring
-580   Wood Composition Flooring
-590   Resilient Wood Flooring Systems
       Cushioned Wood Flooring
       Mastic Set Wood Flooring
       Spring Supported Wood Flooring
       Steel Channel Wood Flooring
       Steel Splined Wood Flooring

09600 **STONE FLOORING**
-610   Flagstone Flooring
-615   Marble Flooring
-620   Granite Flooring
-625   Slate Flooring

09630 **UNIT MASONRY FLOORING**
-635   Brick Flooring
       Chemical Resistant Brick Floorlng
       Industrial Brick Flooring
-640   Pressed Concrete Unit Flooring

09650 **RESILIENT FLOORING**
-660   Resilient Tile Flooring
-665   Resilient Sheet Flooring
-670   Fluid-Applied Resilient Flooring
-675   Static Control Resilient Flooring
       Static Resistant Resilient Flooring

Conductive Resilient Flooring
Static Dissipative Resilient
Flooring
-678   Resilient Base and Accessories

09680   CARPET
-682   Carpet Cushion
-685   Sheet Carpet
-690   Carpet Tile
-695   Wall Carpet
-698   Indoor/Outdoor Carpet

09700   SPECIAL FLOORING
-705   Resinous Flooring
-710   Magnesium Oxychloride Flooring
-720   Epoxy-Marble Chip Flooring
-725   Seamless Quartz Flooring
-730   Elastomeric Liquid Flooring
        Conductive Elastomeric Liquid
        Flooring
-750   Mastic Fills
-755   Plastic Laminate Flooring
-760   Asphalt Plank Flooring

09780   FLOOR TREATMENT
-785   Metallic-Type Static
        Disseminating and Spark
        Resistant Finish
-790   Slip Resistant Finishes

09800   SPECIAL COATINGS
-810   Abrasion Resistant Coatings
-815   High Build Glazed Coatings
-820   Cementitious Coatings
-830   Elastomeric Coatings
-835   Textured Plastic Coatings
-840   Fire Resistant Paints
-845   Intumescent Paints
-850   Chemical Resistant Coatings
-860   Graffiti Resistant Coatings
-870   Coating Systems for Steel
        Exterior Coating System for Steel
        Storage Tanks
        Interior Coating System for Steel
        Storage Tanks
        Coating System for Steel Piping
-880   Protective Coatings for Concrete

09900   PAINTING
-910   Exterior Painting
-920   Interior Painting
-930   Transparent Finishes

09950   WALL COVERINGS

DIVISION 10 — SPECIALTIES

Section Number	Title
10100	**VISUAL DISPLAY BOARDS**
-110	Chalkboards
-115	Markerboards
-120	Tackboards
-130	Operable Board Units
-140	Display Track System
-145	Visual Aid Board Units
10150	**COMPARTMENTS AND CUBICLES**
-160	Metal Toilet Compartments
-165	Plastic Laminate Toilet Compartments
-170	Plastic Toilet Compartments
-175	Particleboard Toilet Compartments
-180	Stone Toilet Compartments
-185	Shower and Dressing Compartments
-190	Cubicles
	Cubicle Curtains
	Cubicle Track and Hardware
10200	**LOUVERS AND VENTS**
-210	Metal Wall Louvers
	Operable Metal Wall Louvers
	Stationary Metal Wall Louvers
	Motorized Metal Wall Louvers
-220	Louvered Equipment Enclosures
-225	Metal Door Louvers
-230	Metal Vents
	Metal Soffit Vents
	Metal Wall Vents
10240	**GRILLES AND SCREENS**
10250	**SERVICE WALL SYSTEMS**
10260	**WALL AND CORNER GUARDS**
	Corner Guards
	Bumper Guards
	Impact Resistant Wall Protection
10270	**ACCESS FLOORING**
-272	Rigid Grid Access Floor Systems
-274	Snap-on Stringer Access Floor Systems
-276	Stringerless Access Floor Systems

10290 PEST CONTROL
-292 Rodent Control
-294 Insect Control
-296 Bird Control

10300 FIREPLACES AND STOVES
-305 Manufactured Fireplaces
Manufactured Fireplace Chimneys
Manufactured Fireplace Forms
-310 Fireplace Specialties and
Accessories
Fireplace Dampers
Fireplace Water Heaters
Fireplace Screens and Doors
Fireplace Inserts
-320 Stoves

10340 MANUFACTURED EXTERIOR
SPECIALTIES
-342 Steeples
-344 Spires
-346 Cupolas
-348 Weathervanes

10350 FLAGPOLES
-352 Ground Set Flagpoles
-354 Wall Mounted Flagpoles
-356 Automatic Flagpoles
-358 Nautical Flagpoles

10400 IDENTIFYING DEVICES
-410 Directories
Electronic Directones
-415 Bulletin Boards
-420 Plaques
-430 Exterior Signs
Dimensional Letter Signs
Illuminated Exterior Signs
Non-illuminated Exterior Signs
Post and Panel/Pylon Exterior
Signs
Electronic Message Signs
-440 Interior Signs
Dimensional Letters
Door Signs
Engraved Signs
Illuminated Interior Signs
Non-Illuminated Interior Signs
Electronic Message Signs

10450 PEDESTRIAN CONTROL
DEVICES
-452 Portable Posts and Railings
-454 Rotary Gates

-456 Turnstiles
-458 Detection Specialties

10500 LOCKERS
-505 Metal Lockers
-510 Wood Lockers
Plastic Laminate Faced Lockers
-515 Coin-Operated Lockers
-518 Glass Lockers

10520 FIRE PROTECTION
SPECIALTIES
-522 Fire Extinguishers, Cabinets, and
Accessories
Fire Extinguishers
Fire Extinguisher Cabinets
-526 Fire Blankets and Cabinets
-528 Wheeled Fire Extinguisher Units

10530 PROTECTIVE COVERS
-532 Walkway Covers
-534 Car Shelters
-536 Awnings
-538 Canopies

10550 POSTAL SPECIALTIES
-551 Mail Chutes
-552 Mail Boxes
-554 Collection Boxes
-556 Central Mail Delivery Boxes

10600 PARTITIONS
-605 Wire Mesh Partitions
-610 Folding Gates
-615 Demountable Partitions
Demountable Gypsum Board
Partitions
Demountable Metal Partitions
Demountable Wood Partitions
-630 Portable Partitions, Screens, and
Panels

10650 OPERABLE PARTITIONS
-652 Folding Panel Partitions
-655 Accordion Folding Partitions
-660 Sliding Partitions
-665 Coiling Partitions

10670 STORAGE SHELVING
-675 Metal Storage Shelving
-680 Storage and Shelving Systems

-683	Mobile Storage Systems
	Motorized Mobile Storage
	Systems
	Manual Mobile Storage Systems
-685	Wire Shelving
-688	Prefabricated Wood Storage
	Shelving

10700	**EXTERIOR PROTECTION**
	DEVICES FOR OPENINGS
-705	Exterior Sun Control Devices
-710	Exterior Shutters
-715	Storm Panels

10750	**TELEPHONE SPECIALTIES**
-755	Telephone Enclosures
-760	Telephone Directory Units
-765	Telephone Shelves

10800	**TOILET AND BATH**
	ACCESSORIES
-810	Toilet Accessories
	Commercial Toilet Accessories
	Detention Toilet Accessories
	Hospital Toilet Accessones
-820	Bath Accessories
	Residential Bath Accessones
	Shower and Tub Doors

10880	**SCALES**

10900	**WARDROBE AND CLOSET**
	SPECIALTIES

DIVISION 11 — EQUIPMENT

Section Number	Title
11010	**MAINTENANCE EQUIPMENT**
-012	Vacuum Cleaning Systems
-014	Window Washing Systems
-016	Floor and Wall Cleaning
	Equipment
-018	Housekeeping Carts
11020	**SECURITY AND VAULT**
	EQUIPMENT
-022	Vault Doors and Day Gates
-024	Security and Emergency
	Systems
-026	Safes
-028	Safe Deposit Boxes
11030	**TELLER AND SERVICE**
	EQUIPMENT
-032	Service and Teller Window Units
-034	Package Transfer Units
-036	Automatic Banking Systems
-038	Teller Equipment Systems
11040	**ECCLESIASTICAL EQUIPMENT**
-042	Baptisteries
-044	Chancel Fittings
11050	**LIBRARY EQUIPMENT**
-052	Book Theft Protection Equipment
-054	Library Stack Systems
-056	Study Carrels
-058	Book Depositories
	Automated Book Storage and
	Retrieval Systems
11060	**THEATER AND STAGE**
	EQUIPMENT
-062	Stage Curtains
-064	Rigging Systems and Controls
-066	Acoustical Shell Systems
-068	Folding and Portable Stages

11070	**INSTRUMENTAL EQUIPMENT**	
-072	Organs	
-074	Carillons	
-076	Bells	

11080	**REGISTRATION EQUIPMENT**

11090	**CHECKROOM EQUIPMENT**

11100	**MERCANTILE EQUIPMENT**
-102	Barber and Beauty Shop Equipment
-104	Cash Registers and Checking Equipment
-106	Display Cases
	Refrigeraed Display Cases
-108	Food Processing Equipment
	Food Weighing and Wrapping Equipment

11110	**COMMERCIAL LAUNDRY AND DRY CLEANING EQUIPMENT**
-112	Washers and Extractors
-114	Dry Cleaning Equipment
-116	Drying and Conditioning Equipment
-118	Finishing Equipment
	Ironers and Accessories

11120	**VENDING EQUIPMENT**
-122	Money Changing Machines
-124	Vending Machines
	Beverage Vending Machines
	Candy Vending Machines
	Cigarette Vending Machines
	Food Vending Machines
	Stamp Vending Machines
	Sundry Vending Machines

11130	**AUDIO-VISUAL EQUIPMENT**
-132	Projection Screens
-134	Projectors
-136	Learning Laboratories

11140	**VEHICLE SERVICE EQUIPMENT**
-142	Vehicle Washing Equipment
-144	Fuel Dispensing Equipment
-146	Lubrication Equipment

11150	**PARKING CONTROL EQUIPMENT**
-152	Parking Gates
-154	Ticket Dispensers

-156	Key and Card Control Units
-158	Coin Machine Units

11160	**LOADING DOCK EQUIPMENT**
-161	Dock Levelers
-162	Dock Lifts
-163	Portable Ramps, Bridges, and Platforms
-164	Dock Seals and Shelters
-165	Dock Bumpers

11170	**SOLID WASTE HANDLING EQUIPMENT**
-171	Packaged Incinerators
-172	Waste Compactors
-173	Bins
-174	Pulping Machines and Systems
-175	Chutes and Collectors
-176	Pneumatic Waste Systems

11190	**DETENTION EQUIPMENT**

11200	**WATER SUPPLY AND TREATMENT EQUIPMENT**
-210	Pumps
	Axial Flow Pumps
	Centrifugal Pumps
	Deepwell Turbine Pumps
	Mixed Flow Pumps
	Vertical Turbine Pumps
-220	Mixers and Flocculators
-225	Clarifiers
-230	Water Aeration Equipment
-240	Chemical Feeding Equipment
	Coagulant Feed Equipment
-250	Water Softening Equipment
	Base-Exchange or Zeolite Equipment
	Lime-Soda Process Equipment
-260	Disinfectant Feed Equipment
	Chlorination Equipment
	pH Equipment
-270	Fluoridation Equipment

11280	**HYDRAULIC GATES AND VALVES**
-285	Hydraulic Gates
	Bulkhead Gates
	High Pressure Gates
	Hinged Leaf Gates
	Radial Gates
	Slide Gates
	Sluice Gates
	Spillway Crest Gates
	Vertical Lift Gates

-295	Hydraulic Valves
	Sutterfly Valves
	Regulating Valves

11300	**FLUID WASTE TREATMENT AND DISPOSAL EQUIPMENT**
-302	Oil/Water Separators
-304	Sewage Ejectors
-306	Packaged Pump Stations
-310	Sewage and Sludge Pumps
-320	Grit Collecting Equipment
-330	Screening and Grinding Equipment
-335	Sedimentation Tank Equipment
-340	Scum Removal Equipment
-345	Chemical Equipment
-350	Sludge Handling and Treatment Equipment
-360	Filter Press Equipment
-365	Trickling Filter Equipment
-370	Compressors
-375	Aeration Equipment
-380	Sludge Digestion Equipment
-385	Digester Mixing Equipment
-390	Package Sewage Treatment Plants

11400	**FOOD SERVICE EQUIPMENT**
-405	Food Storage Equipment
-410	Food Preparation Equipment
-415	Food Delivery Carts and Conveyors
-420	Food Cooking Equipment
-425	Hood and Ventilation Systems
	Surface Fire Protection Systems
-430	Food Dispensing Equipment
-435	Ice Machines
-440	Cleaning and Disposal Equipment
-445	Bar and Soda Fountain Equipment

11450	**RESIDENTIAL EQUIPMENT**
-452	Residential Appliances
-454	Built-In Ironing Boards
-458	Disappearing Stairs

| **11460** | **UNIT KITCHENS** |

11470	**DARKROOM EQUIPMENT**
-472	Transfer Cabinets
-474	Darkroom Processing Equipment
-476	Revolving Darkroom Doors

11480	**ATHLETIC, RECREATIONAL, AND THERAPEUTIC EQUIPMENT**
-482	Scoreboards
-484	Backstops
-486	Gym Dividers
-488	Bowling Alleys
-490	Gymnasium Equipment
-492	Exercise Equipment
-494	Therapy Equipment
-496	Shooting Ranges

| **11500** | **INDUSTRIAL AND PROCESS EQUIPMENT** |

| **11600** | **LABORATORY EQUIPMENT** |

| **11650** | **PLANETARIUM EQUIPMENT** |

| **11660** | **OBSERVATORY EQUIPMENT** |

| **11680** | **OFFICE EQUIPMENT** |

11700	**MEDICAL EQUIPMENT**
-710	Medical Sterilizing Equipment
-720	Examination and Treatment Equipment
-730	Patient Care Equipment
-740	Dental Equipment
-750	Optical Equipment
-760	Operating Room Equipment
-770	Radiology Equipment

| **11780** | **MORTUARY EQUIPMENT** |

| **11850** | **NAVIGATION EQUIPMENT** |

| **11870** | **AGRICULTURAL EQUIPMENT** |

DIVISION 12 — FURNISHINGS

Section Number	Title

12050   **FABRICS**

12100   **ARTWORK**
-110   Murals
       Photo Murals
-120   Wall Decorations
       Paintings
       Prints
       Tapestries
       Wall Hangings
-140   Sculpture
       Carved Sculpture
       Cast Sculpture
       Constructed Sculpture
       Relief Artwork
-160   Ecclesiastical Artwork
-170   Stained Glass Work

12300   **MANUFACTURED CASEWORK**
-301   Metal Casework
-302   Wood Casework
-304   Plastic Laminate Faced Casework
-345   Laboratory Casework
       Laboratory Countertops, Sinks, and Accessones
-350   Medical Casework
       Dental Casework
       Hospital Casework
       Nurse Station Casework
       Optical Casework
       Veterinary Casework
-360   Educational Casework
       Library Casework
-370   Residential Casework
       Bath Casework
       Kitchen Casework
-380   Specialty Casework
       Bank Casework
       Display Casework
       Dormitory Casework
       Ecclesiastical Casework
       Hotel and Motel Casework
       Restaurant Casework

12500   **WINDOW TREATMENT**
-510   Blinds
       Horizontal Louver Blinds
       Vertical Louver Blinds

-515   Interior Shutters
-520   Shades
       Insulating Shades
       Lightproof Shades
       Translucent Shades
       Woven Wood Shades
-525   Solar Control Film
-530   Curtain Hardware
       Curtain Track
-540   Curtains
       Draperies
       Fabric Curtains
       Lightproof Curtains
       Vertical Louver Curtains
       Woven Wood Curtains

12600   **FURNITURE AND ACCESSORIES**
-605   Portable Screens
-610   Open Office Furniture
       Open Office Partitions
       Open Office Work Surfaces
       Open Office Storage Units
       Open Office Shelving
       Open Office Light Fixtures
-620   Furniture
       Classroom Furniture
       Dormitory Furniture
       Ecclesiastical Furniture
       Hotel and Motel Furniture
       Laboratory Furniture
       Library Furniture
       Lounge Furniture
       Medical Furniture
       Office Furniture
       Restaurant Furniture
       Residential Furniture
       Specialized Furniture
-640   Furniture Systems
       Integrated Work Units
-650   Furniture Accessories
       Ash Receptacles
       Clocks
       Desk Accessories
       Lamps
       Waste Receptacles

12670   **RUGS AND MATS**
-675   Rugs
-680   Foot Grilles
-690   Floor Mats and Frames
       Chair Pads
       Entrance Tiles
       Floor Mats
       Floor Runners
       Mat Frames

12700	MULTIPLE SEATING
-705	Portable Audience Seating
	Folding Chairs
	Interlocking Chairs
	Stacking Chairs
-710	Fixed Audience Seating
-730	Stadium and Arena Seating
-740	Booths and Tables
-750	Multiple Use Fixed Seating
-760	Telescoping Stands
	Telescoping Bleachers
	Telescoping Chair Plafforms
-770	Pews and Benches
-775	Seat and Table Systems
	Pedestal Tablet Arm Chairs

12800	INTERIOR PLANTS AND PLANTERS
-810	Interior Plants
-815	Artificial Plants
-820	Interior Planters
-825	Interior Landscape Accessories
-830	Interior Plant Maintenance

DIVISION 13 — SPECIAL CONSTRUCTION

Section Number	Title
13010	AIR SUPPORTED STRUCTURES
13020	INTEGRATED ASSEMBLIES
-025	Integrated Ceilings
13030	SPECIAL PURPOSE ROOMS
-032	Athletic Rooms
-034	Sound Conditioned Rooms
-036	Clean Rooms
-038	Cold Storage Rooms
-040	Hyperbaric Rooms
-042	Insulated Rooms
-046	Shelters and Booths
-048	Planetariums
-050	Prefabricated Rooms
-052	Saunas
-054	Steam Baths
-056	Vaults
13080	SOUND, VIBRATION, AND SEISMIC CONTROL
13090	RADIATION PROTECTION
13100	NUCLEAR REACTORS
13120	PRE-ENGINEERED STRUCTURES
-121	Pre-Engineered Buildings
-122	Metal Building Systems
-123	Glazed Structures
	Greenhouses
	Solariums
	Swimming Pool Enclosures
-124	Portable and Mobile Buildings
-125	Grandstands and Bleachers
-130	Observatories
-132	Prefabricated Dome Structures
-135	Cable Supported Structures
-140	Fabric Structures
-142	Log Structures
-145	Modular Mezzanines

13150	**AQUATIC FACILITIES**
-152	Swimming Pools
	Below Grade Swimming Pools
	On Grade Swimming Pools
	Elevated Swimming Pools
	Recirculating Gutter Systems
	Swimming Pool Accessories
	Swimming Pool Cleaning Systems
-160	Aquariums
-165	Aquatic Park Facilities
	Water Slides
	Wave Pools
-170	Tubs and Pools
	Hot Tubs
	Whirlpool Tubs
	Therapeutic Pools

13175	**ICE RINKS**

13180	**SITE CONSTRUCTED INCINERATORS**
-182	Sludge Incinerators
-184	Solid Waste Incinerators

13185	**KENNELS AND ANIMAL SHELTERS**

13200	**LIQUID AND GAS STORAGE TANKS**
-205	Ground Storage Tanks
-210	Elevated Storage Tanks
-215	Underground Storage Tanks
-217	Tank Lining Systems
-219	Tank Cleaning Procedures

13220	**FILTER UNDERDRAINS AND MEDIA**
-222	Filter Bottoms
-226	Filter Media
	Anthracite Media
	Charcoal Media
	Diatomaceous Earth
	Mixed Media
	Sand Media

13230	**DIGESTER COVERS AND APPURTENANCES**
-232	Fixed Covers
-234	Floating Covers
-236	Gasholder Covers

13240	**OXYGENATION SYSTEMS**
-242	Oxygen Dissolution System
-246	Oxygen Generators
-248	Oxygen Storage Facility

13260	**SLUDGE CONDITIONING SYSTEMS**

13300	**UTILITY CONTROL SYSTEMS**
-310	Water Supply Plant Operating and Monitoring Systems
	Display Panels
	Metering Devices
	Sensing and Communication Devices
-320	Wastewater Treatment Plant Operating and Monitoring Systems
	Control Panels
	Display Panels
	Metering Devices
	Sensing and Communication Devices
-330	Power Generating and Transmitting Control Systems
	Control Panels
	Display Panels
	Meters
	Relays

13400	**INDUSTRIAL AND PROCESS CONTROL SYSTEMS**

13500	**RECORDING INSTRUMENTATION**
-510	Stress Instrumentation
-515	Seismic Instrumentation
-520	Meteorological Instrumentation

13550	**TRANSPORTATION CONTROL INSTRUMENTATION**
-560	Airport Control Instrumentation
-570	Railroad Control Instrumentation
-580	Subway Control Instrumentation
-590	Transit Vehicle Control Instrumentation

13600	**SOLAR ENERGY SYSTEMS**
-610	Solar Flat Plate Collectors
	Air Collectors
	Liquid Collectors
-620	Solar Concentrating Collectors
-625	Solar Vacuum Tube Collectors

-630   Solar Collector Components
Solar Absorber Plates and Tubing
Solar Coatings and Surface Treatment
Solar Collector Insulation
Solar Glazing
Solar Housing and Framing
Solar Reflectors
-640   Packaged Solar Systems
-650   Photovoltaic Collectors

13700 WIND ENERGY SYSTEMS

13750 COGENERATION SYSTEMS

13800 BUILDING AUTOMATION SYSTEMS
-810   Energy Monitoring and Control Systems
-815   Environmental Control Systems
-820   Communications Systems
-825   Security Systems
-830   Clock Control Systems
-835   Elevator Monitoring and Control Systems
-840   Escalators and Moving Walks Monitoring and Control Systems
-845   Alarm and Detection Systems
-850   Door Control Systems

13900 FIRE SUPPRESSION AND SUPERVISORY SYSTEMS

13950 SPECIAL SECURITY CONSTRUCTION

DIVISION 14 — CONVEYING SYSTEMS

Section Number	Title
14100	**DUMBWAITERS**
-110	Manual Dumbwaiters
-120	Electric Dumbwaiters
-140	Hydraulic Dumbwaiters
14200	**ELEVATORS**
-210	Electric Traction Elevators
	Electric Traction Passenger Elevators
	Electric Traction Service Elevators
	Electric Traction Freight Elevators
-240	Hydraulic Elevators
	Hydraulic Passenger Elevators
	Hydraulic Service Elevators
	Hydraulic Freight Elevators
14300	**ESCALATORS AND MOVING WALKS**
-310	Escalators
-320	Moving Walks
14400	**LIFTS**
-410	People Lifts
	Counterbalanced People Lifts
	Endless Belt People Lifts
-420	Wheelchair Lifts
	Inclined Wheelchair Lifts
	Vertical Wheelchair Lifts
-430	Plaform Lifts
	Orchestra Lifts
	Stage Lifts
-440	Sidewalk Lifts
450	Vehicle Lifts
14500	**MATERIAL HANDLING SYSTEMS**
-510	Automatic Transport Systems
	Guided Vehicle Systems
	Track Vehicle Systems
-530	Postal Conveying Systems
-540	Baggage Conveying and Dispensing Systems

-550	Conveyors		**14900**	**TRANSPORTATION SYSTEMS**
	Belt Conveyors		-910	People Mover Systems
	Bucket Conveyors		-920	Monorail Systems
	Container Conveyors		-930	Funicular Systems
	Hopper and Track Conveyors		-940	Aerial Tramway Systems
	Monorail Conveyors		-950	Aircraft Passenger Loading Systems

-550 Conveyors
   Belt Conveyors
   Bucket Conveyors
   Container Conveyors
   Hopper and Track Conveyors
   Monorail Conveyors
   Oscillating Conveyors
   Pneumatic Conveyors
   Roller Conveyors
   Scoop Conveyors
   Screw Conveyors
   Selective Vertical Conveyors

-560 Chutes
   Dry Bulk Material Chutes
   Escape Chutes
   Laundry and Linen Chutes
   Package Chutes

-570 Feeder Equipment
   Apron Feeders
   Reciprocating Plate Feeders
   Rotary Airlock Feeders
   Rotary Flow Feeders
   Vibratory Feeders

-580 Pneumatic Tube Systems

14600 HOISTS AND CRANES
-605 Crane Rails
-610 Fixed Hoists
   Electric Fixed Hoists
   Manual Fixed Hoists
   Air Powered Fixed Hoists

-620 Trolley Hoists
   Electric Trolley Hoists
   Manual Trolley Hoists
   Air Powered Trolley Hoists

-630 Bridge Cranes
   Top Running Overhead Cranes
   Underslung Overhead Cranes

-640 Gantry Cranes
-650 Jib Cranes
-670 Tower Cranes
-680 Mobile Cranes
-690 Derricks

14700 TURNTABLES

14800 SCAFFOLDING
-810 Suspended Scaffolding
   Beam Scaffolding
   Carriage Scaffolding
   Hook Scaffolding

-820 Rope Climbers
   Manual Hope Climbers
   Powered Hope Climbers

-830 Telescoping Platforms
   Electric and Battery Telescoping Plafforms
   Pneumatic Telescoping Plafforms

14900 TRANSPORTATION SYSTEMS
-910 People Mover Systems
-920 Monorail Systems
-930 Funicular Systems
-940 Aerial Tramway Systems
-950 Aircraft Passenger Loading Systems

DIVISION 15 — MECHANICAL

Section Number	Title
15050	**BASIC MECHANICAL MATERIALS AND METHODS**
-060	Pipes and Pipe Fittings
	Aluminum and Aluminum Alloy Pipe and Fittings
	Concrete Pipe and Fittings
	Copper and Copper Alloy Pipe and Fittings
	Ferrous Pipe and Fittings
	Fiber Pipe and Fittings
	Glass Pipe and Fittings
	Hoses and Fittings
	Plastic Pipe and Fittings
	Pre-Insulated Pipe and Fittings
-100	Valves
	Manual Control Valves
	Self Actuated Valves
-120	Piping Specialties
-130	Gages
-140	Supports and Anchors
-150	Meters
-160	Pumps
-170	Motors
-175	Tanks
-190	Mechanical Identification
-240	Mechanical Sound. Vibration, and Seismic Control
15250	**MECHANICAL INSULATION**
-260	Piping Insulation
-280	Equipment Insulation
-290	Ductwork Insulation
15300	**FIRE PROTECTION**
-310	Fire Protection Piping
-320	Fire Pumps
-330	Wet Pipe Sprinkler Systems
-335	Dry Pipe Sprinkler Systems
-340	Pre-Action Sprinkler Systems
-345	Combination Dry Pipe and Pre-Action Sprinkler System
-350	Deluge Sprinkler Systems
-355	Foam Extinguishing Systems
-360	Carbon Dioxide Extinguishing Systems
-365	Halogen Agent Extinguishing Systems

-370	Dry Chemical Extinguishing Systems
-375	Standpipe and Hose Systems
5400	**PLUMBING**
-410	Plumbing Piping
-430	Plumbing Specialties
-440	Plumbing Fixtures
-450	Plumbing Equipment
	Domestic Water Heat Exchangers
	Drinking Water Cooling Systems
	Pumps
	Storage Tanks
	Water Conditioners
	Water Filtrabon Devices
	Water Heaters
-475	Pool and Fountain Equipment
-480	Special Systems
	Compressed Air Systems
	Deionized Water Systems
	Distilled Water Systems
	Fuel Oil Systems
	Gasoline Dispensing Systems
	Helium Gas Systems
	Liquified Petroleum Gas Systems
	Lubricating Oil Systems
	Natural Gas Systems
	Nitrous Oxide Gas Systems
	Oxygen Gas Systems
	Reverse Osmosis Systems
	Vacuum Systems
15500	**HEATING, VENTILATING, AND AIR CONDITIONING**
-510	Hydronic Piping
-515	Hydronic Specialties
-520	Steam and Steam Condensate Piping
-525	Steam and Steam Condensate Specialties
-530	Refrigerant Piping
-535	Refrigerant Specialties
-540	HVAC Pumps
-545	Chemical Water Treatment
15550	**HEAT GENERATION**
-555	Boilers
-570	Boiler Accessories
-575	Breechings, Chimneys, and Stacks
-580	Feedwater Equipment
-590	Fuel Handling Systems
-610	Furnaces

-620   Fuel Fired Heaters
          Duct Furnaces
          Gas Fired Unit Heaters
          Oil Fired Unit Heaters
          Radiant Heaters

15650   REFRIGERATION
-655   Refrigeration Compressors
-670   Condensing Units
-680   Water Chillers
          Absorption Water Chillers
          Centrifugal Water Chillers
          Reciprocating Water Chillers
          Potary Water Chillers
-710   Cooling Towers
          Mechanical Draft Cooling Towers
          Natural Draft Cooling Towers
-730   Liquid Coolers
-740   Condensers

15750   HEAT TRANSFER
-755   Heat Exchangers
-760   Energy Storage Tanks
-770   Heat Pumps
          Air Source Heat Pumps
          Rooftop Heat Pumps
          Water Source Heat Pumps
-780   Packaged Air Conditioning Units
          Computer Poom Air Conditioning
            Units
          Packaged Rooftop Air
            Conditioning Units
          Packaged Terminal Air
            Conditioning Units
          Unit Air Conditioners
-790   Air Coils
-810   Humidifiers
-820   Dehumidifiers
-830   Terminal Heat Transfer Units
          Convectors
          Fan Coil Units
          Finned Tube Padiation
          Induction Units
          Unit Heaters
          Unit Ventilators
-845   Energy Recovery Units

15850   AIR HANDLING
-855   Air Handling Units with Coils
-860   Centrifugal Fans
-865   Axial Fans
-870   Power Ventilators
-875   Air Curtain Units

15880   AIR DISTRIBUTION
-885   Air Cleaning Devices
          Dust Collectors
          Filters
-890   Ductwork
          Metal Ductwork
          Nonmetal Ductwork
          Flexible Ductwork
          Ductwork Hangars and Supports
-910   Ductwork Accessories
          Dampers
          Duct Access Panels and Test
            Holes
          Duct Connection Systems
          Flexible Duct Connections
          Tuming Vanes and Extractors
-920   Sound Attenuators
-930   Air Terminal Units
          Constant Volume
          Variable Volume
-940   Air Outlets and Inlets
          Diffusers
          Intake and Relief Ventilators
          Louvers
          Registers and Grilles

15950   CONTROLS
-955   Building Systems Control
-960   Energy Management and
          Conservation Systems
-970   Control Systems
          Electric Control Systems
          Electronic Control Systems
          Pneumatic Control Systems
          Self-Powered Control Systems
-980   Instrumentation
-985   Sequence of Operation

**15990   TESTING, ADJUSTING, AND
            BALANCING**
-991   Mechanical Equipment Testing,
          Adjusting, and Balancing
-992   Piping Systems Testing,
          Adjusting, and Balancing
-993   Air Systems Testing, Adjusting,
          and Balancing
-994   Demonstration of Mechanical
          Equipment
-995   Mechanical System Startup/
          Commissioning

DIVISION 16 — ELECTRICAL

Section Number	Title

16050 BASIC ELECTRICAL MATERIALS AND METHODS

-110 Raceways
  Cable Trays
  Conduits
  Surface Flaceways
  Indoor Service Poles
  Underfloor Ducts
  Underground Ducts and Manholes

-120 Wires and Cables
  Fiber Optic Cable
  Low Voltage Wire
  600 Volt or Less Wire and Cable
  Medium Voltage Cable
  Undercarpet Cable Systems

-130 Boxes
  Floor Boxes
  Outlet Boxes
  Pull and Junction Boxes

-140 Wiring Devices
  Low Voltage Switching

-150 Manufactured Wiring Systems

-160 Cabinets and Enclosures

-190 Supporting Devices

-195 Electrical Identitication

16200 POWER GENERATION - BUILT-UP SYSTEMS

-210 Generators
  Hydroelectnc Generators
  Nuclear Electric Generators
  Solar Electric Generators
  Steam Electric Generators

-250 Generator Controls
  Instrumentation
  Starting Equipment

-290 Generator Grounding

16300 MEDIUM VOLTAGE DISTRIBUTION

-310 Medium Voltage Substations

-320 Medium Voltage Transformers

-330 Medium Voltage Power Factor Correction

-340 Medium Voltage Insulators and Lightning Arrestors

-345 Medium Voltage Switchboards

-350 Medium Voltage Circuit Breakers

-355 Medium Voltage Reclosers

-360 Medium Voltage Interrupter Switches

-365 Medium Voltage Fuses

-370 Medium Voltage Overhead Power Distribution

-375 Medium Voltage Underground Power Distribution

-380 Medium Voltage Converters
  Medium Voltage Frequency Changers
  Medium Voltage Rectifiers

-390 Medium Voltage Primary Grounding

16400 SERVICE AND DISTRIBUTION

-410 Power Factor Correction

-415 Voltage Regulators

-420 Service Entrance

-425 Switchboards

-430 Metering

-435 Converters

-440 Disconnect Switches

-445 Peak Load Controllers

-450 Secondary Grounding

-460 Transformers

-465 Bus Duct

-470 Panelboards
  Branch Circuit Panelboards
  Distribution Panelboards

-475 Overcurrent Protective Devices
  Circuit Breakers
  Fuses

-480 Motor Control

-485 Contactors

-490 Switches
  Transfer Switches
  Isolation Switches

16500 LIGHTING

-501 Lamps

-502 Luminaire Accessories
  Ballasts
  Lenses
  Lighting Maintenance Equipment
  Light Louvers
  Posts and Standards

-510 Interior Luminaires
  Fluorescent Luminaires
  High Intensity Discharge Luminaires
  Incandescent Luminaires
  Luminous Ceilings

-520 Exterior Luminaires
  Aviation Lighbng
  Flood Lighting
  Navigation Lighting
  Roadway Lighting

	Signal Lighting
	Site Lighting
	Sports Lighting
-535	Emergency Lighting
-545	Underwater Lighting
-580	Theatrical Lighting

16600   **SPECIAL SYSTEMS**
-610   Uninterruptible Power Supply Systems
-620   Packaged Engine Generator Systems
-630   Battery Power Systems
          Central Battery Systems
          Packaged Battery Systems
-640   Cathodic Protection
-650   Electromagnetic Shielding Systems
-670   Lightning Protection Systems
-680   Unit Power Conditioners

16700   **COMMUNICATIONS**
-720   Alarm and Detection Systems
          Fire Alarm Systems
          Smoke Detection Systems
          Gas Detection Systems
          Intrusion Detection Systems
          Security Access Systems
-730   Clock and Program Systems
-740   Voice and Data Systems
          Telephone Systems

	Paging Systems
	Call Systems
	Data Systems
	Local Area Network Systems
	Door Answering Systems
	Microwave and Radio Systems
	Central Dictabon Systems
	Intercommunication Systems

-770   Public Address and Music Systems
-780   Television Systems
          Master Antenna Systems
          Video Telecommunication Systems
          Video Surveillance Systems
          Broadcast Video Systems
-785   Satellite Earth Station System
-790   Microwave Systems

16850   **ELECTRIC RESISTANCE HEATING**
-855   Electric Heating Cables and Mats
-880   Electric Radiant Heaters

16900   **CONTROLS**
-910   Electrical Systems Control
-915   Lighting Control Systems
          Dimming Systems
-920   Environmental Systems Control
-930   Building Systems Control
-940   Instrumentating

EXAMPLE PROJECT

Statement of Work

This example project is an actual project that has been reduced in size and simplified for illustrative purposes. The management of this type of project is discussed in the previous chapters of this book. Chapter 2 presented a discussion of the owner's study, including the needs assessment and project objectives. A discussion of project budgeting based on square foot estimating is presented in Chapter 3. The work breakdown structure and development of the project work plan (Chapter 4), a discussion of project scheduling (Chapter 5), and project tracking (Chapter 6) presented pertinent information for this project.

The project is a service facility that consists of an industrial building (Building A) for servicing equipment and vehicles and an employee's administrative office building (Building B) for management of the operation of the service facility. A warehouse building (Building C) is proposed as a future addition to the project, but is not initially included in the project scope due to constraints in the owner's budget. Site-work consists of grading, drainage, and all on-site utilities that are required for operation of the service facility. The project is located on 100 acres of land. Figure E-1 is a site plan that shows the layout of buildings, driveways, and parking areas.

The scope of work includes engineering, procurement, and construction for the site-work and two buildings. A soil investigation, legal boundary survey, and contour map is provided by the owner. Figure E-2 shows the contour map. Special procurement includes the overhead crane for Building A and the elevator conveying system for Building B. The maintenance building has a 40 foot clear ceiling height, with a 20 ton overhead crane. The owner anticipates 45 employees will be using the building during a day shift and plans expansion of work to include a night shift at a future date. A small office area and a shop with machining equipment is to be located in the maintenance building. A wash-down area is to be provided for washing and servicing of truck vehicles.

The employee's office building is a two-story structure that will be used by 70 employees who will be involved in clerical work. A conference room, training facilities, computer work stations, and small cafeteria are to be included in the building.

All sealed surface paving and parking areas are to be constructed with portland cement concrete. The layout for the crushed aggregate paving area, for storage of major equipment and materials, is shown on the site plan.

The owner's feasibility study involved a needs assessment to produce the project budget that is shown in Figure E-3. Acquisition of land and permits are completed by the owner. Anticipated design fees are included in the total project budget. The owner's required time of completion of the project is 17 months, including engineering, procurement, and construction.

Development of Project Work Plan

The responsibility of the project manager is to develop a comprehensive work plan to guide all aspects of the project. The first step in the process is a detailed review of the two sets of project data: the owner's study that developed the statement of work, budget, and schedule for the project, and the proposal that was approved to issue the contract to the project manager's organization. Ideally, the project manager and key members of his or her project team would have been involved in the development of both of these sets of project data; however, many project managers are assigned the responsibility of managing a project in which they have had no prior involvement.

Chapter 4 presents a discussion of the items to be reviewed by the project manager at the start of a project. A thorough review must be performed so the project manager has a clear understanding of the work that must be accomplished. In particular, the project budget must be evaluated to ensure it is realistic, and the project schedule must be evaluated to ensure it is reasonably attainable.

After the project manager's initial review, he or she develops a work breakdown structure (WBS) in sufficient detail to identify major areas of work to be performed. The purpose of this initial development of the WBS is to define the required disciplines for selection of project team members. The project manager must work with the managers of the different disciplines to staff the project based upon available resources from the organizational breakdown structure (OBS). For this example project, the design work for Building B is to be assigned to an outside design organization because the building requires architectural expertise that is not available in the project manager's organization and the time constraints that would be placed on in-house personnel to accomplish the work.

Figure E-4 shows the WBS for the project, which indicates the tasks to be performed, the grouping of the tasks, and the person responsible for each part of the project. Each project team member is responsible for development of a work package for the work that he or she is to perform. The format for the contents of a work package is shown in Figure E-5. The total cost of the project is derived from the sum of the costs of the work packages from all team members.

As discussed in Chapter 5, a project schedule (CPM) is developed by the project manager in cooperation with the team members based upon an integration of the schedule of the work packages, reference Figure E-6. The project manager works with the team members to develop a coding system for the project to sort and report project reports. The coding system for the example project is shown in Figure E-7.

A complete listing of all computer input data for the project is shown in Figure E-8. The information that is contained in Figure E-8 is the project data that is used to generate all of the reports that are shown in the remainder of this appendix. These reports are illustrative examples of typical project reports. The title at the top of each report identifies the contents of the report.

FIGURE E-1
Site Plan for EPC Project.

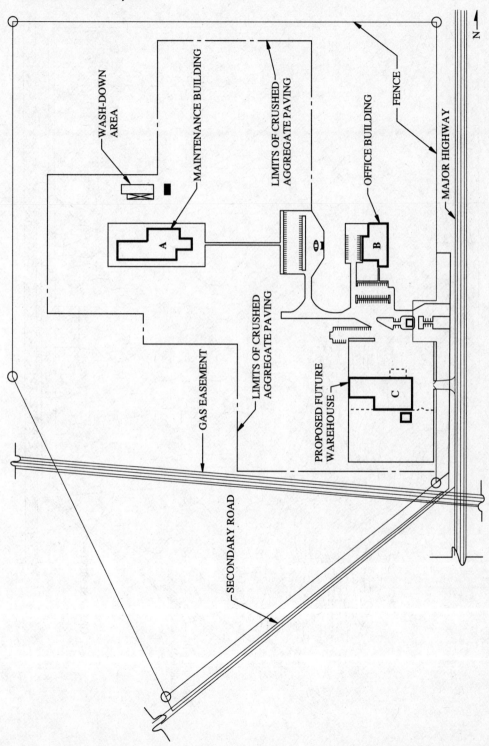

FIGURE E-2
Contour Map for Project.

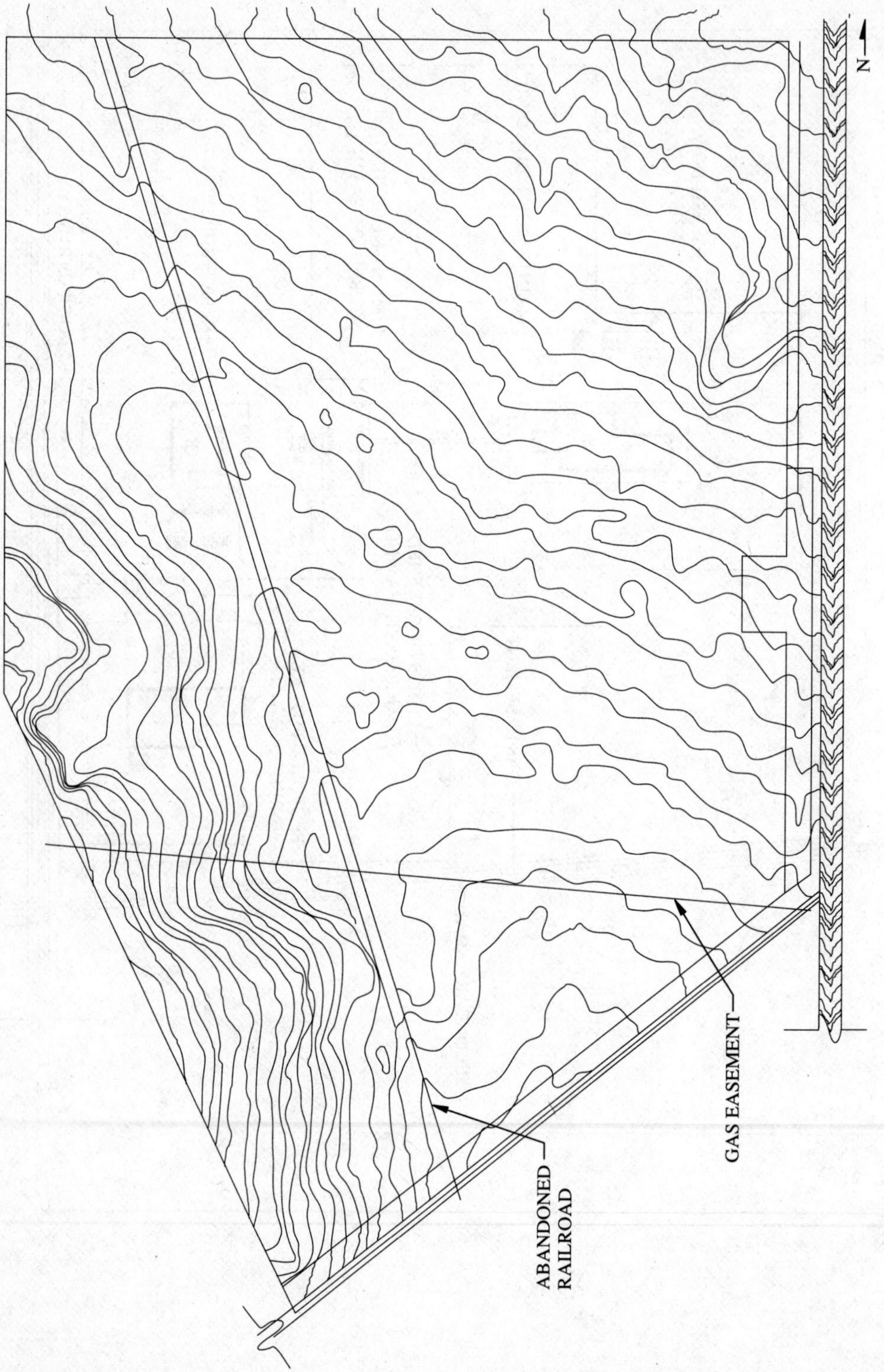

N

ABANDONED
RAILROAD

GAS EASEMENT

FIGURE E-3
Approved EPC Project Budget.

Facility	Budget
Site-work	$522,400
Grading	
Paving	
Landscape	
On-Site Utilities	$173,700
Stormwater	
Sanitary Sewer	
Domestic Water	
Underground Electrical	
Natural Gas	
Maintenance Building A	$1,083,600
Architectural	
Structural	
Electrical	
Plumbing	
Heat & Air	
Maintenance Building B	$1,097,100
Architectural	
Structural	
Electrical	
Plumbing	
Heat & Air	
Project Management	$19,350
Clerical	
Procurement	$157,000
Crane	
Elevators	
Construction Bids	

Total Directs = $3,053,150

Contingency $150,000

Total Approved Budget = $3,203,150

FIGURE E-4
Work Breakdown Stucture for Service Facility Project.

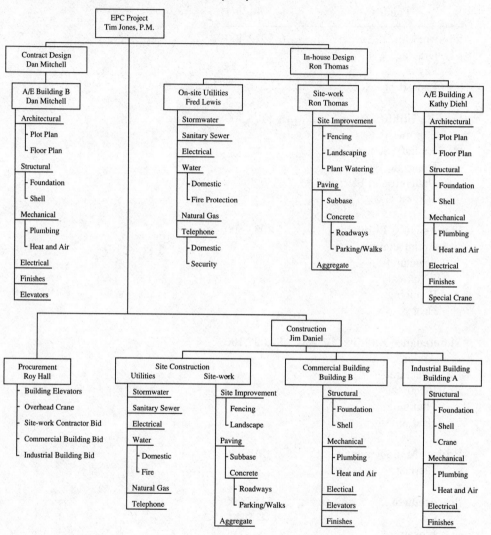

FIGURE E-5
Team Member's Work Package.

WORK PACKAGE

Title: _____

WBS Code: _____

1. SCOPE

Required Scope of Work: _____
_____
_____

Services to Be Provided: _____
_____
_____
_____
_____
_____

2. BUDGET

			CBS			
	Work		Code	Computer Services		
Personnel Assigned to Job	Hours	$ Cost	Acct	Type	Hours	$ Cost
_____	___	___	___	___	___	___
_____	___	___	___	___	___	___
_____	___	___	___	___	___	___
_____	___	___	___	___	___	___

Total Work Hours = ____   Personnel Costs = $ ____

Computer Hours = ____   Computer Costs = $ ____

Travel Expenses		Reproduction Expenses		Other Expenses	
_____	+	_____	+	_____	= $ ____

Total Budget = $-Labor + $-Computer + $-Travel + $-Other = $ _____

3. SCHEDULE

OBS Code	Work Task	Responsible Person	Start Date	End Date
___	_____	_____	___	___
___	_____	_____	___	___
___	_____	_____	___	___
___	_____	_____	___	___

Work Package: Start date: _____ End date: _____

ADDITIONAL COMMENTS: _____
_____
_____
_____

Prepared by: _____ Date: _____

Approved by: _____ Date: _____

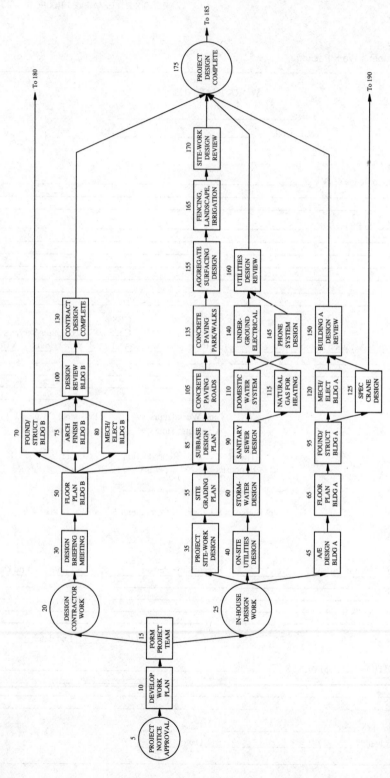

FIGURE E-6A
CPM Diagram for EPC Service Facility Project (continued on next page).

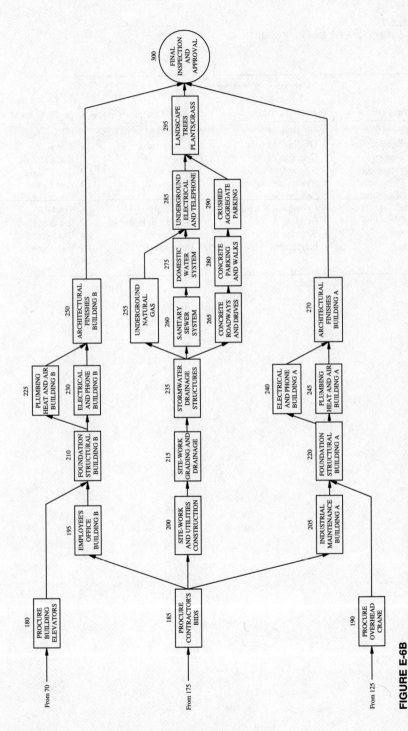

FIGURE E-6B

CPM Diagram for EPC Service Facility Project (continued from previous page).

255

FIGURE E-7
Coding System for EPC Service Facility Project.

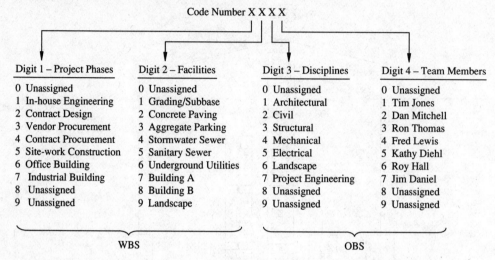

Code Number X X X X

Digit 1 – Project Phases	Digit 2 – Facilities	Digit 3 – Disciplines	Digit 4 – Team Members
0 Unassigned	0 Unassigned	0 Unassigned	0 Unassigned
1 In-house Engineering	1 Grading/Subbase	1 Architectural	1 Tim Jones
2 Contract Design	2 Concrete Paving	2 Civil	2 Dan Mitchell
3 Vendor Procurement	3 Aggregate Parking	3 Structural	3 Ron Thomas
4 Contract Procurement	4 Stormwater Sewer	4 Mechanical	4 Fred Lewis
5 Site-work Construction	5 Sanitary Sewer	5 Electrical	5 Kathy Diehl
6 Office Building	6 Underground Utilities	6 Landscape	6 Roy Hall
7 Industrial Building	7 Building A	7 Project Engineering	7 Jim Daniel
8 Unassigned	8 Building B	8 Unassigned	8 Unassigned
9 Unassigned	9 Landscape	9 Unassigned	9 Unassigned

WBS   OBS

FIGURE E-8A

Computer Input Data for Generation of Project Reports that are shown on the following pages in this appendix (continued on next page).

```
*************************
**   INPUT DETAILS   **
*************************
```

PROJECT NAME: SERVICE MAINTENANCE FACILITY

ACTIVITY NUMBER	CODE	DESCRIPTION	DURATION	COST	ASSIGNED START
5	71	PROJECT NOTICE APPROVAL	3	$ 500.	
10	71	DEVELOP WORK PLAN	7	$ 12000.	
15	71	FORM PROJECT TEAM	5	$ 850.	
20	2872	DESIGN CONTRACTOR'S WORK	2	$ 3000.	
25	1073	IN-HOUSE DESIGN WORK	3	$ 1500.	
30	2872	DESIGN BRIEFING MEETING	1	$ 1200.	
35	1073	PROJECT SITE-WORK DESIGN	1	$ 1400.	
40	1624	ON-SITE UTILITIES DESIGN	1	$ 1200.	
45	1715	A/E DESIGN BUILDING A	1	$ 1500.	
50	2812	FLOOR PLAN BUILDING B	10	$ 9900.	
55	1123	SITE GRADING PLAN	12	$ 14000.	
60	1424	STORM-WATER DESIGN	10	$ 2000.	
65	1715	FLOOR PLAN BUILDING A	15	$ 26000.	
70	2832	FOUND/STRUCT BUILDING B	45	$ 31200.	
75	2812	ARCH FINISHES BUILDING B	30	$ 49500.	
80	2842	MECH/ELECT BUILDING B	45	$ 37300.	
85	1123	SUBBASE DESIGN PLAN	5	$ 4000.	
90	1524	SANITARY SEWER DESIGN	10	$ 12000.	
95	1735	FOUND/STRUCT BUILDING A	30	$ 92700.	
100	2871	DESIGN REVIEW BUILDING B	10	$ 8000.	
105	1223	CONCRETE PAVING ROADS	20	$ 12000.	
110	1624	DOMESTIC WATER SYSTEM	7	$ 9000.	
115	1624	NATURAL GAS SYSTEM	8	$ 6000.	
120	1745	MECH/ELECT BUILDING A	30	$ 22200.	
125	1735	SPECIAL OVERHEAD CRANE	11	$ 10800.	
130	2872	CONTRACT DESIGN COMPLETE	1	$ 1000.	
135	1223	CONCRETE PAVING PARKING/WALKS	10	$ 7000.	
140	1654	UNDERGROUND ELECTRICAL	14	$ 12000.	
145	1654	UNDERGROUND TELEPHONE SYSTEM	4	$ 3000.	
150	1771	BUILDING A DESIGN REVIEW	3	$ 5000.	
155	1323	AGGREGATE SURFACING DESIGN	8	$ 6000.	
160	1677	UTILITIES DESIGN REVIEW	1	$ 1100.	
165	1963	FENCING/LANDSCAPE/IRRIGATION	14	$ 28000.	
170	1071	SITE-WORK DESIGN REVIEW	5	$ 7000.	
175	71	PROJECT DESIGN COMPLETE	1	$ 1000.	
180	3876	PROCURE BUILDING ELEVATORS	25	$ 95000.	
185	4076	PROCURE CONTRACTOR'S BIDS	20	$ 7000.	
190	3776	PROCURE OVERHEAD CRANE	40	$ 55000.	
195	6887	EMPLOYEE'S OFFICE BUILDING B	3	$ 1000.	
200	5087	SITE-WORK/UTILITIES CONSTRUCTION	4	$ 1500.	
205	7787	INDUSTRIAL/MAINTENANCE BLDG A	2	$ 1400.	
210	6882	FOUND/STRUCT BUILDING B	45	$ 195000.	
215	5083	SITE-WORK/GRADING/DRAINAGE	18	$ 85000.	
220	7785	FOUND/STRUCT BUILDING A	110	$ 390000.	
225	6882	PLUMBING, HEAT, & AIR BLDG B	75	$ 285000.	
230	6882	ELECTRICAL/PHONE BUILDING B	60	$ 215000.	
235	5484	STORMWATER/DRAINAGE STRUCTURES	15	$ 22000.	
240	7785	ELECTRICAL/PHONE BUILDING A	65	$ 167000.	
245	7785	PLUMBING, HEAT, & AIR BLDG A	85	$ 192000.	
250	6882	ARCH FINISHES BUILDING B	50	$ 260000.	
255	5684	UNDERGROUND NATURAL GAS	5	$ 10500.	
260	5584	SANITARY SEWER SYSTEM	21	$ 33200.	
265	5283	CONCRETE PAVING ROADS & DRIVES	60	$ 185000.	
270	7785	ARCH FINISHES BUILDING A	30	$ 175000.	
275	5684	DOMESTIC WATER SYSTEM	7	$ 13200.	
280	5283	CONCRETE PARKING & WALKWAYS	15	$ 35000.	
285	5684	UNDERGROUND ELECT & PHONE	14	$ 47000.	
290	5383	CRUSHED AGGREGATE PARKING	40	$ 76000.	
295	5983	LANDSCAPE TREES/PLANTS/GRASS	20	$ 62000.	
300	9977	FINAL INSPECTION & APPROVAL	3	$ 3500.	

FIGURE E-8B

Computer Input Data for Generation of Project Reports that are shown on the following pages in this appendix (continued from previous page).

```
      SEQUENCE ORDER
      ****************

  I NODE     J NODE
  --------   --------
       5         10
      10         15
      15         20
      15         25
      20         30
      25         35
      25         40
      25         45
      30         50
      35         55
      40         60
      45         65
      50         70
      50         75
      50         80
      50         85
      55         85
      60         90
      65         95
      70        100
      70        180
      75        100
      80        100
      85        105
      90        110
      90        115
      95        120
      95        125
     100        130
     105        135
     110        140
     110        145
     115        140
     115        145
     120        150
     125        150
     125        190
     130        175
     135        155
     140        160
     145        160
     150        175
     155        165
     160        175
     165        170
     170        175
     175        185
     180        210
     185        195
     185        200
     185        205
     190        220
     195        210
     200        215
     205        220
     210        225
     210        230
     215        235
     220        240
     220        245
     225        250
     230        250
     235        255
     235        260
     235        265
     240        270
     245        270
     250        300
     255        285
     260        275
     265        280
     270        300
     275        285
     280        290
     285        295
     290        295
     295        300
```

```
     PROJECT START DATE:  5/26/93
 **  NO HOLIDAYS REPORTED FOR THE PROJECT  **
```

FIGURE E-9
Schedule of All Activities for EPC of Service Facility Project.

```
*****************************
**   ACTIVITY  SCHEDULE   **
*****************************
```

PROJECT: SERVICE MAINTENANCE FACILITY
SCHEDULE FOR ALL ACTIVITIES - ISSUED TO TIM JONES ON 4/15/93   ** PAGE 1 **
                                                                              ACTIVITY SCHEDULE

	ACTIVITY NUMBER	DESCRIPTION	DURA-TION	EARLY START	EARLY FINISH	LATE START	LATE FINISH	TOTAL FLOAT	FREE FLOAT
C	5	PROJECT NOTICE APPROVAL	3	26MAY93 1	28MAY93 3	26MAY93 1	28MAY93 3	0	0
C	10	DEVELOP WORK PLAN	7	31MAY93 4	8JUN93 10	31MAY93 4	8JUN93 10	0	0
C	15	FORM PROJECT TEAM	5	9JUN93 11	15JUN93 15	9JUN93 11	15JUN93 15	0	0
	20	DESIGN CONTRACTOR'S WORK	2	16JUN93 16	17JUN93 17	25JUN93 23	28JUN93 24	7	0
C	25	IN-HOUSE DESIGN WORK	3	16JUN93 16	18JUN93 18	16JUN93 16	18JUN93 18	0	0
	30	DESIGN BRIEFING MEETING	1	18JUN93 18	18JUN93 18	29JUN93 25	29JUN93 25	7	0
	35	PROJECT SITE-WORK DESIGN	1	21JUN93 19	21JUN93 19	25JUN93 23	25JUN93 23	4	0
	40	ON-SITE UTILITIES DESIGN	1	21JUN93 19	21JUN93 19	9AUG93 54	9AUG93 54	35	0
C	45	A/E DESIGN BUILDING A	1	21JUN93 19	21JUN93 19	21JUN93 19	21JUN93 19	0	0
	50	FLOOR PLAN BUILDING B	10	21JUN93 19	2JUL93 28	30JUN93 26	13JUL93 35	7	0
	55	SITE GRADING PLAN	12	22JUN93 20	7JUL93 31	28JUN93 24	13JUL93 35	4	0
	60	STORMWATER DESIGN	10	22JUN93 20	5JUL93 29	10AUG93 55	23AUG93 64	35	0
C	65	FLOOR PLAN BUILDING A	15	22JUN93 20	12JUL93 34	22JUN93 20	12JUL93 34	0	0
	70	FOUND/STRUCT BUILDING B	45	5JUL93 29	3SEP93 73	22JUL93 42	22SEP93 86	13	0
	75	ARCH FINISHES BUILDING B	30	5JUL93 29	13AUG93 58	12AUG93 57	22SEP93 86	28	15
	80	MECH/ELECT BUILDING B	45	5JUL93 29	3SEP93 73	22JUL93 42	22SEP93 86	13	0
	90	SANITARY SEWER DESIGN	10	6JUL93 30	19JUL93 39	24AUG93 65	6SEP93 74	35	0
	85	SUBBASE DESIGN PLAN	5	8JUL93 32	14JUL93 36	14JUL93 36	20JUL93 40	4	0
C	95	FOUND/STRUCT BUILDING A	30	13JUL93 35	23AUG93 64	13JUL93 35	23AUG93 64	0	0
	105	CONCRETE PAVING ROADS	20	15JUL93 37	11AUG93 56	21JUL93 41	17AUG93 60	4	0
	115	NATURAL GAS SYSTEM	8	20JUL93 40	29JUL93 47	7SEP93 75	16SEP93 82	35	0
	110	DOMESTIC WATER SYSTEM	7	20JUL93 40	28JUL93 46	8SEP93 76	16SEP93 82	36	1
	145	UNDERGROUND TELEPHONE SYSTEM	4	30JUL93 48	4AUG93 51	1OCT93 93	6OCT93 96	45	10
	140	UNDERGROUND ELECTRICAL	14	30JUL93 48	18AUG93 61	17SEP93 83	6OCT93 96	35	0
	135	CONCRETE PAVING PARKING/WALKS	10	12AUG93 57	25AUG93 66	18AUG93 61	31AUG93 70	4	0
	160	UTILITIES DESIGN REVIEW	1	19AUG93 62	19AUG93 62	7OCT93 97	7OCT93 97	35	35
C	120	MECH/ELECT BUILDING A	30	24AUG93 65	4OCT93 94	24AUG93 65	4OCT93 94	0	0
	125	SPECIAL OVERHEAD CRANE	11	24AUG93 65	7SEP93 75	31AUG93 70	14SEP93 80	5	0
	155	AGGREGATE SURFACING DESIGN	8	26AUG93 67	6SEP93 74	1SEP93 71	10SEP93 78	4	0
	100	DESIGN REVIEW BUILDING B	10	6SEP93 74	17SEP93 83	23SEP93 87	6OCT93 96	13	0
	180	PROCURE BUILDING ELEVATORS	25	6SEP93 74	8OCT93 98	22DEC93 151	25JAN94 175	77	23
	165	FENCING/LANDSCAPE/IRRIGATION	14	7SEP93 75	24SEP93 88	13SEP93 79	30SEP93 92	4	0
	190	PROCURE OVERHEAD CRANE	40	8SEP93 76	2NOV93 115	15SEP93 81	9NOV93 120	5	5

FIGURE E-9 (*Continued*)
Schedule of All Activities for EPC of Service Facility Project.

```
PROJECT: SERVICE MAINTENANCE FACILITY
SCHEDULE FOR ALL ACTIVITIES - ISSUED TO TIM JONES ON 4/15/93                    ** PAGE  2 **
                                                                               ACTIVITY SCHEDULE
```

	ACTIVITY NUMBER	DESCRIPTION	DURA-TION	EARLY START	EARLY FINISH	LATE START	LATE FINISH	TOTAL FLOAT	FREE FLOAT
	130	CONTRACT DESIGN COMPLETE	1	20SEP93 84	20SEP93 84	7OCT93 97	7OCT93 97	13	13
	170	SITE-WORK DESIGN REVIEW	5	27SEP93 89	1OCT93 93	1OCT93 93	7OCT93 97	4	4
C	150	BUILDING A DESIGN REVIEW	3	5OCT93 95	7OCT93 97	5OCT93 95	7OCT93 97	0	0
C	175	PROJECT DESIGN COMPLETE	1	8OCT93 98	8OCT93 98	8OCT93 98	8OCT93 98	0	0
C	185	PROCURE CONTRACTOR'S BIDS	20	11OCT93 99	5NOV93 118	11OCT93 99	5NOV93 118	0	0
	195	EMPLOYEE'S OFFICE BUILDING B	3	8NOV93 119	10NOV93 121	21JAN94 173	25JAN94 175	54	0
	200	SITE-WORK/UTILITIES CONSTRUCTION	4	8NOV93 119	11NOV93 122	24JAN94 174	27JAN94 177	55	0
C	205	INDUSTRIAL/MAINTENANCE BLDG A	2	8NOV93 119	9NOV93 120	8NOV93 119	9NOV93 120	0	0
C	220	FOUND/STRUCT BUILDING A	110	10NOV93 121	12APR94 230	10NOV93 121	12APR94 230	0	0
	210	FOUND/STRUCT BUILDING B	45	11NOV93 122	12JAN94 166	26JAN94 176	29MAR94 220	54	0
	215	SITE-WORK/GRADING/DRAINAGE	18	12NOV93 123	7DEC93 140	28JAN94 178	22FEB94 195	55	0
	235	STORMWATER/DRAINAGE STRUCTURES	15	8DEC93 141	28DEC93 155	23FEB94 196	15MAR94 210	55	0
	255	UNDERGROUND NATURAL GAS	5	29DEC93 156	4JAN94 215	28JUL94 211	3AUG94 270	151	23
	260	SANITARY SEWER SYSTEM	21	29DEC93 156	26JAN94 176	27JUN94 284	25JUL94 304	128	0
	265	CONCRETE PAVING ROADS & DRIVES	60	29DEC93 156	22MAR94 215	16MAR94 211	7JUN94 270	55	0
	225	PLUMBING, HEAT, & AIR BLDG B	75	13JAN94 167	27APR94 241	30MAR94 221	12JUL94 295	54	0
	230	ELECTRICAL/PHONE BUILDING B	60	13JAN94 167	6APR94 226	20APR94 236	12JUL94 295	69	15
	275	DOMESTIC WATER SYSTEM	7	27JAN94 177	4FEB94 183	26JUL94 305	3AUG94 311	128	0
	285	UNDERGROUND ELECT & PHONE	14	7FEB94 184	24FEB94 197	4AUG94 312	23AUG94 325	128	73
	280	CONCRETE PARKING & WALKWAYS	15	23MAR94 216	12APR94 230	8JUN94 271	28JUN94 285	55	0
	240	ELECTRICAL/PHONE BUILDING A	65	13APR94 231	12JUL94 295	11MAY94 251	9AUG94 315	20	20
C	245	PLUMBING, HEAT, & AIR BLDG A	85	13APR94 231	9AUG94 315	13APR94 231	9AUG94 315	0	0
	290	CRUSHED AGGREGATE PARKING	40	13APR94 231	7JUN94 270	29JUN94 286	23AUG94 325	55	0
	250	ARCH FINISHES BUILDING B	50	28APR94 242	6JUL94 291	13JUL94 296	20SEP94 345	54	54
	295	LANDSCAPE TREES/PLANTS/GRASS	20	8JUN94 271	5JUL94 290	24AUG94 326	20SEP94 345	55	55
C	270	ARCH FINISHES BUILDING A	30	10AUG94 316	20SEP94 345	10AUG94 316	20SEP94 345	0	0
C	300	FINAL INSPECTION & APPROVAL	3	21SEP94 346	23SEP94 348	21SEP94 346	23SEP94 348	0	0

```
***************************************************  END OF SCHEDULE  ***************************************************
```

FIGURE E-10
Monthly Distribution of Costs for All Activities of EPC Service Facility Project

```
                          *******************************
                          **  MONTHLY COST SCHEDULE  **
                          *******************************
PROJECT: SERVICE MAINTENANCE FACILITY                              MONTHLY COST SCHEDULE
SCHEDULE FOR ALL ACTIVITIES - ISSUED TO TIM JONES ON 4/15/93        - For all activities -
                       START : 26 MAY 93    FINISH : 23 SEP 94
```

NO.	MONTH YEAR	EARLY START COST/MON	EARLY START CUMULATIVE COST	LATE START COST/MON	LATE START CUMULATIVE COST	TARGET SCHEDULE COST/MON	TARGET SCHEDULE CUMULATIVE COST	%TIME	%COST
1	MAY 93	$ 2214.	$ 2214.	$ 2214.	$ 2214.	$ 2214.	$ 2214.	1.1%	.1%
2	JUN 93	$ 50556.	$ 52770.	$ 36359.	$ 38573.	$ 43457.	$ 45672.	7.5%	1.5%
3	JUL 93	$ 168792.	$ 221562.	$ 95992.	$ 134566.	$ 132392.	$ 178064.	13.8%	5.8%
4	AUG 93	$ 139053.	$ 360614.	$ 136051.	$ 270616.	$ 137552.	$ 315615.	20.1%	10.3%
5	SEP 93	$ 166931.	$ 527545.	$ 160525.	$ 431141.	$ 163728.	$ 479343.	26.4%	15.7%
6	OCT 93	$ 65805.	$ 593350.	$ 60334.	$ 491475.	$ 63069.	$ 542413.	32.5%	17.8%
7	NOV 93	$ 183637.	$ 776987.	$ 65957.	$ 557432.	$ 124797.	$ 667210.	38.8%	21.9%
8	DEC 93	$ 247116.	$ 1024103.	$ 111945.	$ 669377.	$ 179531.	$ 846740.	45.4%	27.7%
9	JAN 94	$ 308169.	$ 1332272.	$ 168332.	$ 837710.	$ 238251.	$ 1084991.	51.4%	35.5%
10	FEB 94	$ 334785.	$ 1667058.	$ 238998.	$ 1076708.	$ 286892.	$ 1371883.	57.2%	44.9%
11	MAR 94	$ 317029.	$ 1984086.	$ 233279.	$ 1309986.	$ 275154.	$ 1647036.	63.8%	53.9%
12	APR 94	$ 231428.	$ 2215515.	$ 230945.	$ 1540931.	$ 231187.	$ 1878223.	69.8%	61.5%
13	MAY 94	$ 262417.	$ 2477932.	$ 318499.	$ 1859431.	$ 290458.	$ 2168681.	76.1%	71.0%
14	JUN 94	$ 282817.	$ 2760749.	$ 329191.	$ 2188622.	$ 306004.	$ 2474685.	82.5%	81.1%
15	JUL 94	$ 98089.	$ 2858838.	$ 306575.	$ 2495196.	$ 202332.	$ 2677017.	88.5%	87.7%
16	AUG 94	$ 109145.	$ 2967983.	$ 356587.	$ 2851783.	$ 232866.	$ 2909883.	95.1%	95.3%
17	SEP 94	$ 85167.	$ 3053150.	$ 201367.	$ 3053150.	$ 143267.	$ 3053150.	100.0%	100.0%

```
*************************************************  END OF MONTHLY COST SCHEDULE  *************************************************
```

FIGURE E-11
S-Curve for Design Activities Only (Sort by Code Digit 1 Greater Than 0 and Less Than 3).

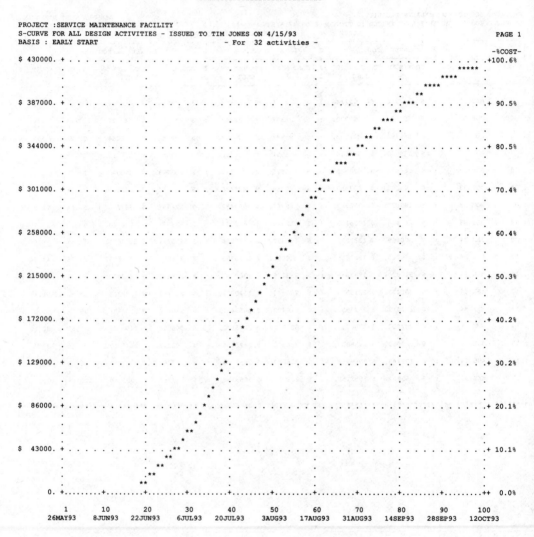

```
                          ******************************
                          **  CUMULATIVE COST CURVE  **
                          ******************************

PROJECT :SERVICE MAINTENANCE FACILITY
S-CURVE FOR ALL DESIGN ACTIVITIES - ISSUED TO TIM JONES ON 4/15/93                    PAGE 1
BASIS : EARLY START                        - For  32 activities -
                                                                                    -%COST-
 $ 430000. + . . . . . . . . . . . . . . . . . . . . . . . . . . . . . . . . . .+100.6%
           .                   .                   .               .    *****   .
           .                   .                   .               .  ****      .
           .                   .                   .               .****        .
 $ 387000. + . . . . . . . . . . . . . . . . . . . . . . . . . . .***. . . . . .+ 90.5%
           .                   .                   .           .**               .
           .                   .                   .         ***                 .
           .                   .                   .       **                    .
 $ 344000. + . . . . . . . . . . . . . . . . . . .** . . . . . . . . . . . . . .+ 80.5%
           .                   .                  .**                            .
           .                   .               *** .                             .
           .                   .              **   .                             .
 $ 301000. + . . . . . . . . . . . . . . . .** . . . . . . . . . . . . . . . . .+ 70.4%
           .                   .           **      .                             .
           .                   .          *        .                             .
           .                   .         *         .                             .
 $ 258000. + . . . . . . . . . . . . . .*. . . . . . . . . . . . . . . . . . . .+ 60.4%
           .                   .      **           .                             .
           .                   .      *                                          .
 $ 215000. + . . . . . . . . . .*. . . . . . . . . . . . . . . . . . . . . . . .+ 50.3%
           .                   *                                                 .
           .                  *                                                  .
 $ 172000. + . . . . . . . . .*. . . . . . . . . . . . . . . . . . . . . . . . .+ 40.2%
           .                 *                                                   .
           .                *                                                    .
 $ 129000. + . . . . . . .*. . . . . . . . . . . . . . . . . . . . . . . . . . .+ 30.2%
           .              *                                                      .
           .             *                                                       .
 $  86000. + . . . . . .*. . . . . . . . . . . . . . . . . . . . . . . . . . . .+ 20.1%
           .           *                                                         .
           .         **                                                          .
           .        *                                                            .
 $  43000. + . . .**. . . . . . . . . . . . . . . . . . . . . . . . . . . . . .+ 10.1%
           .    **                                                               .
           .   **                                                                .
           . **                                                                  .
       0. +.........+.........+.........+.........+.........+.........+.........+.........+.........+.........++ 0.0%
         1        10        20        30        40        50        60        70        80        90       100
      26MAY93   8JUN93   22JUN93   6JUL93   20JUL93   3AUG93  17AUG93  31AUG93  14SEP93  28SEP93  12OCT93
```

FIGURE E-12
Daily Distribution of Costs for Design Work Only (Sort by Code Digit 1 Greater Than 0 and Less Than 3).

```
****************************
**   COST EVERY DAY CURVE   **
****************************
```

PROJECT: SERVICE MAINTENANCE FACILITY
DISTRIBUTION OF COSTS FOR ALL DESIGN WORK - ISSUED TO TIM JONES ON 4/15/93   PAGE 1
BASIS : EARLY START   - For 32 activities -

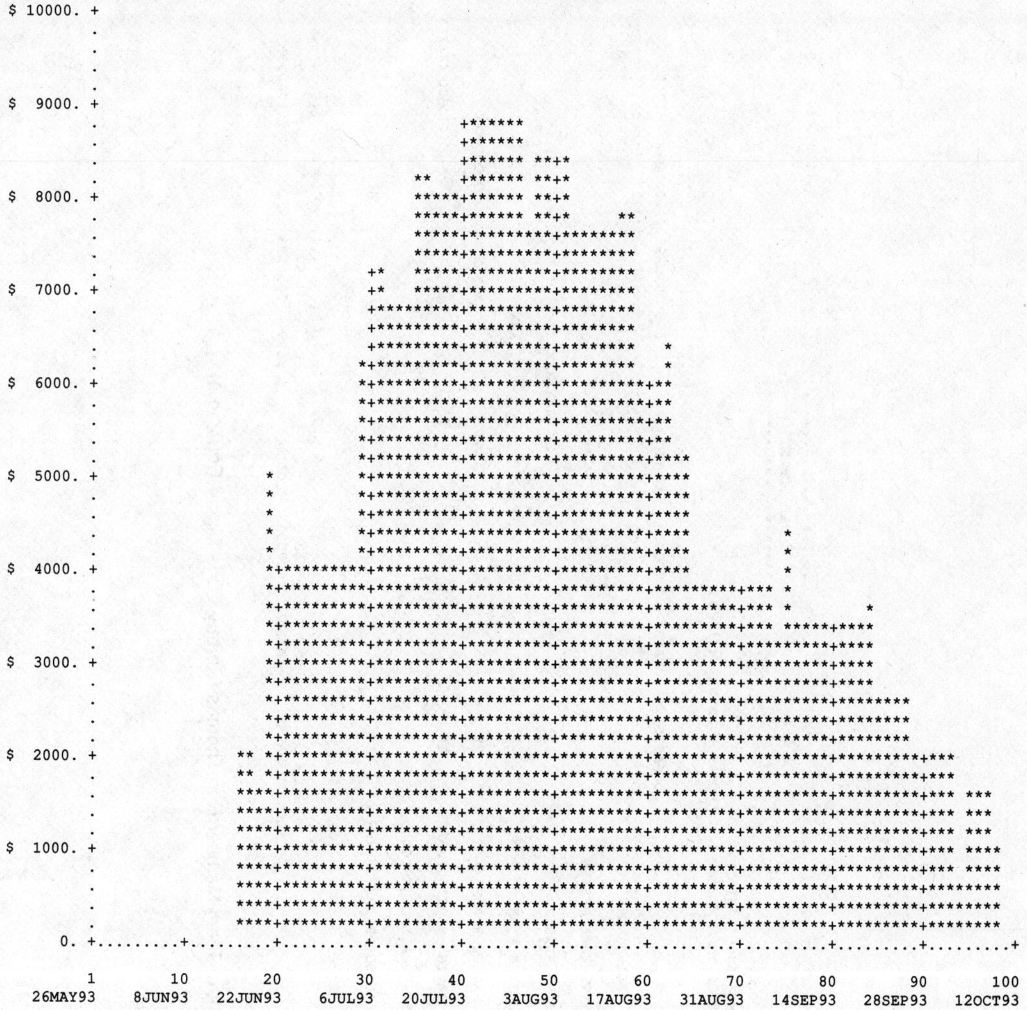

```
$ 10000. +
         .
         .
         .
         .
$  9000. +
         .                                    +******
         .                                    +******
         .                                    +****** **+*
         .                           **    +****** **+*
$  8000. +                           *****+****** **+*
         .                           *****+****** **+*     **
         .                           *****+**********+*********
         .                           *****+**********+*********
         .                        +*  *****+**********+*********
$  7000. +                        +*  *****+**********+*********
         .                        +**********+**********+*********
         .                        +**********+**********+*********
         .                        +**********+**********+*********          *
         .                       *+**********+**********+*********          *
$  6000. +                       *+**********+**********+*********+**
         .                       *+**********+**********+**********+**
         .                       *+**********+**********+**********+**
         .                       *+**********+**********+**********+**
         .                       *+**********+**********+**********+****
$  5000. +            *          *+**********+**********+**********+****
         .            *          *+**********+**********+**********+****
         .            *          *+**********+**********+**********+****
         .            *          *+**********+**********+**********+****          *
         .            *          *+**********+**********+**********+****
$  4000. +          *+**********+**********+**********+**********+**********+***  *
         .          *+**********+**********+**********+**********+**********+*** *     *
         .          *+**********+**********+**********+**********+**********+*** *****+****
         .          *+**********+**********+**********+**********+**********+**********+****
$  3000. +          *+**********+**********+**********+**********+**********+**********+****
         .          *+**********+**********+**********+**********+**********+*********
         .          *+**********+**********+**********+**********+**********+*********
         .          *+**********+**********+**********+**********+**********+*********
         .          *+**********+**********+**********+**********+**********+*********
$  2000. +       ** *+**********+**********+**********+**********+**********+**********+***
         .       ** *+**********+**********+**********+**********+**********+**********+***
         .       ****+**********+**********+**********+**********+**********+**********+*** ***
         .       ****+**********+**********+**********+**********+**********+**********+*** ***
         .       ****+**********+**********+**********+**********+**********+**********+*** ***
$  1000. +       ****+**********+**********+**********+**********+**********+**********+*** ****
         .       ****+**********+**********+**********+**********+**********+**********+*** ****
         .       ****+**********+**********+**********+**********+**********+**********+*********
         .       ****+**********+**********+**********+**********+**********+**********+*********
         .       ****+**********+**********+**********+**********+**********+**********+*********
      0. +........+.........+.........+.........+.........+.........+.........+.........+.........+.........+
         1        10        20        30        40        50        60        70        80        90       100
      26MAY93   8JUN93   22JUN93   6JUL93   20JUL93   3AUG93   17AUG93  31AUG93  14SEP93  28SEP93  12OCT93
```

```
                          *******************
                          **  BAR CHART   **
                          *******************

PROJECT: SERVICE MAINTENANCE FACILITY                                                                    ** PAGE 1.1 **
SCHEDULE FOR ALL WORK OF TEAM MEMBER RON THOMAS - ISSUED 4/15/93                                            BAR CHART

                                                  1       10      20      30      40      50      60      70      80      90
ACTIVITY   DESCRIPTION               DURATION   26MAY93  8JUN93 22JUN93  6JUL93 20JUL93  3AUG93 17AUG93 31AUG93 14SEP93 28SEP93
                                               +.....+.....+.....+.....+.....+.....+.....+.....+.....+.....+.....+.....+.....+.....+.....+.....+.....+.....+
C   25     IN-HOUSE DESIGN WORK          3      XXX      .     .     .     .     .     .     .     .     .
    35     PROJECT SITE-WORK DESIGN      1          X    .     .     .     .     .     .     .     .     .
    55     SITE GRADING PLAN            12           XXXXXXXXXXX  .     .     .     .     .     .     .
    85     SUBBASE DESIGN PLAN           5                      XXXXX  .     .     .     .     .     .
   105     CONCRETE PAVING ROADS        20                           XXXXXXXXXXXXXXXXXXXX  .     .     .
   135     CONCRETE PAVING PARKING/WALKS 10                                         XXXXXXXXXX  .     .
   155     AGGREGATE SURFACING DESIGN    8                                                   XXXXXXXX  .
   165     FENCING/LANDSCAPE/IRRIGATION 14                                                         XXXXXXXXXXXXXX
                                               +.....+.....+.....+.....+.....+.....+.....+.....+.....+.....+.....+.....+.....+.....+.....+.....+.....+.....+
                                     WORK DAYS    1       10      20      30      40      50      60      70      80      90
                                 CALENDAR DATES 26MAY93  8JUN93 22JUN93  6JUL93 20JUL93  3AUG93 17AUG93 31AUG93 14SEP93 28SEP93
```

FIGURE E-13

Bar Chart for all Work of Team Member Ron Thomas (Sort by Code Digit 4 Equal to 3).

```
*************************
**  ACTIVITY SCHEDULE  **
*************************
```

PROJECT: SERVICE MAINTENANCE FACILITY
SCHEDULE FOR ALL ACTIVITIES RELATED TO BUILDING A - ISSUED TO KATHY DIEHL ON 4/15/93

ACTIVITY SCHEDULE

```
*******************************************************************************************
```

ACTIVITY NUMBER		DESCRIPTION	DURA-TION	EARLY START	EARLY FINISH	LATE START	LATE FINISH	TOTAL FLOAT	FREE FLOAT
C	45	A/E DESIGN BUILDING A	1	21JUN93 / 19	21JUN93 / 19	21JUN93 / 19	21JUN93 / 19	0	0
C	65	FLOOR PLAN BUILDING A	15	22JUN93	12JUL93	22JUN93	12JUL93	0	0
C	95	FOUND/STRUCT BUILDING A	30	20 / 13JUL93 / 35	34 / 23AUG93 / 64	20 / 13JUL93 / 35	34 / 23AUG93 / 64	0	0
C	120	MECH/ELECT BUILDING A	30	24AUG93 / 65	4OCT93 / 94	24AUG93 / 65	4OCT93 / 94	0	0
C	125	SPECIAL OVERHEAD CRANE	11	24AUG93 / 65	7SEP93 / 75	31AUG93 / 70	14SEP93 / 80	5	19
C	190	PROCURE OVERHEAD CRANE	40	8SEP93 / 76	2NOV93 / 115	15SEP93 / 81	9NOV93 / 120	5	5
C	150	BUILDING A DESIGN REVIEW	3	5OCT93 / 95	7OCT93 / 97	5OCT93 / 95	7OCT93 / 97	0	0
C	205	INDUSTRIAL/MAINTENANCE BLDG A	2	8NOV93 / 119	9NOV93 / 120	8NOV93 / 119	9NOV93 / 120	0	0
C	220	FOUND/STRUCT BUILDING A	110	10NOV93 / 121	12APR94 / 230	10NOV93 / 121	12APR94 / 230	0	0
C	240	ELECTRICAL/PHONE BUILDING A	65	13APR94 / 231	12JUL94 / 295	11MAY94 / 251	9AUG94 / 315	20	20
C	245	PLUMBING, HEAT, & AIR BLDG A	85	13APR94 / 231	9AUG94 / 315	13APR94 / 231	9AUG94 / 315	0	0
C	270	ARCH FINISHES BUILDING A	30	10AUG94 / 316	20SEP94 / 345	10AUG94 / 316	20SEP94 / 345	0	0

```
*******************************************************************************************
```

END OF SCHEDULE

```
*******************************************************************************************
```

FIGURE E-14
Schedule for All Activities Related to Building A (Sort by Code Digit 2 Equal to 7).

INDEX